The Essentials of Meeting Management

Richard A. Hildreth, Ph.D.

A National Publishers Book
Prentice Hall, Englewood Cliffs, New Jersey 07632

Library of Congress Cataloging-in-Publication Data

Hildreth, Richard A.
The essentials of meeting management / Richard A. Hildreth.
p. cm.
"A National Publishers book."
Includes bibliographical references.
ISBN 0-13-284480-X
1. Meetings--Planning--Handbooks, manuals, etc. 2. Congresses and conventions--Planning--Handbooks, manuals, etc. I. Title.
AS6.H55 1990
658.4'56--dc20 89-49652
CIP

Editorial/production supervision
and interior design: *Denise Gannon*
Cover design: *George Cornell*
Manufacturing buyer: *David Dickey*

Printed in the United States of America
10 9 8 7 6 5 4 3 2 1

ISBN 0-13-284480-X

Prentice-Hall International (UK) Limited, *London*
Prentice-Hall of Australia Pty. Limited, *Sydney*
Prentice-Hall Canada Inc., *Toronto*
Prentice-Hall Hispanoamericana, S.A., *Mexico*
Prentice-Hall of India Private Limited, *New Delhi*
Prentice-Hall of Japan, Inc., *Tokyo*
Simon & Schuster Asia Pte. Ltd., *Singapore*
Editora Prentice-Hall do Brasil, Ltda., *Rio de Janeiro*

The Essentials of Meeting Management

Contents

Acknowledgments

Many individuals have contributed their time, effort, and thought to the production of this book. It is impossible to acknowledge everyone, particularly the hundreds of students at Metropolitan State College who used the original draft and who were kind, demanding, and extremely perceptive in their comments, evaluations, and suggestions.

My family has been tolerant, patient, and helpful. Therefore, this book is dedicated to my wife, Paulette, my son, Rick, and his wife, Junella, and my grandson, Kitt, who with great effort, managed to restrain his nine-year-old exuberance so I could write.

My thanks to Alma Galindo-Anguiano, my staff assistant, who typed the original manuscript, and to Betty G. Richardson, who meticulously edited that original manuscript.

It is a privilege to work in an industry with professionals who are willing to take their valuable time to share ideas and experience and to read the original manuscript. Their suggestions have been carefully incorporated so that this book contains not only my own ideas but the thinking and experience of these industry leaders. My appreciation goes to Susan Armstrong, Public Information Manager, Battelle Project Management (Ohio); Lincoln Colby,* Director, Field Communications, Merck, Sharp & Dohme (Pennsylvania); Dave Countin, Vice President, MMC (Kentucky); Lucy Elliott Enterprises (Florida), James Goebel,* Manager, Education-Training Department, Wisconsin Credit Union League (Wisconsin); Raymond Hall,* CEO and Executive Vice President, Electronic Representatives Association (Illinois); James Jones,* President, James E. Jones Associates (Connecticut); Damian Mogilka, Operation Meeting Planner, Eaton Corporation (Wisconsin); and Rudy Wright,* Managing Director, International Conference Consortium (California).

*Past president, Meeting Planners International

A publication in the area of meeting management should not fail to acknowledge the helpfulness of the hundreds of hotel and convention bureau professionals who tolerate the idiosyncrasies of meeting planners. They have played an invaluable role in my education as well as the education of other meeting managers.

To all, thank you.

Richard A. Hildreth, Ph.D.

Introduction

". . . and when Ur spake, the Kings seated around him listened and also spake . . ."

from the *Ballad of Sumer and Akkad*

We can speculate about what procedures, what problems, and what techniques the people responsible for organizing and facilitating the meetings of King Ur might have used in 4000 B.C. One thing is certain: Penalties for poor planning or the appearance of Murphy's Law were swift and fatal.

Meetings have been a part of people's lives since earliest recorded history. From the *Ballads of Sumer and Akkad,* through the *Eloquent Peasant* of ancient Egypt, the peoples' forums in Greece and Rome, King Arthur's Round Table, religious meetings in all faiths, and in governmental bodies, to modern times, meeting, in one form or another, have been an integral part of our human life. We have been, and are, social animals.

Despite its long history, meeting planning as a recognized and organized career did not begin to materialize until three farsighted individuals, "Buzz" Bartow, Marion Kershner, and Jay Lurye, provided the concept of an umbrella organization (rather than the small, specialized groups that had existed) for the meeting profession. Founded during the World Meeting Planners Congress in Chicago in 1972, the organization became known as Meeting Planners International (MPI).

One hundred twenty planners and suppliers attended the first meeting. (It is interesting to note, in view of the number of women currently in the profession, that there were only two women in the original membership.)

The first board of directors of MPI, under the leadership of Bartow, Kershner, and the second president, Paul Barsaloux, conceived and assisted in the development, from 1973 to 1976, of the first academic meeting planning program. This program, formally approved by the State of Colorado, September 24, 1976, was implemented at Metropolitan State College in Denver. This first program was followed closely by a meeting program at Northeastern Oklahoma State University in Tahlequah.

Two factors contributed to a rapid development of both industry workshops and academic programs during the 1980s. The first factor was the development and implementation of the Certified Meeting Professional (CMP) examination and designation by the Convention Liaison Council (CLC). This certification gives both status and credence to the person who achieves it.

A second factor was the development of a "model" meeting curriculum by the Professional Convention Management Association (PCMA) under the leadership of Roy Evans and Ed Polivka. PCMA, once it had a model curriculum, actively pursued the inauguration of its program in several colleges and universities. Along with the model curriculum came accreditation.

PCMA has become the accrediting agency for academic meeting management programs. Accreditation means the academic institution must meet standards of excellence in quality, breadth, and professionalism in courses, course content, instructors, and resources. As with any professional program (engineering, medicine, accounting, and so on), a student pursuing an academic program in meeting management should seek out those colleges and universities that have been accredited. To determine if an academic institution has an accredited program in meeting management, contact PCMA in Birmingham, Alabama.

To the Reader

This book is based upon my 35 years of academic instruction and professional meeting planning experience. Throughout, I have worked to combine the theoretical with its practical application.

The original version of the book was developed in 1983 for the use of meeting planning students at Metropolitan State College, Denver. It was also used in seminars and workshops for meeting professionals. Each time it was used, the students, whether professionals or collegians, submitted written evaluations on content, readability, and practicality. Their comments and suggestions, along with those of my colleagues in the meeting profession, have been incorporated into the present edition.

I believe meeting management draws upon two basic areas, communication theory and business management. You will find communication theory serves as the theoretical basis in the book, whereas business provides the application procedures and management techniques.

Lastly, you should know that the book is designed to provide the *basic* knowledge necessary for the Certified Meeting Professional examination. Before taking the examination, you should supplement your preparation by reading two additional publications: *Professional Meeting Management,* published by the Professional Convention Management Association (PCMA), and *Handbook for Meeting Professionals,* published by Meeting Planners International (MPI).

The CMP examination covers 25 meeting planning functions and 17 independent conditions that affect meeting planning functions:

Meeting Planning Functions	**Independent Condition**
1. Establishing meeting design and objectives	1. Time of year
2. Selecting site and facilities	2. Labor conditions
3. Negotiating with facilities	3. Length of meeting

4. Budgeting
5. Handling reservations and housing
6. Choosing from transportation options
7. Planning program
8. Planning guidebook/staging guide/documentation of specifications
9. Establishing registration procedures
10. Arranging for and using support services
11. Coordinating with convention center or hall
12. Planning with convention services manager
13. Briefing facilities staff
14. Shipping
15. Planning function room setup
16. Managing exhibits
17. Managing food and beverage
18. Determining audiovisual requirements
19. Selecting speakers
20. Booking entertainment
21. Scheduling promotion and publicity
22. Developing guest and family programs
23. Producing and printing meeting materials
24. Distributing gratuities
25. Evaluating—postmeeting

4. Size of attendance
5. Site/facility location and type
6. Objective
7. Type of organization
8. Location or geography
9. Budget
10. Participant funding
11. Management responsibility
12. Space requirements
13. Transportation variables
14. Participant demographics
15. Social events
16. Special requirements
17. Weather

When you are ready to apply for the CMP examination, write to:

Convention Liaison Council
P.O. Box 1738
Alexandria, VA 22320

I do not attempt to cover all the functions and conditions of the examination in this book, since it is designed as a starting point in preparation for both the meeting profession and the examination.

At the end of each chapter, you will find a Chapter Summary, specific statements of What You Should Have Learned from the chapter, Review Questions, and Application Exercises. These are all designed to assist you in learning the most possible information from the book.

The best of luck to you, and I hope to meet each of you at a meeting of meeting professionals.

Chapter 1

The Meeting Profession: An Orientation

This chapter defines what a meeting is and what the meeting profession is. The status of meetings, the levels and duties of the meeting professional, and the approximate salaries of those engaged in the development and presentation of meetings are discussed. A quick reference to Appendix A will show the major organizations in the field that permit specific focuses for the meeting industry.

Meeting Defined

Broadly speaking, a *meeting* is an encounter between entities, not necessarily between people; that is, "I met the *idea* in Peter Drucker's book," or "I met the bear in the woods," or "We met at the dance last night," or "I met with the Affirmative Action officer."

However, for our purposes, a meeting is defined more specifically. *A meeting is a planned communication encounter between two or more persons for a common purpose.* Although still broad, the definition permits us to focus on two key ideas: people and common purpose.

People, according to experts in psychology and sociology, have the unique combined abilities of memory, thinking, and communication. Further, people react to emotions and intellectual stimuli based upon their particular needs or desires.

Thus, the meeting for the meeting professional, becomes *the communication of intellectual and emotional stimuli to two or more people in a manner designed to secure the accomplishment of the peoples' common purpose. Common purpose* simply means they are at the meeting to learn something, to influence each other, to be entertained, or to solve a problem through communication.

The Meeting Professional

The meeting professional is a communication expert who analyzes a communication situation and then selects, plans, and uses, in a cost-conscious manner, those communication techniques needed to influence people who attend in order to accomplish a purpose.

If a meeting professional used communication techniques to influence humans to accomplish a purpose, he or she is practicing manipulation. The word *manipulation* has a connotation of unethical behavior. However, popularization has clouded the layperson's perspective. Influencing through communication is a human characteristic as old as humans themselves. For instance, a baby begins to use influence when it cries for food or a change of diapers.

Influencing people through one or many forms of communication is, and will be, with us. (Such management terms as discipline, leadership, direction, persuasion, motivation, management-by-objective, marketing, and advertising show this.) All would be impossible without some form of verbal or nonverbal communication used to influence. The problem lies *not* with influencing people but with the *ethics* of the *means* and the *consequences* of striving to meet the objective.

Thus, the meeting professional, if he or she is a professional, must constantly review communication techniques, new or old, in terms of his or her personal ethics, the meeting situation, and the *consequences* of the techniques.

This information may be helpful for those readers whose intellectual curiosity prompts them to raise the question, "Are these meeting professionals *artists* or *scientists?*"

Most authors believe that science is a body of knowledge based on empirical data, whereas art is the application of knowledge. Also, most authorities (business and nonbusiness alike) view business as an *art*. Meetings today are big business, as discussed in the next section. You, the reader, should make your own decision as to the *art* or *science* question.

The Status of Meetings Today

A description of the meeting industry today is a challenging and complex task. We must look at the current economic conditions of the business, predictions for the future, and the job requirements and conditions surrounding the job. Also, most readers will wish to have some indication of salaries. Each of these areas is covered in this section.

Present and Future Economic Conditions

As with most analyses of economic conditions, there are contradictions, depending upon the orientation of the source making the analysis. For instance, *Meetings & Conventions Magazine,* which previewed its biannual "Trends in the Meeting Market" at the April 1988 ITIX Show in Chicago, indicated a decrease in convention spending from $34.6 billion in 1985 to $31.9 billion in 1987. You should note that *Meetings & Conventions* conducted its study, for the most part, prior to the October 1987 stock market drop.

On the other hand, *Meeting News,* in its May 1988 issue, took exception to the report and solicited statements from industry leaders of convention and visitors bureaus and the trade show industry. These leaders were in agreement that spending had increased from, or at least maintained, its 1985 level.

The Association of Convention and Visitors Bureaus (ACVB) reported that expenditures by convention attendees increased from $464.16 in 1985 to $526.92 in 1986, the latest year that data were compiled. Trade show attendee expenditures showed a similar increase.

One conclusion is obvious. Meetings and conventions are big business and represent a major economic gain for the communities and facilities where the meetings are held. What about the future of meeting management? Two fundamental factors give every indication that meetings, as a form of communication, have an excellent future.

The first factor is the increasing need for education and training as the world becomes more specialized in its demands upon people. Workers and managers alike constantly need to upgrade their skills and knowledge. Meetings, whether conventions or specialized seminars and workshops, provide a relatively inexpensive way of providing this information to a large number at a low per-person cost. For example, if you need information, you could read a book or listen to a sound cassette or watch a videocassette. If you are an employee of an organization, the same information could be provided to 20 or more of you in an interactive meeting format with one or more experts to answer your questions. The organization reaps the advantage, similar to volume buying.

The second factor is that we have become an information rather than industrialized society. Dr. Marvin Cetron, cited in *Meetings & Conventions,* has found that "85% of all information today is transferred not through college courses or books but via meetings."[1]

There is a logic to this. A much-quoted maxim in adult education is that "adults learn with their feet." This is a way of saying that as adults we learn more effectively if we can use a hands-on approach, asking questions as we go and relating the materials to our own or peers' experiences. The common student reaction among adults in college and business alike is, "Give us an example." A person with experience in the subject can provide realistic examples on-the-spot that are not available on cassettes or in books.

These two factors are interrelated. An information society requires more and more specialization from its people, and meetings provide the interactive communication medium for transmission and learning of the required information and skill.

The essential unknown for the meeting industry is the cost factor. Meetings cost money, and many corporate and organization chief executive officers (CEOs) are not convinced of the cost-effectiveness of professional meeting management; hence resistance to hiring a consulting firm may be very high. However, when an accountant sits down with the accounting section of the organization, analyzes direct and indirect costs of previous meetings with them, and submits a proposal "guaranteeing" a 10% reduction in costs or a fee waiver, the resistance disappears. When the reduction is accomplished, contract renewal for additional meetings is automatic.

As the introduction pointed out, meetings incorporate both communication theory and management theory. Thus, in summary of the present and future economic status of the industry, we can say that meetings will continue to exist and have a major role in our economy. However, the role of the meeting manager will depend upon the orientation, knowledge, and skill of the managers. The role of the meeting professional will depend upon *you,* the future generation, and how well prepared you are to be managers, not just facilitators.

The next subsection looks specifically at the job requirements and the psychological, sociological, and financial conditions that surround the job.

The Job, or Position, of Meeting Management

As recently as 1978, many executives "held meetings" because it was traditional to do so; they would call in a secretary and say, "I want to have a meeting—get me a hotel, some meeting space, and some food and drinks."

Those days are almost gone. The modern executive identifies a problem and calls a meeting that is expected to yield returns for the dollars spent. Whether an in-house employee or an outside consulting firm plans the meeting, the bottom line has become return on investment. You may have the glamour and the frills, but the results you get are what determine your success or failure or, for that matter, your job retention.

There are two labels used in the meeting industry that, at present, are merely labels: *planner* and *professional.* The term professional is gradually approaching an accepted meaning through the Certified Meeting Professional examination, the educational programs from seminars and workshops of the industry, and academic programs. However, planner has not achieved that much status.

For example, the 25 functions and 17 conditions on the Certified Meeting Professional exam do not include *planning* per se, but rather indicate *arranging.* When *Successful Meetings* magazine published the study by Susan Hatch, [2], it listed 25 areas of planner responsibility, which were compared to "average expertise." Again, planning as an area of responsibility or expertise was not included. When other job areas using the term planning are considered, such as urban planning and environmental planning, intensive academic and industry programs are directed specifically to planning.

Planning is defined in this book as anticipatory decision making, and a chapter is included on methods and procedures for organized anticipatory decision making that range from checklists to manual and computerized approaches such as the Program Evaluation Review Technique (PERT) and the Critical Path Method (CPM). This has been done in the belief that the meeting manager needs to master such approaches if the term planning is to be used and if the industry wishes to increase its image and status among chief executive officers. Otherwise, the industry will be using the seat-of-the-pants method of flying a sophisticated jet aircraft.

If we exclude planner and professional, there are three *levels* of jobs in the meeting field: facilitator, manager, and administrator.

1. *The facilitator.* About 50% to 60% of the people engaged in the conduct of meetings are facilitators. Their ranks include the secretary called upon to set up a meeting for the boss, the convention services manager in a hotel or convention bureau, ground operators, travel agents, and others in the industry whose duties are generally limited to: reserving a property, sleeping rooms, food and beverage functions, audiovisual equipment, air and ground transportation, pre- and postmeeting tours, on-site registration, special events (sports contests, entertaining speakers, bands, singers, casino parties, and so on), and being a "gofer" (a flunky) during the meeting.

There are many jobs at this level. Salaries are generally in the $12,000 to $22,000 range. Consulting firms in this category average between $1000 and $15,000 per meeting, depending upon duties requested. Decorating firms fulfill many of these needs for trade shows and exhibits at association meetings. Their margin of profit is similar to that of the meeting consulting firm but is dependent upon the services provided and the size of the show.

The facilitator is the important and essential level of meeting management, and people at higher levels of the meeting industry need, employ, and respect the work done by quality facilitators.

2. *The meeting manager.* About 25% to 35% of people in the meeting industry are at this level. Their duties may include determining objectives for the meeting, projecting and managing budgets, developing agendas and meeting patterns, planning on-site registration, performing site inspections, contract negotiations, on-site management, postmeeting evaluations, and the like.

The salary range for this level generally falls within the range $20,000 to $75,000, with an average around $35,000. However, there are exceptions where managers earn as much as $150,000 per year.

3. *The meeting administrator.* About 5% to 10% of people in the industry could be classified at this level. Their duties include most of the management functions. They have a thorough knowledge of effective communication theory and techniques, learning and programming approaches, and problem-solving group methods and, in reality, are organizational communication, and behavior-modification experts. Most hold advanced degrees in communication, business, adult learning, or some aspect of psychology.

This person is more highly qualified than people at the other levels, may have been with the organization longer, may become appreciated for the breadth, depth, and quality of ability, and may have administrative duties that encompass more than meeting management, since there will be others available to the organization to perform facilitation and management duties: thus the salary level will be considerably higher. The few administrators who were willing to share salary information indicate a salary level in excess of $100,000.

Roles of the Meeting Specialist

Duties and salaries were discussed in the previous section. However, a duty is different from a role. An example from the theater makes this clear. Acting is both an *art* and *craft*. A person must master the art and craft. However, the art and craft must be put to work in a performance (duty). The master of the art must assume many "roles" during a career. So it is with the meeting manager during each meeting. In performing the duties of manager, the person assumes many roles. Although no list could be complete, the following list includes a few roles and their related job requirements.

1. *Communication Specialist*
   a. Knowledge of learning theory, principles, and practices of how people learn and change.
   b. Knowledge of effective presentation methods to meet the objectives of each session and the meeting. (People attending meetings will not be

inspired, motivated, changed, "buy" an idea, or produce unless they learn something from the experience.)

2. *Manager-Planner*
   a. Application of administrative skills
      (i) Recruit, select, and develop a staff.
      (ii) Plan programs.
      (iii) Set up the process of coordination and communication.
      (iv) Carry out financial planning for the meeting.
      (v) Perform other related functions of a staff manager.
   b. Plan for achieving goals and objectives
      (i) Agree on and understand the goals and objectives of the organization.
      (ii) Gather information on the nature of the current situation, prospective available resources, and future requirements (forecasting).
      (iii) Involve others in the process.
      (iv) Diagnose needs and set planning objectives and goals.
      (v) Choose alternative courses of action.
      (vi) Decide upon responsibility for action.
      (vii) Prepare the plan.
      (viii) Secure approval of the final plan.

3. *Information Specialist*
   a. Identify information needed.
   b. Clarify information.
   c. Synthesize information.
   d. Reality-test the information.
   e. Distribute the information.
   f. Act as an organization communication link.
      (i) Be accessible to those who are working on the meeting.
      (ii) Develop trust between yourself and others concerned.
      (iii) Be truthful with people about plans and problems.
      (iv) Keep objectives in mind and ensure the staff does also.
      (v) Define the responsibilities of others in terms of the meeting.
      (vi) Develop listening skills.

4. *Consultant to Management*
   a. The problem-solving function (Know the ecology of the organization environment.)
      (i) Help management to examine organizational problems.
      (ii) Help management to examine the contribution of the proposed meeting to solve identified problems.
      (iii) Help examine the long- and short-range objectives of the meeting at the end of the meeting.
      (iv) Explore, with management, alternatives to holding a meeting.
      (v) Develop the meeting plan within the organization policies and guidelines.
      (vi) Explore appropriate resources to implement the plan.
      (vii) Provide consultation for management on evaluation and review of the planned program.
      (viii) Explore, with management, the follow-up steps necessary to reinforce problem solutions and outputs from a meeting.

b. The internal consultant function
   (i) Provide direct consultation to the organization.
      (a) As an expert: Give advice to management.
      (b) As an advocate: Persuade management as to a proper approach.
      (c) As an identifier of alternatives: Provide alternatives to management.
   (ii) Provide nondirect consultation to the organization.
      (a) As a process specialist: Assist in problem solving.
      (b) As a reflector: Serve as a catalytic agent in solving problems.

These are some of the internal duties and roles a meeting manager must assume. Next is some advice to both the beginner and the experienced manager on choosing a position to take at any given time when you are called upon to serve as a consultant in management, particularly within your own organization. *Choosing your position is governed by several factors:*

1. Personal factors:
   a. Your skills as a person
   b. Your ability to work with others
   c. Your experience in the areas of the problems
   d. Your self-image
   e. Your level of knowledge and skill in the area in which you consult
2. Factors in the relationship between management and yourself:
   a. Your status in the organization
   b. Your previous role in management problem solving
   c. Your familiarity with organization history and objectives
   d. Your ability to influence management
   e. Your previous successes and failures working with other elements of the organization
   f. Organization expectations of you
3. Factors in the problem situation:
   a. Your knowledge of the content of the problem
   b. The time available for solution
   c. Your ability to see alternatives

Finally, don't consult just to consult. You can ruin your career!

Environmental Factors in Meeting Management

The challenges of meeting new people, travel to many areas in and out of the country, and the variety of tasks faced by a meeting manager are stimulating and interesting. However, as with any occupation, you should be familiar with potentially negative aspects.

Meeting management is stressful. Murphy's Law is often quoted: Anything that can go wrong, will go wrong. The more experience you gain, the more you become aware of potential problems. For instance, suppose you had scheduled a meeting in a country in which a sudden outburst of terrorist attacks occurred. Your organization decided it did not wish to run the risk of meeting in that country and asked you to reschedule. Or, suppose you had scheduled a meeting in a state where the governor abolished a holiday important to all, particularly minorities, and your organization insisted on moving the meeting to another state just two months before the date of the meeting. Or, suppose all the luggage of the chairman of the board of your organization was lost on the way to the meeting.

Another aspect that can be very stressful is the pressure placed on the marriage or romantic involvement of the meeting manager. If one partner has to stay at home while the manager is constantly traveling to out-of-town meetings, extreme pressure is placed on the relationship.

A final aspect is the "boom-bust" cycles. As the meeting approaches, duties and responsibilities mount, the on-site management is a pressure-cooker situation where the manager may get as little as three or four hours of sleep per night for several nights. Then, the meeting is over, evaluation is completed, and you don't have another meeting scheduled immediately. There is a letdown.

All these environmental conditions, and more, require that the meeting manager have both psychological and physiological endurance. Unless you have this endurance and can tolerate "living out of a suitcase," there are many less stressful occupations you should consider.

WHAT YOU SHOULD HAVE LEARNED FROM THIS CHAPTER

1. A definition of a meeting.
2. A definition of a meeting professional.
3. The effect of fluctuations in the economy on meetings.
4. The potential for increase in the demand for and the number of meetings, regardless of economic fluctuations.
5. The current image of the meeting professional.
6. The levels of jobs in the meeting industry: facilitator, manager, administrator.
7. The duties and responsibilities of each of the meeting job levels.
8. The salary ranges of each of the meeting job levels.
9. The roles and related job and personal requirements in the meeting industry.
10. Some suggestions and ideas on the meeting professional's role as a consultant to an organization.
11. Psychological and sociological factors that can affect a person in the meeting industry.

References

1. Susan Crystal. "Into the Future: The Complex Meeting Mosaic." *Meetings & Conventions* 22, no. 11 (December 1987): 30.
2. Susan Hatch. "How Good Do You Have to Be?" *Successful Meetings* (March 1988): pp. 22–27.

REVIEW QUESTIONS

1. Are meeting professionals artists or scientists? Explain your answer.
2. What impact has the Certified Meeting Professional designation had upon the meeting industry?
3. What are the three levels of the meeting profession?
4. Which of the roles of the meeting professional would most frequently be involved in the job of the meeting facilitator? In the job of the meeting manager?
5. List what you believe are the advantages of being a meeting professional. List what you believe are the greatest disadvantages of being a meeting professional.
6. Your organization executives ask for your advice on an organization policy. What factors should you consider before giving that advice?
7. What are the differences and similarities between the roles of communication specialist and information specialist?
8. How do you believe the term planner relates (if it does) to the meeting facilitator, manager, and administrator?
9. What do you believe is the future of the meeting profession?
10. How would you define the term meeting specialist?

Chapter 2

Phases of Professional Meeting Development

This chapter presents the reader with an overview of the *phases* that are concerns of the meeting professional during the process of meeting conceptualization and production. Phases are not steps, since they may be developed at the same time. Places in which a sequence is fundamental to successful planning—for example, a site should not be inspected or selected before the meeting pattern has been determined—are suggested.

This discussion begins with a visual representation of how the phases relate to chapters in the book, functions and conditions covered on the Certified Meeting Professional (CMP) examination, and what makes an effective meeting.

As you read, remember that each of the functions and conditions may not be developed in enough depth to permit success on the CMP examination. However, enough coverage is given to provide adequate background understanding to guide your further reading. Also, remember there are management chapters in the book, such as Chapter 6, "Models for Developing Meeting Plans," Chapter 13, "The Law and the Meeting Professional," and Chapter 15, "Computers and the Meeting Professional," that go beyond the CMP examination and are essential to the professional meeting manager today and into the future. Turn to Diagram I before reading further to make certain you understand the interrelationships among phases, chapters, functions, and conditions.

PHASE I: Group History and Analysis

Probably the basic principle of meeting planning most universally accepted by professionals is "know your group."

While professionals may vary in their approaches to collecting and analyzing group data, four general categories are common: (1) personal characteristics and preferences, (2) geographical characteristics, (3) previous meeting

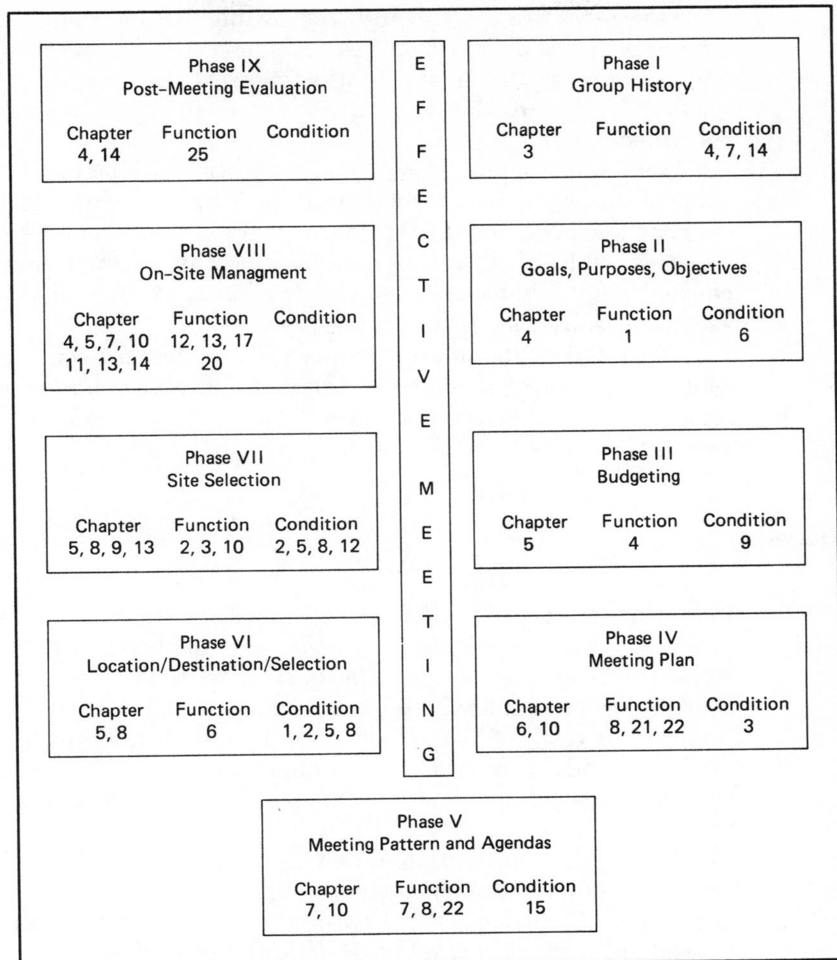

Diagram 1 Interrelationships of planning phases, text chapters, CMP functions, CMP conditions, and an effective meeting.

characteristics, and (4) policy characteristics and their interpretation by the organization.

These four general categories are treated in detail in Chapter 3. However, an emerging concept is that data on the organization should be capable of being stored on a computer for quick reference and analysis.

PHASE II: Establishment of Organization and Meeting Goals, Purposes, and Objectives

Goals and purposes of a meeting are usually dictated by organization policy and/or tradition.

Briefly, *goals* are long-range targets—sometimes spelled out five or more years in advance. Corporations frequently have strategic planning sections, and as a meeting professional, you will have ready access to corporate goals by contacting this division of the Research and Development (R&D) division.

Purposes are generalized, immediate (tactical) targets. Accomplishment of purposes should lead the organization along a continuum toward achieving its goals. Purposes generally fall into categories of enlightenment, problem solving, motivation, and persuasion.

Objectives are specific and measurable. An individual meeting will have *one and only one* primary, or first-level, objective that is measurable—that is, increase sales by 10% in six months following the meeting. The primary objective is so important that failure to accomplish it probably means the meeting has failed.

Accomplishment of the primary objective is dependent on meeting a multitude of sublevels. Large conventions may have as many as 30 sublevels (from level 2 to level 30), and the total measurable sublevels may be several hundred. All these sublevel objectives may be stored in a computer and the results of measurement (Chapters 4, 14, and 15) added at the end of the meeting, analyzed, and stored for future reference.

Actual phrasing of all objectives is a critical aspect that must take place before the planning process can begin. The process and techniques of developing and phrasing objectives and arranging them into an *objective tree* is covered in Chapter 4.

PHASE III: Budgeting

Budgeting is vital to the success of a meeting. Once the objectives have been clearly stated (note there is a *sequence* here of phases, which yields steps), it is necessary to develop a *preliminary* budget. It is almost axiomatic that the meeting professional will be given a total budget figure with which to work. Pinpointing costs of individual objectives will give you essential costs and provide a guide to fixed and variable costs you will be using when you build your *spreadsheet* for budget management during planning and meeting management.

Note that a *preliminary* budget is developed. A *final* meeting budget cannot be completed until the *critical path* (discussed in Chapter 6) has been determined. Once the critical path is discovered and resources reallocated to its accomplishment, a final budget can be produced.

Accounting procedures will vary with the organization represented by the meeting professional, and the only recommendation that can be given is that you anticipate some form of double-entry system. Normally the professional should keep a record of income and expenses (preferably in a spreadsheet showing cash flow) to check against the organization's accounting system and, more importantly, to keep a running tabulation of expenditures for each activity conducted for the objective tree. This permits more effective management of the parts and whole of the meeting production. The JOE Spreadsheet (cost, about $30) computer software program is a relatively simple approach to use for both budget projections and budget management. However, there are numerous spreadsheet software programs on the market, and most will work effectively for this vital meeting process.

Budgeting and a suggestion for projecting a preliminary budget are discussed in Chapter 5.

PHASE IV: Producing a Meeting Plan

A difficult task for the meeting amateur is the development of a meeting plan. Many people in the meeting industry do not develop a plan. They go by experience or by using guesswork. However, as the industry becomes more demanding and more sophisticated, the need and demand for plans are increasing.

There are general models, discussed in Chapter 7, in use by meeting professionals today. These are, in order of precision and sophistication from lowest to highest, (1) Checklist, (2) Gantt, (3) PERT, (4) Critical Path/PERT.

1. *Checklist.* The checklist model is the least precise of the models and has been in use, in one form or another, for years. Airlines, hotels, associations, the Convention Liaison Council, and many authors of books and manuals have published their own. There are several checklists in the appendix, but you will not find a *planning* checklist, since the emphasis here is on the more sophisticated and less familiar approach.

   There are three values of the checklist: (a) you have a "memory jogger" to make certain nothing has been omitted, (b) sections of the checklist can be given subordinates as a "job description" for a meeting, and (c) it provides the basis for determining activities for the more precise and sophisticated models.
2. *Gantt.* The Gantt model adds time of accomplishment, usually represented by a form of bar graph, to the checklist. Time intervals are usually represented on the y-axis and items (activities) to be accomplished on the x-axis.

   The Gantt adds the valuable concept of *target time* to the checklist. A planner anticipates a necessary completion date prior to the meeting and makes it visible as an ongoing memory jogger. Given to subordinates, a Gantt chart gives them both a target *and* accountability. A manager's job is thus facilitated because the subordinate has *written communication* and less grounds for quibbling if the task is not progressing or completed in the time schedule.
3. *PERT (Program Evaluation Review Technique).* PERT was developed in 1956 and adopted by the U.S. Navy for use with its missile-planning program in 1958. Today much government planning requires PERT, and corporate strategic planning sections utilize it for precise project plans in the construction, manufacturing, marketing, banking, and other industries.

   Essentially, PERT is a system calling for listing activities, sequencing activities to produce events (a completed activity), and drawing a *bubble chart.* Mathematical calculations are used to predict times for accomplishment of activities. The mathematical approach provides a higher degree of accuracy than the time projections used in Gantt.

   Another approach in meeting planning has been the use of mini-PERTs for planning of lower-level objectives, placing each on floppy disks and monitoring accomplishment of each objective on its own disk. The overall plan, however, must still be monitored, which can be done through several PERT software programs on the market.
4. *Critical Path/PERT.* Critical path/PERT is the most sophisticated of the planning models. The critical path can be computer-determined, and the entire meeting plan can be continuously monitored on terminals.

Essential details of all four models are covered in Chapter 7, as already noted. Do not expect to find the computer programs, since the programs are copyrighted. However, Chapter 16 gives a brief description of some of the software available.

PHASE V: Meeting Pattern and Agenda

Two different items are contained in this phase, and each needs definition to clarify relationships.

Meeting Pattern. The meeting pattern is the entire sequence of meeting events from arrival to departure. It encompasses check-in, hospitality and food functions, recreation and entertainment, and the general and break-out sessions. Even though it is listed first, it *cannot be accomplished until you have completed the agenda.*

Meeting Agenda. The meeting agenda is the educational, motivational, problem-solving, and business session "meat" of the meeting. A large part of the on-site success of the meeting is determined by the sessions that make up the meeting agenda.

Both the meeting pattern and the meeting agenda grow out of the meeting plan.

Normally a meeting manager or meeting administrator is not capable of performing this essential task and assigns agenda development to a person knowledgeable in adult learning theory and group communication theory.

Development of agenda content and presentation is relatively new in the meeting industry. It is the result of organizations' (particularly corporations) demands, as discussed in Chapter 1, for cost-effective meetings.

Associations may have program committees made up of people knowledgeable in content. In such situations, the meeting professional is being called on as a communication expert to guide presenters in the most effective methods for communicating their knowledge to the meeting attendees. Chapter 7 and materials contained in the bibliography (see the appendices) discuss this phase in greater detail.

Phase V is crucial to the meeting. Normally the critical path of the meeting plan will involve the agenda and usually the entire meeting pattern.

PHASE VI: Location Determination

Many times the meeting location (geographical area) is predetermined by the organization. However, when the professional has established confidence among organization executives that knowledge of how to determine the location is important, the meeting manager will gain the responsibility of selecting meeting locations.

Four factors determine a meeting location: transportation, climate, past meeting history, and facility adequacy. Chapter 8 examines various approaches valuable in making location determinations. However, *location selection should never be done until Phases I through V have been completed.* The meeting professional does not have adequate information to make a decision until these phases have been completed.

PHASE VII: Site Selection

Site selection is the most commonly thought-of portion of the meeting professional's duties and responsibilities. The site provides the communication arena for the meeting. Its facilities, services, and decor exist, for the meeting professional, for one purpose—to facilitate effective communication during the meeting.

The meeting manager needs to guard against allowing beauty, the glamorous atmosphere, or the charm of the service to distract him or her from the concept that a *facility is the communication arena, and all facilities, services, and decor exist only to further communication.*

Basically, site selection involves sleeping space, meeting space, service and accessibility, and food and beverage capability.

Sleeping Space. Although room rates are an important factor in many meeting budgets, the principle to remember is: *What you get for your money is more important than the price.*

This principle needs explanation. For instance, if you want double occupancy, does the room have two double beds or one? Most unrelated attendees do not like to sleep in the same bed. A twin double is better than a single double.

Is the room clean? Look for dirt and lint in the air conditioner vents and under the bed. Is the caulking around the tub and shower intact and is it clean? Caulking picks up mildew, which is readily visible.

If you need double occupancy, are there two sinks? Hotels tend to limit themselves to one sink per bath for economic reasons. The meeting professional needs to weigh the service and convenience for the attendee. A tight meeting pattern might require extra early wake-up calls for double-occupancy attendees if only one sink exists in the rooms and both need to do their makeup or shave before breakfast and the meeting. Many people would prefer to pay extra dollars per room night to secure double sinks for double occupancy.

Consider the amenities in the room—for instance, shampoo, deodorant and nondeodorant soap, facial tissue, shoe-polishing cloths, and a telephone in the bath area (or at least with a long-enough cord enabling the guest to place it in the bath area). If you have been shaving or putting on makeup and have been in a hurry to get to breakfast or your first session and have had to drop everything to run to the traditional telephone area by or between beds, you see the point.

Television, radio, city directories of events and entertainment, and easy-to-understand directories of hotel services are expected today.

Check the lighting. Are the light switches an electrician's prank requiring the flip of switches at a door and table or bedside, or are the switches hidden? Will applying makeup and shaving be done by the touch system? Don't be fooled by the wattage in the bath. *How that wattage is directed on the mirror user is more important.*

The hotel room has been discussed in terms of what you get for your money, but there are other services to research, usually in return for a higher rate. A large number of arrivals at one period of time may require extra desk clerks. Conversely, a heavy departure schedule may require additional cashiers. Will there be adequate bellpeople at times when your group arrives or departs? *What you get* for the price of hotel rooms should be foremost in your mind.

Meeting Space. The actual space in which the meeting is held creates the communication ambiance for the session. Is the space adequate for the room setup? *Remember:* a room is set up in terms of the type of communication you will be using in the meeting. Chapter 8 gives a chart showing square footage per person for each room setup. The chart allows for adequate fire and other emergency exit space. Meeting Planners International has a space calculator that provides less per-person space and makes hotels happy because they can get more people in a room when meeting your space needs. As the professional gains experience, judgments on space can be made more easily.

Other factors governing the meeting space are acoustics, ceiling height, wall decor and/or coloring, lighting, windows, drapes, mirrors, audiovisual capabilities, and light and temperature controls.

Service. Meeting attendees need "stroking." The knowledge and practice of human relations by owners, managers, and facility staff members is vital. Facilities as well as meeting professionals are in a service industry.

As a meeting professional, you look for the services the facility has and is willing to offer. For any writer to attempt to list all possible services is impossible, because hotel and convention people are constantly creating new and unique ideas. However, there are some fundamental services you should examine. Is transportation and/or shuttle service from air, train, or bus terminals provided without charge? If not, what is the charge? Can additional transportation be negotiated at reasonable or no cost? Interhotel and convention complex shuttles can also frequently be negotiated with convention bureaus and/or local transportation authorities.

Front desk, cashier, and bellpeople service has already been discussed. Other services are number of covers per waiter (*covers* refers to the place settings or people to be served by each waiter), kinds and types of nutrition-break foods—for instance, fresh fruit or soft ice cream—prekeying for rapid check-in, direct billing for the master account, on-site audiovisual equipment and service, and recreational facility access and charges.

Food and Beverage. Modern food preparation and storage equipment have greatly expanded hotel food-service capability. In fact, the only remaining factors that limit the hotel are how busy the property is, the creativity of the chef, the flexibility of the food and beverage policy, and the food-service space and location.

A *chef* (as differentiated from a cook) is often considered to be an important determinant for selecting a site. The reason for this is that true chefs are creative artists who can make food functions memorable occasions. Food and beverage and catering managers do not necessarily have the creative capacity of a chef. With a chef at the property, you have greater flexibility for your food functions.

Costs of food and beverage operations can have a major impact on a meeting budget. For the property, profit margins on food are minimal. Therefore, a meeting professional would be well advised to acquire a knowledge of portion control and menu development.

Hospitality functions (cocktail parties of one kind or another) provide a major profit margin for the property. The meeting manager needs to learn dram and grog (liquor) laws of the area where the property is located; that is, can partial bottles of the same brand be "married" at the end of the function? Are there corkage charges (a price charged per bottle for bottles brought into the property from outside for meeting functions)? Further, it is necessary to determine the property's policies on bartender charges and minimum consumption. What about tax and gratuities? One major property in downtown Denver, Colorado charges gratuity on taxes. They justify it by a loophole in the law. Most meeting managers abhor paying gratuity on tax, but if all other site conditions are perfect, it might be worth the money.

Accessibility. As a meeting professional, you need to examine all air and ground transportation to and from the property. A resort served by a single commuter airline and/or bus may be satisfactory for a small group, but if you have several hundred attendees, it would not be advisable unless the majority would be driving personal cars. In a major city, taxi fares of $25 and up might be prohibitive for individuals in your group. (*Remember:* Know your group.) Rental of buses could become necessary, which would impact your budget.

Traffic flow in a meeting site is frustrating to both meeting manager and hotel professionals. All too frequently hotels are designed by architects who produce a beautiful exterior facade with little thought or knowledge of the functionality of the interior.

Meeting rooms may be on several levels with limited escalator, elevator, or stairway connections. Several meeting rooms of 250-person capacity may open onto a hall space 20 feet wide. Imagine five such rooms emptying into this hallway with nutrition-break tables set up in the same area. How can 1000 people crowd into the hall, get their food, and still return to their meeting rooms during a 15-minute break?

Even worse, what about restrooms? It has been statistically established that the average turn-around time is 5 minutes for women and three minutes for men using restrooms. Suppose our hallway, described above, has a women's restroom with six stalls and a men's room with four urinals and one stall. If our 1000 people are equally divided between the sexes, simple arithmetic makes a 15-minute break an impossibility. Additional restrooms must be close and quickly accessible, or your entire meeting pattern will have to be changed.

You have been given a quick introduction to the fundamental areas of site selection, which is covered in detail by Chapter 9. This section began with a principle of communication as the key to site selection. A final summary principle of site selection is: *Never approach a site until you know all your meeting-site needs.*

PHASE VIII: On-Site Management

A meeting has been called Murphy's Law to the tenth power (if anything can go wrong, it will). On-site management has to deal with problems in order to ensure a smooth and effective meeting.

Careful attention to Phases I through VII assists the professional in anticipating and preparing for on-site problems. However, *experience* is the only consistently reliable guide both to anticipating and handling on-site problems.

Two suggestions that may be of assistance are (1) perform daily audits of the master account to save time when the meeting is over and to discover immediately any unusual charges, and (2) ensure the property has a cooperative, knowledgeable, and efficient convention-services person to work with you. Chapter 11 gives suggestions and ideas for working with on-site personnel.

Chapters 4, 5, 7, 11, and 15 give additional insights for on-site management. Appendix H has suggestions for securing accuracy of food and beverage guarantees—an on-site management problem.

PHASE IX: Postmeeting Evaluation

When a meeting manager goes to his or her superior with a meeting evaluation, the manager's job may be on the line. Evaluation is one of the most difficult tasks facing the meeting professional. Ideally, evaluations should be based upon a statistical analysis. (One meeting manager was terminated because her *opinions* differed from those of her superior and she had no solid data to back up her evaluation.) However, there are many intangible and subjective factors that affect meeting success, many not measurable by objective methods. Thus, a meeting evaluation form that permits objective evaluation *plus* space for subjective individual comment is recommended. Sometimes you may wish to determine salience as well as ambiance.

Ambiance. In this case, ambiance refers to the *attitude* or *belief* of the person completing the form.

Salience. We are referring now to the *strength* of the attitude or belief of the person completing the form.

An additional consideration is *when* to evaluate. Evaluations may be performed (1) at the end of a *session,* (2) at the end of the *meeting,* or (3) *after* the meeting by a mailed questionnaire. Evaluation is discussed in greater depth in Chapter 14.

We have now discussed the nine phases of meeting development. Diagram I illustrated how the phases create the environment surrounding an effective meeting. Each of these nine phases is presented in greater detail in the following chapters.

WHAT YOU SHOULD HAVE LEARNED FROM THIS CHAPTER

1. The nine phases of meeting development.
2. The content of each phase.
3. The interrelationships of the phases, book, CMP functions, CMP conditions, and an effective meeting (Diagram I).
4. A basic knowledge of how each of the phases is used in the development of the meeting.
5. Some guidelines and warnings about use of the phases.

REVIEW QUESTIONS

1. What are the nine phases of meeting development?
2. Relate each phase of meeting development to the functions described for the Certified Meeting Professional examination.
3. As the term is used in the book, are phases the same or different than steps?" Justify your answer.
4. What is a *primary* objective and why is it important to the success of a meeting?
5. What is the most basic principle of meeting management?

6. What are the three general models for developing a meeting plan?
7. How are an agenda and a meeting pattern different?
8. According to the chapter, a room is set up in terms of what key element of agenda success?
9. Site selection involves *four elements*. What are they?
10. What is the relationship of accessibility to destination and site selection?

Chapter 3

Group History and Analysis

This chapter will discuss three aspects of group history and analysis: (1) Why we must analyze our group, (2) what data are needed, and (3) what approaches we may take to collect group data.

Why We Must Analyze Our Group

Let's begin by asking you some questions.

1. Do all people in the medical profession have the same specialization? Do they all play handball or tennis?
2. Do all people in the legal profession watch the same television program? Are they all of the same age and sex?
3. Do you belong to an organization? Are all members of your organization of the same religious convictions? Do they all eat the same food? Do they all dance to the same style of music?

These simple questions should give you an idea of the need for the meeting manager to *know the group.*

For instance, how do you begin planning without knowing what members of your group need and want to know? How could you know whether they will attend unless you know how to create a program they would appreciate?

First, the analysis of the knowledge or skill needs of your attendees is probably most important because you cannot discover precisely how to create a program that would meet organization goals and objectives and individual knowledge levels without this information.

Second, a knowledge of the economic status of your people can be of value to you in selecting a destination for your meeting, selecting a property, and selecting menus. If attendees must pay their own expenses, then transportation, lodging, and food costs must be economically feasible for them. If, on the other hand, the organization pays all but personal expenses, the economic condition of the organization is a determining factor.

Third, political and religious preferences, educational levels, age, sex, music, food, and recreation preferences assist you in planning your meeting pattern and your agenda.

There is no need to belabor the point about the importance of a thorough knowledge of a group. You will see the importance of further data than that mentioned when we cover the kinds and extent of needed data in the next section.

Data Needed

The extent and depth of data needed before beginning your planning makes any listing incomplete because it will vary from organization to organization and possibly from meeting to meeting. You are better off having too much data than not enough. In this section, parts of the form in Appendix B on Group and Organization Analysis will be used to not only guide your thinking about the data but also to guide you toward a tabulation approach that might be utilized for computer storage.

Personal characteristics of attendees may be collected in a form similar to Table I. (*Note:* You will have to expand the spacing on the form for effective use.)

The age categories in Table I are arbitrary and may be adapted to your needs. However, you will find the categories used here do reflect characteristics of the age groups. Most young professionals fall within Category 3 (ages 26–45) and are people out to achieve and gain status. They are adventuresome and are eager for new ideas and approaches to aid them in their searches for success.

Category 4 (ages 46–65) are those who have gained a degree of success and have become more conservative. Security and ways to protect their achievements and status are important.

Category 5 (ages over 65) represent successful people ready to retire or already retired. They are more conservative and frequently suggest that they worry about the younger generation and where the young are leading the world and the organization. Their tastes in music are different and many are on low-cholesterol diets. Food is important. See Table II.

As you can see, Table II on food preference is longer than Table I but still not complete. However, collection of such data, with lettered or numbered

TABLE I PERSONAL ATTENDEE DATA: AGE

Category	No. of Males	No. of Females	Total Number
1. Under 18	____	____	____
2. 19–25	____	____	____
3. 26–45	____	____	____
4. 46–65	____	____	____
5. Over 65	____	____	____

TABLE II PERSONAL ATTENDEE DATA: FOOD PREFERENCES

Category	No. of Males	No. of Females	Total Number
1. Breakfasts			
Continental	____	____	____
Dietetic	____	____	____
Eggs and meat	____	____	____
Hotcakes/waffles	____	____	____
Gourmet (croissants, pastries, etc.)	____	____	____
Vegetarian	____	____	____
Kosher	____	____	____
Dislikes	____	____	____
	____	____	____
2. Lunches			
Salads	____	____	____
Sandwiches	____	____	____
Fruit	____	____	____
Substantial (meat, potatoes, etc.)	____	____	____
Dietetic	____	____	____
Vegetarian	____	____	____
Kosher	____	____	____
Dislikes	____	____	____
	____	____	____
3. Dinners			
Fish	____	____	____
Ham	____	____	____
Beef	____	____	____
Lamb	____	____	____
Poultry	____	____	____
Shellfish	____	____	____
Vegetables			
Corn	____	____	____
Peas	____	____	____
Beans	____	____	____
Carrots	____	____	____
Beets	____	____	____
Cauliflower	____	____	____
Broccoli	____	____	____
Desserts			
Ice cream	____	____	____
Fruit pies	____	____	____
Cream pies	____	____	____
Cakes	____	____	____
Mousse	____	____	____
Custards	____	____	____
Fresh fruit	____	____	____
Cheeses	____	____	____
Dietetic	____	____	____
Vegetarian	____	____	____
Kosher	____	____	____
Dislikes	____	____	____
	____	____	____

(continued)

TABLE II *(Continued)*

Category	No. of Males	No. of Females	Total Number
Nutrition breaks			
Beverages			
Coffee	_____	_____	_____
Decaffeinated coffee	_____	_____	_____
Iced coffee	_____	_____	_____
Tea			
Iced	_____	_____	_____
Hot	_____	_____	_____
Soft drinks			
Regular	_____	_____	_____
Diet	_____	_____	_____
Food			
Sweet rolls	_____	_____	_____
Toast	_____	_____	_____
Vegetables	_____	_____	_____
Chips	_____	_____	_____
Soft ice cream	_____	_____	_____
Fruit cocktail (fresh)	_____	_____	_____
Fresh fruit	_____	_____	_____
Other			
__________	_____	_____	_____
__________	_____	_____	_____
Dislikes			
__________	_____	_____	_____
__________	_____	_____	_____

subpoints, can be entered into a computer and later shared with a chef. Such information can be a valuable asset in menu planning as well as in negotiating food functions.

Another table, equally long, could be developed for hospitality functions and cover alcoholic and nonalcoholic beverages.

There are, of course, other general preferences that may be included. You should note that some of these data can be used in planning activities for families or companions. After securing data on meeting attendees from several organizations, a comparison of the findings is interesting and frequently startling. In all cases these data are extremely valuable in planning meeting patterns and agendas, especially when the data are related to data from Table IV on geographical backgrounds.

Table IV provides invaluable data for travel arrangements, the need for interpreters and simultaneous translation (an item not found in many continental United States properties although common in other countries), a guide for times to start and terminate your meetings, and, finally, information on geographical differences you might anticipate.

America's highly mobile population has tended to eliminate many geographical differences. However, there are still noticeable characteristics. For example, East Coast residents tend to be more formal in both dress and behavior than do the casual West Coast inhabitants. People from predominantly agricultural areas have a greater tendency toward conservatism than do urban people.

As the meeting professional becomes more familiar with his or her orga-

TABLE III PERSONAL ATTENDEE DATA: GENERAL PREFERENCES

Category	No. of Males	No. of Females	Total Number
1. Music			
Classical	_____	_____	_____
Semiclassical	_____	_____	_____
Pop	_____	_____	_____
Rock	_____	_____	_____
Hard rock	_____	_____	_____
Disco	_____	_____	_____
Country and western	_____	_____	_____
Ballroom	_____	_____	_____
Dislikes			
__________	_____	_____	_____
__________	_____	_____	_____
2. Recreation			
Team sports			
__________	_____	_____	_____
__________	_____	_____	_____
Individual sports			
Golf	_____	_____	_____
Tennis	_____	_____	_____
Swimming	_____	_____	_____
Racquetball	_____	_____	_____
Handball	_____	_____	_____
Shuffleboard	_____	_____	_____
Skiing	_____	_____	_____
Fishing	_____	_____	_____
Sailing	_____	_____	_____
Other			
__________	_____	_____	_____
__________	_____	_____	_____
3. Political			
Democrat	_____	_____	_____
Independent	_____	_____	_____
Libertarian	_____	_____	_____
Republican	_____	_____	_____
Other			
__________	_____	_____	_____
__________	_____	_____	_____
4. Speaker			
Humorous	_____	_____	_____
Motivational	_____	_____	_____
Subject content	_____	_____	_____
Other			
__________	_____	_____	_____
__________	_____	_____	_____
5. Religious			
Agnostic	_____	_____	_____
Atheist	_____	_____	_____
Catholic	_____	_____	_____
Fundamentalist	_____	_____	_____
Jewish	_____	_____	_____

(continued)

TABLE III *(Continued)*

Category	No. of Males	No. of Females	Total Number
Protestant	_____	_____	_____
Other			
__________	_____	_____	_____
__________	_____	_____	_____
6. Tours			
Historical	_____	_____	_____
Landscape	_____	_____	_____
Museum	_____	_____	_____
Hiking	_____	_____	_____
Jeep	_____	_____	_____
Shopping	_____	_____	_____
River rafting	_____	_____	_____
Other tours			
__________	_____	_____	_____
__________	_____	_____	_____
7. Cultural			
Musical concerts	_____	_____	_____
Painting	_____	_____	_____
Sculpture	_____	_____	_____
Theatre	_____	_____	_____
Other			
__________	_____	_____	_____
__________	_____	_____	_____

nization, other geographical differences peculiar to the group may appear. If the organization has geographical administrative units, such as chapters or regional offices, the data collected may serve as a basis for on-site competition among regions.

Finally, a geographical analysis can provide an essential tool for determining travel factors for both budgeting and location selection. Applications of the use of these data can be found in Chapters 5 and 9.

Individual preferences, characteristics, and geographical location are but one-half of the knowledge the meeting planner needs. The other half relates to the history and policies of the organization for whom the planner works. Table V gives three types of data inputs: (1) a history of the organizations's meetings, (2) a guide to destination selection (because the organization probably does not wish to repeat a destination for several years), and (3) a guide to the value of maintaining an accurate history of previous meetings for use in planning future meetings.

Rather than extend Table V, we list some additional items you may wish to consider when you collect data on previous meetings: registration area size, registration tables, registration equipment, registration personnel used, interpreters, simultaneous translators, buses used for shuttle and tours, ground operators used (with phone numbers and addresses plus evaluative comments), and convention bureau personnel used (plus comments). The list could continue on but will depend on you and the meeting(s) you will be planning and managing.

Although Table V is extensive and could be expanded, there is one area

TABLE IV PERSONAL ATTENDEE DATA: GENERAL GEOGRAPHICAL DATA

Category	No. of Males	No. of Females	Total Number
1. Home residence			
Urban	____	____	____
Small city (under 50,000)	____	____	____
Rural	____	____	____
Suburban	____	____	____
2. Home point of origin			
United States			
East Coast	____	____	____
Northeast	____	____	____
Southeast	____	____	____
Midwest	____	____	____
Rocky Mountain	____	____	____
Southwest	____	____	____
West Coast	____	____	____
Alaska	____	____	____
Hawaii	____	____	____
Puerto Rico	____	____	____
European country			
__________	____	____	____
__________	____	____	____
__________	____	____	____
Middle Eastern country			
__________	____	____	____
__________	____	____	____
African country			
__________	____	____	____
__________	____	____	____
Central/Latin American/Caribbean country			
Mexico	____	____	____
__________	____	____	____
__________	____	____	____
Asian country			
Japan	____	____	____
China	____	____	____
Taiwan	____	____	____
__________	____	____	____
Australia	____	____	____
New Zealand	____	____	____

about which no table can ever provide information, and yet it is an area no meeting manager can ignore. That area is *organization policy.*

Organizations are as different in policy as they are diverse in product, purpose, membership, and title. The meeting professional must be aware of these policies because they impact almost every aspect of the meeting from location to program content. One problem might involve corporate dress policies. For example, one publishing firm expected completely casual attire for all sessions except hospitality and evening dinners. Another publishing firm, meeting in the same location and property, required suits and ties for men and

TABLE V ORGANIZATION DATA: PREVIOUS MEETINGS

Organization: ______________________ Address: ______________________

____ Phone: __________

1. General data
   a. Location and sites of previous two meetings (include evaluative notes)
   b. Length of previous two meetings (days/nights)
   c. Decision maker: (Give name, title, phone number)
   d. Committees: _____ used _____ not used
      (Give committee names and chairperson names.)
   e. Methods of evaluation used
   f. Transportation to site (Who paid costs—organization, individual, combination? Were group rates used? What percent of meeting budget was used for transportation of attendees, meeting staff, executives, shipping, and freight?)
   g. How far in advance were
      Meetings scheduled: ______________________
      Meetings planned: ______________________
      Sites selected: ______________________
2. Objectives of the meeting (list for each meeting)
3. Attendance
   a. Preregistered
      (i) General sessions
      (ii) Break-out sessions
      (iii) Companions
      (iv) Entertainment
      (v) Food functions
         (a) Breakfasts
         (b) Lunches
         (c) Dinners
         (d) Banquets
      (vi) Hospitality functions
      (vii) Recreation
      (viii) Tours
      (ix) Premeeting events
      (x) Postmeeting events
   b. Walk-in (on-site) registration
      (i) General sessions
      (ii) Break-out sessions
      (iii) Companions
      (iv) Entertainment
      (v) Food functions
         (a) Breakfasts
         (b) Lunches
         (c) Dinners
         (d) Banquets
      (vi) Hospitality functions
      (vii) Recreation
      (viii) Tours
      (ix) Premeeting events
      (x) Postmeeting events
   c. Average age
   d. Sex: male _____ female _____

(continued)

TABLE V (*Continued*)

Organization: ______________________ Address: ______________________
____ Phone: ____________

4. Equipment used
   a. Audiovisual

Types	Number
_____	_____

   b. Office equipment

Typewriters	_____	Telephones	_____
Reproduction	_____	Beepers	_____
Paper (reams)	_____	Walkie-talkie	_____
Carbon	_____	Recorders	_____
Pens	_____	Computers	_____
Pencils	_____	Name badges	_____
__________	_____	__________	_____

5. Facilities used

		Cost
Sleeping rooms		Cost
Singles	_____	_____
Doubles	_____	_____
Queen suites	_____	_____
King suites	_____	_____
Parlors	_____	_____
Meeting rooms		Cost
Break-outs	_____	_____
General session	_____	_____
Food functions	_____	_____

6. Group
   Special likes
   Special dislikes
   Special characteristics
7. Attach policy data

suits (with skirts) for women during all sessions, except after all scheduled day and evening sessions had been completed or for recreation events. Both groups had planned recreation events, so the meeting pattern required time to change clothes for the second group. Needless to say, when the policy of the second group became known, there was a scramble to realign the meeting pattern in order to allow such time.

Although this example involved a minor problem, the meeting manager who violates a basic organization policy (or crosses a chief executive officer's personal code) may be immediately seeking new employment.

There are no universally usable forms to determine policies. However, as a guide, it is suggested you should examine the organizations's bylaws, particularly under the article or section dealing with *purposes*. This can be followed by interviews with your superiors. In some cases, your study of previous meeting histories may raise some questions concerning why such functions took place. As a final suggestion, when you have completed your meeting pattern, have it reviewed by your immediate superiors, and have them *initial* the written pattern as *approved*.

When you have worked with an organization for a year, you should know the policies. However, it is still a good idea to (1) have a written statement of the policies as a reference and (2) have the meeting pattern approved.

After—and only after—you have collected all possible data and stored them in a computer you are ready to begin the planning of the meeting. But, how do you approach collection of so much information? The next section of this chapter addresses that problem.

Approaches to Data Collection

Undoubtedly a major reason many meeting managers don't collect adequate data on their groups, although they say "knowing your group" is important, is that group data collection seems a difficult and time-consuming task. It can be difficult and it can be time-consuming if you don't approach it in an organized manner. This section covers some helpful approaches and an approach you may want to avoid.

Questionnaires. Questionnaires can be developed using techniques similar to those of Tables I through V but adapted to your organization. When a cover letter is included indicating you are asking the respondents' help in developing a meeting that meets their needs and that will be both enjoyable and profitable, you will be amazed at the high number of responses. (A survey of one organization of 12,000 members generated 5600 responses. Evaluations of the meeting showed significantly higher appreciation and effectiveness ratings than any previous meeting.)

A questionnaire permits respondents to remain anonymous while feeling they are a valuable part of the organization. There are two keys to getting a good response: (1) the cover letter, which must have a strong appeal, and (2) a simple questionnaire requiring no more than minimal effort checking responses. Also, the tables in this chapter are only examples. You need to leave more space when developing your questionnaire. Items must be spaced in such a way that *visually* the respondent does not feel it is going to take much time or effort.

You might want to consider, though it may increase costs, writing a preliminary letter to each potential respondent and asking their participation by returning a stamped postcard. Questionnaires are then mailed only to those who returned the cards. Still another consideration would be the use of sampling techniques, where you mail to a statistically valid sample. Most books on market research give relatively simple equations to use in computing sizes and types of samples.

Interviews. The interview approach does not generally give a valid sample and is very costly in terms of the amount of your time involved. Any interview should be approached with a questionnaire in your possession so that you cover the same questions with all interviewees. It is often preferable to use the interview with organization executives only—and only those executives who can supply information on policy or information to assist in developing objectives.

Under no circumstances should telephone interviews be used. There are two reasons: (1) People are being buried under a deluge of telemarketing phone calls asking for a "few minutes of their time," which usually ends up being many minutes. (2) There is an attitude developing that phone interviews are an invasion of privacy. Attitudes toward your meeting may be clouded by placing it in the category of the telemarketing survey. The telephone interview is the approach you may want to avoid.

Analysis of Previous Meeting Data. If you are fortunate enough to follow a meeting professional who collected and stored data on previous meetings, including evaluation results, your work is reduced significantly. You will need to use questionnaires to survey only new members who have joined since the last meeting. In fact, you might not need to do this if the membership application form has adequate data and the forms have been stored—preferably in a computer.

Computer Searches. A computer search is the fastest and usually the most effective approach. If previous data are in the computer, you need to learn only how to access the data. However, if you are starting data collection for the first time, you need to develop data-collection and data-storage formats compatible with the software available to you in the organization. Chapter 15, "Computers and Meeting Management," should be of assistance in identifying software that will work for your needs or in purchasing software to meet your computer needs.

WHAT YOU SHOULD HAVE LEARNED FROM THIS CHAPTER

1. The importance of securing and analyzing data on your group, your organization, and on previous meetings.
2. The types of attendee data you need to collect:
   a. Personal
   b. Preferences
   c. Geographic and demographic
   d. Organizational
3. The kind of previous meeting data you need to collect.
4. The importance and types of data on organization policy.
5. Approaches to collecting data.
6. The application of collected data to the planning and management process.

REVIEW QUESTIONS

1. Why are group history and analysis important to effective meeting management?
2. How may a knowledge of attendee geographical data aid a meeting manager?
3. How does organization policy influence meeting planning?
4. Even though you have worked with an organization for a year or more, the chapter suggests the meeting manager should have two things in hand before going ahead with the meeting. What are they?
5. What are the four approaches a meeting manager may use in data collection?
6. What kind of previous meeting data should be collected?
7. Chapter 3 provided a checklist for kinds of previous meeting data. How-

ever, it said there are "other" types of data you might wish to collect. What are those additional data items?

8. How do you believe a knowledge of individual recreation preferences of attendees can be of value to a meeting manager? Be as specific as possible.
9. How would you use economic data on your group in planning a meeting?
10. What kind of group data should you collect?

APPLICATION EXERCISES

(Results gained from these exercises should be shared with others to provide comparisons and greater insight.)

1. If you are in a class or seminar, select *one* of the attendee forms, Tables II through IV, and use it to analyze members of the class or seminar. Then, analyze the data you have collected to determine: (a) What kinds of food you would serve the group, (b) what kinds of entertainment you would provide for the group, and (c) what kind of recreation you would provide for the group. Present your results and analysis for comparative discussion with other members of the group.
2. If you are not in a class, select an organization to which you belong and then use one or more of the forms in Tables II through IV, and analyze a cross section (sample) of the organization to determine the kinds of food, recreation, and speakers you would provide for a meeting of the organization.

Chapter 4

Establishing, Writing, and Organizing Objectives

Chapter 4 deals with the second most fundamental aspect of planning an effective meeting (knowing your group is first)—establishing objectives.

In this chapter we will begin with the question, Why should goals, purposes, and objectives be identified and written? Then we consider definitions and examples. However, since goals, purposes, and objectives have little value to a meeting manager until they are systematically organized, we give an approach to organizing called an *objective tree,* which has the additional value of establishing a basis for constructing a Gantt or PERT, covered in detail in Chapter 6, "Models for Developing Meeting Plans." Also, in this chapter, we will begin to use a hypothetical meeting from Appendix C.

Why Should Goals, Purposes, and Objectives Be Identified and Written?

You have all seen an organizational chart that shows the boss at the top and two, three, or more subordinates in boxes below the boss. Establishment of goals, purposes, and objectives is the first step in making that chart work. They provide for orderly development and management of the organization and, for us, the planning and management of a meeting. They indicate, by means of statements, what is expected from everyone involved and supply the basis for measurement and evaluation of what is achieved.

Additionally, goals, purposes, and objectives help overcome typical management problems. For example:

1. They enhance the possibility of coordinated effort and teamwork.
2. They provide a means of measuring the true contribution of ideas and people.

3. They help define the major areas of responsibilities and tasks (job descriptions).
4. They provide a basis for the process of achieving results desired for the organization, the meeting, and the individuals involved.
5. They provide guidelines for delegation of *tasks* to subordinates during the planning, programming, and managing aspects of the meeting. (*Remember:* Responsibility is yours as the meeting manager and cannot be delegated.)

Admittedly, the writing of goals, purposes, and objectives is not an easy task until you gain practice and experience. However, once you master the art, the results are well worth your effort. This book, as you will discover, will give you practice both in writing and then in using objectives in planning, programming, managing, and evaluating.

A case study of an actual situation (modified to protect those involved) will provide you an example-answer to the question, Why should goals, purposes, and objectives be identified and written?

Case Study: A Chapter of a Professional Organization

1. New officers and board members are elected.
2. The new president gives a speech indicating his or her course of action for the year.
3. The chapter and national bylaws state the organization's educational purpose.
4. A program chairman is appointed for the year.
5. The program chairman decides upon a series of speaker programs based upon whom the chairman has heard are good speakers on subjects related to the organization.
6. The meeting pattern is: program, cocktails, dinner.
7. Officers and board members have a preprogram meeting to conduct chapter business and solve problems that may have developed.
8. The board meetings usually run overtime, so the board adjourns for cocktails rather than interrupt the program by walking in late.
9. Members discover the board is having cocktails rather than attending the program and join the board in the bar.
10. Program attendance dwindles to a few dedicated professionals who really want to learn something.
11. Programs are limited to one hour, in order not to delay cocktails and dinner being served by a property—regardless of the speaker's subject.
12. Evaluations show the membership feels they get little except socializing and business contacts for their membership dollars.

Of course, you can see many things wrong with this case. Let us examine the case under the microscope of a meeting professional.

CASE ANALYSIS

1. The new president probably did not set a *goal* for the year. (The usual explanation is a *theme* that, though needed, does not set a clear direction for the organization.)
2. The bylaws set a purpose of *education*. Education is designed to meet

identified needs. The case seems to indicate no organized attempt was made to identify *current* needs of the chapter membership. (It was probably done by the divine inspiration of the program chairman or officers.)

3. The officers, board members, and program chairman apparently shirked their responsibilities as follows:
   a. They failed to provide clear objectives for the program chairman.
   b. The program chairman did not bother to write related objectives for each program. (The speakers would have enjoyed knowing why and for what purpose they were being asked to speak.)
   c. The program chairman apparently selected speakers by hearsay rather than having made an effort to personally hear the speakers or listen to a cassette recording of their presentations.
   d. The programs were not designed to meet measurable objectives based on identified *current* needs of the membership.
   e. They did not establish a meeting pattern that was realistic in terms of time allocations.
   f. They did not establish board meetings at a reasonable time—earlier or on a different day—or have a rule for a time of adjournment or to recess until after the program and dinner.
   g. The executive director of the chapter, if it has one, or the management company, if such was used, was not consulted or failed to provide the necessary needs assessment and advice.
   h. The chapter needs a meeting professional who can set up meetings clearly designed to accomplish the organization's purpose.

Underlying the identified problems in the case study is a lack of knowledgeable use of effective management techniques. Obviously a major portion of the problems identified stem from the officers and board members. Planning, if any, was done very casually. There was little *thinking* performed in systematically selecting courses of action and possible outcomes for monthly meetings. Provision for solution-choice was not made, and most importantly, goals, purposes, and objectives were not clearly identified, specified in writing, and communicated.

This is a case of poor management. Planning and specifying goals, purposes, and objectives are inherent elements of management. But, you must also recognize that officers and board members who volunteer their services to an organization, while excellent managers on their jobs, frequently do not carry this competence over to the organization. Further, many individuals covet the titles for their own egos or for use on their résumés.

A meeting professional needs to recognize these human failings and plan to overcome them. This understanding and the use of planning is the *art* of the profession. Anticipatory decision making, the thinking process, and provision for solution-choice are covered under the planning models in Chapter 7.

Definition and Examples of Goals, Purposes, and Objectives

Goals. Goals, as stated in Chapter 2, are long-range and may be projected from 1 to 50 years or more in the future. A goal for a corporate sales training meeting might be

> To provide the information necessary for accomplishment of salesperson motivation to produce a sales volume increase of 5 percent per year for the next three years, or,

> To provide an understanding of company policy and problems so sales personnel feel involved in the company to the point where sales force attrition is reduced to 3%.

The president and board, in our case study, might have given a one-year direction to the chapter by providing a goal like this:

> To develop a series of enlightenment-motivational meetings to aid chapter members in better professional performance of their data-management duties.

Such a goal would specify a series of meetings with a clear purpose of *enlightening* and/or *motivating*. Most importantly, it targets one subject area, data management, for the meetings. (This, of course, would have been based upon analysis of group needs.)

Purposes. Once a goal has been established, we look at *purposes*. Purposes are usually more specific than goals and are frequently incorporated into both goals and objectives. In the preceding case study goal, the word enlightenment and motivation are the words identifying purpose.

Purposes are related to the *impact* of the meeting and meeting content *on the attendees*. Meeting purposes, directed toward the impact on the attendee rather than the intent of the planner/programmer, are

1. To secure enlightenment
2. To secure belief
3. To solve problems
4. To secure motivation
5. To secure enjoyment
6. To influence behavior

Enlightenment. The primary concern of enlightenment is that the attendees will have more *usable* knowledge about a subject *after* the meeting than they had *before* the meeting. To accomplish such a purpose the programmer must have a knowledge of the information level already possessed by the attendees—knowing the group. (Refer to Chapter 3 and the methods of data collection.)

Belief. Attendees must accept and acknowledge as correct the concepts and/or information presented during the meeting. The meeting professional must have an accurate premeeting assessment of attitudes and beliefs to program a meeting (or speaker) to accomplish this purpose—again, knowing your group. (Refer to Chapter 3.)

Problem Solving. Whether the focus is on a single problem or single or multiple solutions to multiple problems depends on the organization's and/or executives' policies. Problem solving affords the meeting programmer numerous alternatives in terms of approaches and techniques and gets the attendees *involved* usually to a greater extent than the other purposes. The meeting professional needs a thorough background in problem-solving techniques best found in communication and management publications.

Motivation. "Let's turn them on." This purpose directs itself toward getting the attendee intellectually and emotionally aroused so that he or she leaves the meeting ready and willing to accomplish the tasks selected by the organization policymakers.

Enjoyment. This is the clearest of the purposes cited, but many times it is one of the most difficult to accomplish because so many little things can interfere. For instance, a poor travel connection, a delay in registering at the meeting hotel, or a noncommunicative bellperson can all get a meeting off on a bad note that cannot be overcome, so the "enjoyment" purpose is defeated at the very beginning of the meeting.

Properly done, any meeting should be enjoyable to some degree. Therefore, most meetings produced by a professional will list enjoyment not as a primary purpose but as a joint purpose with another purpose such as enlightenment or belief.

Influence Behavior. This purpose is inherent in all the other purposes, although it is usually not identified because it smacks of manipulation. When influencing behavior is identified, it is in sales or motivational meetings with a format of getting attendees to lose their inhibitions.

Communication itself is generally for purposes of influencing behavior and, therefore, should appear in all meetings, as we discovered in the introduction to this book.

Returning to our case study, the officers and board members could have given guidelines for the program chairman by specifying a number of meetings for each of several purposes. This would have been a good management technique because it would have provided a continuity to the programs and would have placed more accountability on the program chairman.

Objectives

Objectives are short-range, apply to the immediate meeting, and may cover planning, management, or the *program*. Program objectives are slightly different than planning or management objectives and will be covered in Chapter 7, "Programming: Agenda and Meeting Pattern."

Guidelines for Writing Objectives. The following ground rules will aid in the writing of objectives. A given objective does not necessarily have to conform to all the criteria. However, be absolutely certain that your situation really permits you to bypass a guideline.

Remember *simplicity* is the key to well-stated objectives. Also, a good objective does not have to be defensible in the eyes of all who see it—just those who must approve it or use it.

The Characteristics of Good Objectives

A. Objectives should relate to the job to be done.

B. Objectives should *always* be written. (This prevents problems, since there is a point of reference that cannot be disputed.)

C. Objectives must be measurable. (This provides for postevaluation that is meaningful.)

D. Objectives must consider *all* organizational variables, including personnel—particularly supervisors.

E. Objectives should serve as guides to action in planning and management.

How to Write Good Objectives

1. Objectives should start with the word *to* followed by an *action* verb (an infinitive).

   Examples: To enlighten, to produce, to achieve

2. Objectives should specify a single key result.

   Examples: To increase sales 3%. To produce higher job evaluations for members. To create four new markets for the corporation. To achieve a 5% membership increase.

3. Objectives should specify a target date for completion (as with a PERT Chart).
   Examples: To increase sales by 3% not later than January 1 of the new fiscal year. To increase membership 5% by July 1 of this membership year. To produce a gross sales volume of $50 million in fiscal year 19—.
4. Objectives should specify maximum cost factors (labor hours, dollars, materials).
   Examples: To plan a sales meeting by November 15 at a planning cost not to exceed $50,000. To complete planning of meeting space requirements using 5.4 worker days by September 3, 19—. To project a meeting budget by August 4, using two worker days and the in-house mainframe computer.
5. Objectives must be specific and measurable.
   Examples: To secure a sales increase of 3% one year after completion of the meeting. To secure salary increases for members that average 1.5% above the average of the year 19—. To conduct three site inspections by August 1, 19—, at a cost of $2500.
6. Objectives should specify *only* the "what" and "when." (Avoid "why" and "how" because they lead to disputes.)
   Examples: *Did you catch the mistake in Guideline 4, which said "using two worker days and the in-house mainframe computer"?* By stating *how,* you limit yourself in alternatives in the event you discover a new or different way. Do the other examples have errors?
7. Objectives should relate directly to the accountable manager's role and to higher-echelon missions, purposes, and objectives.
   Examples: The sales increase of 3% *must* relate to organization marketing goals. Or, the membership increase must conform to the organization's policy. Our case study could well have such an objective for the chapter *if* it did not come at the expense of quality programs.
8. Objectives must be easily understood by those who have to contribute to their accomplishment.
   Examples: Facilitators, custodians, managers, part-time help, and so on. You may have a variety of educational levels, and this must be kept in mind when writing.
9. Objectives must be realistic and attainable.
   Examples: Is the 1.5% salary increase above average realistic? Do you think the membership could really achieve this, given possible economic fluctuations? *The best principle here is to be fair but make it a challenge.*
10. Objectives should avoid dual accountability for achievement when more than one person is involved in accomplishing the objective.
   Examples: Do you think two committees can effectively be responsible for planning one dinner? What about two people responsible for planning one program and ending up with two program groups or speakers showing up? Can you imagine the arguments? Or, can you imagine one person leaving the job to the other when the second person thought the first would do it? Laugh if you will, but it happens all too frequently when there is no statement of responsibility in the objective.
11. Objectives should be recorded in writing; copies should be made and re-

ferred to periodically by you and the staff. This guideline is the *communication* guideline, which is so essential.

Examples: We have all been members of groups where something is decided and then we never come back to it until it is too late to accomplish it. As a manager, guard against procrastination in both yourself and others; a good *written* objective helps.

Testing Objectives

Example Objective

To spend a maximum of $42,000 to motivate publisher representatives at a 3-day session to produce a 5% sales volume increase during fiscal 19— by enlightening them about six newly published books designed for a new market.

Tests for Evaluating Objectives

Apply these tests to this example objective.

1. Is the objective statement constructed properly? To (action verb) (single key result) by (target date) at (cost).
2. Is the objective measurable?
3. Does it relate to the manager's roles and mission and to higher-level roles, missions, and objectives?
4. Can it be easily understood by those who must implement it?
5. Is the objective a realistic and attainable one that still represents a challenge? (The example objective presents a problem since you're not familiar with the company or the situation; but *yes,* it did present a challenge and it was accomplished.)
6. Will the result, when achieved, justify the expenditure of time and resources required to achieve it?
7. Is the objective consistent with basic company and organization policies and practices?
8. Can the accountability for final results be clearly established?

Now that we have a background understanding of goals, purposes, and objectives, it is time to examine a process of organizing them in such a way that we can use them effectively in planning and management. The system we'll use is called an *objective tree.*

Developing an Objective Tree

Objective Tree Defined

An objective tree is the following:

1. A process to provide the planner a means of determining if all feasible objectives for a given meeting have been anticipated.
2. A thinking process that systematically determines targets for accomplishment in the course of planning a meeting.
3. A visual process that graphically relates objectives to each other.

Use the following steps to approach the objective tree process:

1. Develop a *primary* objective. (The primary objective, when accomplished, means the meeting has succeeded.) The example objectives given in the preceding section are the kind used as *primary objectives. Note:* Many people prefer to use the term *first-level* objective. Either term is acceptable.
2. Develop secondary (second-level) objectives. These are the major categories involved in meeting planning. Turn to the part of Appendix D titled "Planning Checklist." You will note that there are major categories of planning, with each identified by a roman numeral—for example, Administration, Food and Beverage, Space Requirements, Program, and Transportation.

   All these major categories may serve as secondary objectives (second-level). However, for *management* reasons, it is preferable to have only *one* secondary objective. Administration is a good secondary objective. This will permit you, if a staff is used, to indicate that *all* planning done by others *must* flow through you so that you have the final check and approval of their work. Even when working alone, use Administration as your secondary objective so that you will have to double-check all your work. *However, many meeting managers use all the categories as secondary.* This is permissible, since an objective tree *must* fit the individual manager and the meeting situation. You should feel free to use the system that works most effectively for you.
3. Develop tertiary (third-level) objectives. Again refer to Appendix D. The items shown on the checklist under the major categories will serve as a source for third-level objectives. In order to distinguish the most important objectives that should be third-level rather than fourth-, fifth-, or sixth-level, write an objective for each item in the checklist and then arrange them through "mind geometry," as explained in the following section. Also, look at each item and ask yourself "*how* will I be able to do this or accomplish this or *what* must I do to accomplish this?"

   When you ask yourself these questions you will discover that some items cannot be done until you have done something else first. If you cannot do or plan something until something else is done first, that which you cannot do until something else is done is a *higher-level* objective. For instance, you can't go to work until you are dressed. Thus, going to work is a higher level than getting dressed.

   An example from the checklist is budget approval. Before you can have a budget you must have a preliminary budget, a final budget, and an accounting system. Thus, "budget approval" could be a third-level objective, whereas "final budget" would be fourth-level and "preliminary budget" and "accounting" would be fifth-level objectives. (Note that "administration" is a secondary, or second-level, objective in this example.)
4. Develop all necessary fourth-, fifth-, or sixth-level objectives using the checklist or your experience for ideas.

Are You Confused?

The problem people encounter with the objective tree is that they forget the idea of a *tree*. The lower levels of objectives may be compared to the roots of a tree. As the tree grows, it is fed by the roots. Thus, when we reach the crown of the tree we have the roots, the trunk, the branches, and—finally—the crown. The crown may be compared to the primary objective, the trunk and branches to second- and third-level objectives, and the roots to the lower-level objectives. As with a tree, you can't have a crown until you have roots, a trunk, and branches.

Now that you understand the concept, let's see if we can build an objective tree.

Constructing the Objective Tree

1. Develop a *set* of objectives:
   a. From previous meetings
   b. From scratch using a checklist
   c. From group brainstorming
   Warning! Do not restrict yourself by trying to see relationships such as rank or time.
2. Write the objectives on 3-by-5-inch cards, one to a card.
3. Place the cards on a cork board, wall, or wherever you can sit back and *look*.
4. Use "mind geometry." Arrange and rearrange the cards until they fall into a logical order for you. When you are done you should have something that looks like this:

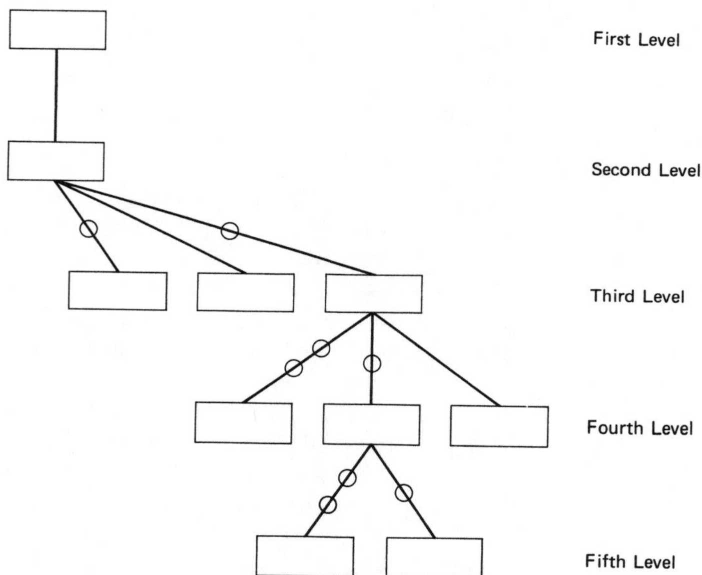

Your objective trees will probably have many more second-, third-, fourth-, fifth-, and sixth-level objectives and occupy much more space.

Many planners color code the objectives by *level* for quick identification. *Barriers* may also be color coded.

5. When gaps are discovered in your tree, you will have to create new objectives.
6. The more levels you get, the more detail you will have anticipated.

7. After completing the tree, start at the bottom and ask "why?" You may discover *unnecessary* objectives.
8. Put in *barriers* to each objective as you visualize them. *Barriers are circumstances or events that might prevent you from accomplishing an objective.* For instance, a speaker shows up intoxicated (it has happened). Or, an airline strike might cause you to reroute several attendees. By anticipating barriers you can help prevent Murphy's Law from striking so frequently. Also, the more experience you get, the more barriers you will be able to anticipate, thus helping you to preplan alternatives.
9. Put in hints for *barrier solution.*
10. Photograph or draw the tree you have created. This permits the tree to:
    a. Have semipermanence,
    b. Be communicated to others, and
    c. Serve as a ready reference when applying it to the planning design for this meeting.

Although some planners believe the creation of an objective tree requires considerable time and effort, the trade-off when selecting and implementing a planning model for a meeting will become apparent. Some of you may be old enough to remember when teachers became very upset at the idea of using lesson plans, audiovisual, and television as aids for effective teaching. Now these aids have proved themselves and are readily accepted and used.

Applying the Theory to Corporate Meeting 1, Appendix C

We can see that Meeting 1 is a regional meeting, which will cut down on transportation costs and help our meeting schedule, since there won't be major time differences for departures from points of origin. We have been given purpose, goal, destination, and dates as well as the food and beverage functions. There is one transportation problem. Organizations, particularly corporations, do not like to have their VIPs on one flight, so we know we'll have to arrange separate flights; there is no reason however, that executives cannot travel on flights with sales personnel. We know we begin planning *a minimum* of six months before the meeting and preferably even sooner.

As we begin, we immediately become concerned with *times* and *costs*. Because we are in the preliminary stages, we can leave target dates and costs as blanks when writing our objectives. (These will be filled in after completing the meeting plan by dates and costs discovered through the Gantt or PERT, which is done later.)

Primary Objective (1)

To plan a three-day meeting by (date) to enlighten and motivate sales personnel to produce $1 million in new-book gross sales in one year following completion of the meeting at a meeting cost of $__________.

Secondary (Second-Level) Objective (2)

To develop a plan by (date) to administer the planning, budgeting, transportation, space, programming, and food and beverage for a three-day meeting in Denver, Colorado, February 19—, at a cost not to exceed $__________.

Tertiary (Third-Level) Objectives (3a, 3b, 3c, 3d, 3e, 3f)

Write the third-level objectives based on what you have been given in the secondary (second-level) objective (planning, budgeting, transportation, space, programming, and food and beverage).

Now, create an objective tree from the preceding objectives. (*Note:* The numbers in the boxes correspond to numbers by the objectives.)

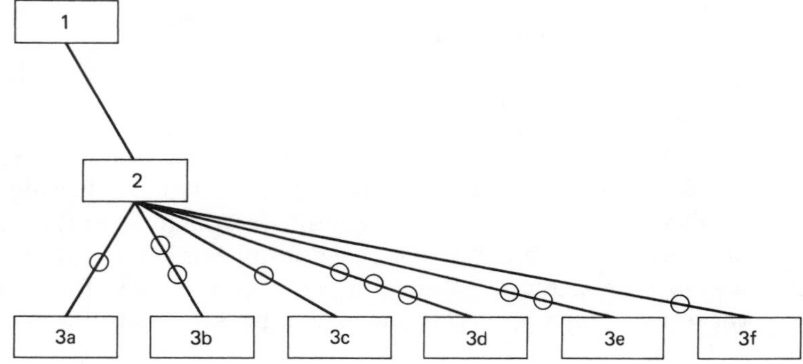

(Any lower-level objectives would be added in this format.)

Summary

This chapter has answered the question of *why* objectives should be developed, written, and used, as well as defining and giving examples of goals, purposes, and objectives. It also discussed the objective tree as a system for organizing objectives to make them useful for management. The material in this chapter will be used again in Chapter 6, "Models for Developing Meeting Plans."

WHAT YOU SHOULD HAVE LEARNED FROM THIS CHAPTER

1. Why objectives are important in meeting planning and management.
2. What goals, purposes, and objectives are and how they relate to each other.
3. How goals, purposes, and objectives are *used* in planning and management of meetings.
4. How to write and test planning objectives for a meeting.
5. What an objective tree is and how it can be developed and used in the process of planning a meeting.
6. How to arrange your own objectives into an objective tree.

REVIEW QUESTIONS

1. Define, in your own words (a) goal, (b) purpose, (c) objective.
2. What kinds of *purposes* are there? Define each.
3. What, in your own words, is an objective tree?
4. How do goals, purposes, and objectives help overcome management problems?
5. Give two examples from your own experience where the use of objectives could have made an event more effective.
6. What are the characteristics of a good objective?
7. Apply the tests of an objective to the primary and secondary objectives given for Corporate Meeting 1. If the objectives do not meet the tests, rewrite the objectives so they will meet the test. Can you justify your rewritten objectives?
8. List ten possible barriers to accomplishment of meeting objectives. How would you overcome these barriers?

APPLICATION EXERCISE

Turn to Appendix C and read Corporate Meeting 2. Write objectives for the first, second, third, and fourth levels. Arrange the objectives into an objective tree. Identify and list as many barriers as you can for each objective.

Chapter 5

Projecting and Controlling Meeting Budgets

Projecting meeting budgets is performed *after* the establishment of meeting objectives, since it is very difficult to determine costs until we know what we intend to accomplish with the meeting.

You will notice that there are two parts to the title of this chapter: projecting meeting budgets and controlling meeting budgets. The projection of meeting budgets has two steps: (1) developing a preliminary, or guide, budget, and (2) conducting cost research within the guidelines of the preliminary budget to set the final, or operating, budget. Controlling the operating budget becomes financial management, which requires a knowledge of some basic accounting and a system for managing the budget. This book will lead you through the *basics* of both accounting and budget management, but you should either take a course in the areas or do extensive reading before you begin independent operation. Controlling the budget can make or break you as a meeting manager.

You will remember that the use of a planning checklist was recommended for developing objectives. A similar recommendation is made to you for the development of your preliminary and final budgets. However, you now need to turn to the All-purpose Checklist (Appendix D) so you have more detailed specifics for operation than the Planning Checklist (Appendix D) we used in Chapter 4. The All-purpose Checklist must be used extensively in projecting the *final* budget.

Projecting the Preliminary Budget

A history of previous meeting budgets is the ideal starting point for projecting a preliminary budget. Unfortunately we do not always have this type of information available to us. In the event that we have no previous budget, we develop a guide, or pie, budget from our objective tree. We use only the secondary objectives for the pie budget. These secondary objectives serve as a handy check when we have completed our projections and as a basis for budget control discussed in the next section.

The Pie Guide Budget

Look at the example of a pie guide budget. You will discover *percentages* of total costs have been used to decide upon the size of the *slices* of the pie. These percentages have been computed over a period of years from the budgets for approximately 1000 corporate and association meetings. These percentages vary from meeting to meeting, and that is why *range* has been used. As you gain experience, you will be able to create your own range based upon *your* style of operation and changing economic conditions.

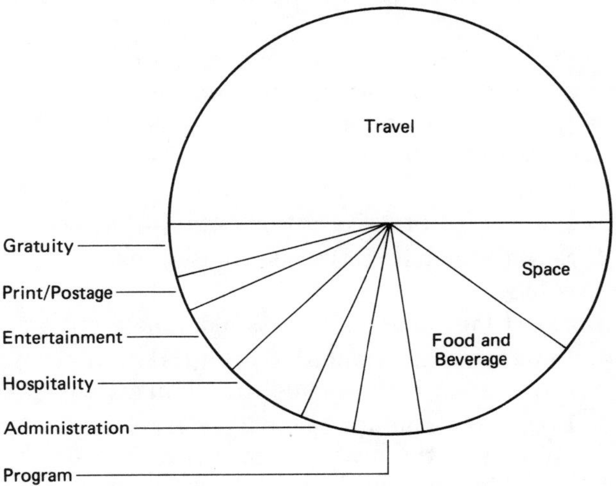

The percentages shown are from an actual meeting. However, a range is more valuable than only one example budget.

The table of percentage ranges uses the four objectives given as secondary and tertiary objectives on the example objective tree from Chapter 4.

BUDGET ITEM PERCENTAGE RANGES

Item	Percentage range
Travel	35–60
Space	10–25
Food and beverage	25–35
Program	5–20
Administration	3–12
Hospitality	2–4
Entertainment	5–12
Printing and postage	1–7
Gratuity*	2–12

*Here the percentage is of the total meeting budget and should include gratuities on food and beverage.

However, some additional items that affect the preliminary budget to a significant degree have been added.

As you begin to work with a pie budget you will discover that the key is the amount of money allocated to travel. Following is an example using travel as 50%, 40%, and 35%:

Travel as 50%	=	$125,000
Total budget	=	$250,000
Travel as 40%	=	$125,000
Total budget	=	$312,500
Travel as 35%	=	$125,000
Total budget	=	$357,100

You notice the total budget *increases* as the *percentage for travel decreases*. Conversely, the total budget *decreases* as the *percentage for travel increases*. As you will see, this variation based on travel will have an influence on destination selection.

Our first step in projecting a pie budget is the determination of travel costs. Recognize that whether the organization (usually in corporations) pays for the travel or the individual pays for travel, we still use travel as the basis for projecting the budget.

1. Plot the points of origin of potential attendees (use a map).
2. Select possible destinations based upon your objectives and organization policy.
3. Select four or five airports most distant from *one of the destinations*.
4. Determine the number of potential *local* attendees (those whose points of origin are within a 100-mile radius of the destination).
5. Determine round-trip airfares from each of the selected most distant airports to the destination. [I use the *official airline guide* (*OAG*). However, you may ask a travel agency that is willing to cooperate.] *Since airfares vary almost weekly, use the best available information, since specific fares can be determined at the time of the final budget.*
6. Determine the number of potential attendees located within a 100-mile radius of each distant airport.
7. Multiply the *airfare* of each distant airport by the *number of attendees* around that airport (step 6 × step 5).
8. Add the totals for *each distant* airport (from step 7) together.
9. Add the *total number of attendees from each distant airport* (discovered in step 6) to the *total local attendees* (discovered in step 4).
10. Divide the *total airfares* (step 8) by the *total attendees* (step 9). This gives an *approximate* average airfare.
11. Multiply the *average airfare* by the *total potential attendees* to be at the meeting.
12. Multiply the total from step 11 by 2. (If you are using travel as 50% this gives you a projected total meeting budget.)

We will use this *projected total budget* in projecting other meeting costs. But first, let us apply the theory.

Using Corporate Meeting 2, Appendix C (Greatest Corporation)

Notice that the information needed to project a pie budget is given to you. First, there is the list of attendees with their points of origin. At the end of the meeting description, notice that most distant and nearest cities have been selected, and an airfare to a destination (Mazatlan, Nassau, San Jose) is given. This is an international meeting, given to illustrate that the pie procedure works just as well for international meetings as for domestic meetings. The only change for international meetings is that we have selected nearest cities rather than local cities and we use only three distant and nearest cities rather than four or five distant cities and one local city, as with a domestic meeting.

We will use Mazatlan for the example; later you will have an opportunity to practice by projecting budgets for Nassau and San Jose and selecting a destination from among the three based upon a *projected budget.*

1. Plot the points of origin of potential attendees (given by the meeting description).
2. Select possible destinations based upon your objectives and organization policy (given by the meeting description, Mazatalan, Nassau, San Jose).
3. Select four or five airports most distant from *one of the destinations* (given as Boston, New York, and Washington, D.C.). Remember: Use only three locations because three nearest cities are used rather than one local city.
4. Determine the number of potential *local* attendees. (Given. We use nearest cities for international meetings: Phoenix—5, Los Angeles—14, San Francisco—10; *total:* 29.)
5. Determine round-trip airfares from each of the selected most distant airports to the destination (given: Boston, $1350; New York, $1250; Washington, D.C., $1050).
6. Determine the number of potential attendees located within a 100-mile radius of each distant airport (given: Boston—9, New York—11, Washington, D.C.—9; *total* = 29).
7. Multiply the *airfare* of each distant airport by the *number of attendees* around that airport.

Boston: $1350 × 9	= $12,150
New York: $1250 × 11	= $13,750
Washington, D.C.: $1050 × 9	= $ 9,450
Total:	$35,350

8. Add the totals for *each distant* airport (from step 7) together (from step 7: $35350).
9. Add the *total number of attendees from each distant airport* (discovered in step 6) to the *total local attendees* (discovered in step 4).

Distant:	29
Nearest:	29
Total:	58

10. Divide the *total airfares* (step 8) by the *total attendees* (step 9). This gives an *approximate* average airfare.

$$\frac{\$35{,}350}{58} = \$609.48^*$$

11. Multiply the average airfare by the *total potential attendees* to be at the meeting (total potential attendees given as 110).

$$110 \times \$609.48 = \$67{,}042.80$$

12. Multiply the total from step 11 by 2. (If you are using travel as 50%, this gives you a projected total meeting budget.)

$$\$67{,}042.80 \times 2 = \$134{,}086 \text{ total meeting budget.}^\dagger$$

The second step in projecting a pie budget is the determination of other meeting costs. Other meeting costs will depend upon whether the *organization or the individual pays.*

We must now go back to our objective tree and examine the second- and third-level objectives to see if the organization will pay these or the individual will pay. However, we are fortunate in that the pie budget will work in the same way whether costs are paid by the organization or the individual. If the individual pays some of the costs, then we will: (1) have an indication of what individual costs will be, and (2) be able to extract those costs *we* must cover through our budget sources such as registration fees, exhibits, or organization funds. If the organization pays costs, then we have determined what we must budget for the organization.

We will now continue with Corporate Meeting 2 and project a preliminary budget based on its international meeting.

In the objective tree set up in Chapter 4, administration was used as the secondary objective and planning, budgeting, transportation, space, programming, and food and beverage as third-level objectives.

The budget item percentage ranges given earlier do not include planning and budgeting. However, administration *is* included and planning and budgeting are administrative functions which can be provided for in the administration percentage.

We are now ready to project the other meeting costs for Corporate Meeting 2:

1. Travel	50%	× $134,085.60	=	$67,042.80
2. Space	10%	× $134,085.60	=	13,408.56
3. Food and beverage	25%	× $134,085.60	=	33,521.40
4. Program	0%‡	× $134,085.60	=	0.00
5. Administration	6%**	× $134,085.60	=	8,045.14
6. Hospitality	1%	× $134,085.60	=	1,340.86
7. Entertainment	3%	× $134,085.60	=	4,022.57
8. Printing and postage	2%	× $134,085.60	=	2,681.71
9. Gratuity	3%	× $134,085.60	=	4,022.57
		Total	=	$134,085.61

*Round *up* when 5 or over and round *down* when under 5.

†If travel is 35%, you would divide $67,042.80 by 0.35. If travel is 40%, you would divide $67,042.80 by 0.4. Follow this pattern for other travel percentages.

‡Program presentation by in-house executives.

**Many administrative costs performed by departments in-house and charged to department budgets.

Note: The $.01 difference in total is due to rounding and is not significant at this stage of budget projection.

Summary Visual Showing Projected Costs

Numbers in the "slices" of the pie correspond with the preceding item numbering.

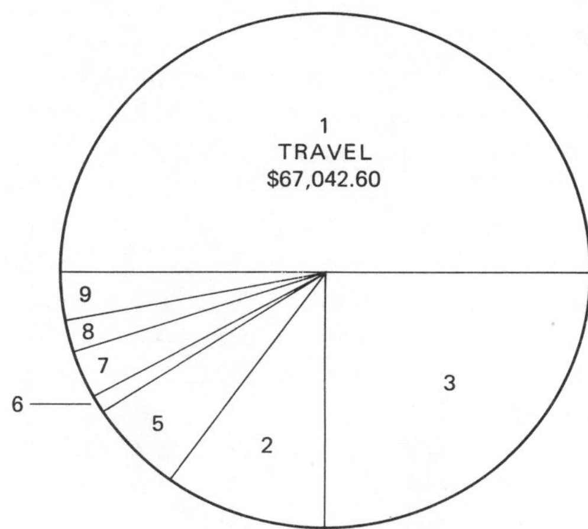

Researching for the Guide Budget

Once we have established parameters for our budget we must do research to determine if specific costs will permit us to work within the guide budget or if we have to make modifications. Here is where the financial history of previous meetings can be very beneficial.

A well-kept history (including operating spreadsheets, cash-flow charts, lists of direct and indirect costs, fixed, variable and semivariable costs, income and expense statements, and charts of account) give us quick references as we relate these previous meetings to our current guide budget.

Experience is also extremely helpful. It is particularly helpful to have financial records of previous meetings. The table containing budget item percentage ranges was compiled from about 1000 meetings of all types. You need to develop your own detailed data and ranges because then the data will be current for you, your management approach and style, and the economic conditions prevailing while you are gaining experience.

The last task, one that requires the most effort (particularly your first time), is physically collecting the needed data. There are several kinds of data that must be collected.

1. Hotel space and food and beverage data should be secured directly from the hotels in the destination area you select. As you begin to become known in the industry, hotels will innundate you with brochures, which you may collect and file systematically. There are publications available in most hospitality/tourism libraries, such as *The Hotel-Motel Redbook, The Official Meeting Facilities Guide, Meetings & Conventions Gavel, Successful Meetings Sourcebook,* and *The Hotel and Travel Index*. These pub-

lications give the name and address of the property, usually an 800 telephone number, contact person, number of rooms and suites, meeting room numbers, and various data on recreation, facilities for the handicapped, and, most importantly, ranges of rates for guest rooms.

A follow-up phone call can give you more specific data. But remember, the rates quoted are subject to negotiation and are designed to give you a starting point on cost data. *If you are a buyer and not a critical shopper, you will have a difficult time staying within your budget guidelines.*

2. Printing costs may be secured by three bids from printers or from your in-house printing department. Remember to include the cost of paper and artwork in your printing research.

   Postage costs should be carefully researched with the postal service, since you may be eligible for a metered postage machine with a bulk rate.

3. Program costs are sometimes difficult to determine. However, if you intend to use an outside speaker, there are many speakers' bureaus that send free brochures on many of their speakers. When you join a professional meeting organization, these brochures come to you without request and should be catalogued and filed.

   Audiovisual costs vary with the type of program. Costs also vary with the area where you may be holding your meeting. If you have some in-house equipment, it may be less expensive to ship or carry the equipment to the meeting. (If you ship, get *quality* insurance.)

4. Entertainment can be the proverbial "can of worms." Not only do the types and quality of entertainment vary, but so do the responsibility levels of those handling the entertainment. Use a *reputable agent-broker* when contracting for entertainment. (Many a novice has learned the hard way by listening to someone say that he or she has a "contact" and can get this or that famous person at a low cost.) Talk to an agent or the Convention Bureau or property at your tentative destination(s).

5. The cost of hospitality is relatively easy to determine. See Appendix E for a size of drink guide and then discover destination properties' by-the-drink, by-the-bottle, consumption, and corkage charges. Don't forget the hors d'oeuvre. Usually bulk or volume purchase of hors d'oeuvre is less expensive (that is, by the hundred) unless you want to purchase by the piece and have them served.

6. General administrative costs can be estimated in different ways. Frequently, when you have subscriptions to such journals as *Meetings & Conventions, Successful Meetings,* and *Meeting News,* you will periodically receive packets of advertising cards from suppliers of various types of equipment and supplies.

   Also, you will be added to the mailing lists of various venders of meeting supplies such as binders, name badges, and folders. These suppliers send catalogs of the products they offer along with the prices. These prices can be compared to those of local stores. Include in your comparison the cost of shipping from an out-of-town or out-of-state vendor. Other administrative costs may include personnel, shipping of supplies to the destination, accounting, fees to attorney and consultants, administrative travel, and so forth.

Comparing Researched Costs with the Pie Budget

We are now ready to *compare* the costs we found with the parameters set by the pie budget. We may find that certain costs exceed those projected by the pie budget.

What Do You Do if Total Costs Exceed the Pie? Remember, changing the cost for travel affects the total. If you allocate *less* to travel, you *increase* the amount available for other areas. You may discover that no amount of changing percentages will permit you to stay within your projected total budget. Here is where you may have to make a tough decision. Can you justify increasing the total budget and allow travel costs to remain the same? Someone will have to approve your budget; if you believe you can sell the larger budget to the person(s) who approve, try increasing the budget. Or, can you find other sources of income to cover the costs such as exhibits, or can you ask the attendees to pay more? Or, can you reduce some of the individual costs enough to reduce the total budget without losing the *quality* of the meeting? Can you find other destinations that meet your requirements and require less travel cost?

These are alternatives you can use in making your decision. In general, try to increase the total budget first. If this can't work, look for other sources of income. As a third choice, reduce one or more individual costs; as a last resort, change destinations. These are general suggestions. *Your actual choices depend on your group and the situation.*

What Do You Do if an Individual Cost Exceeds the Pie Projection? This is the easiest of the two questions. For instance, if space or food and beverage is too large, look at additional properties or plan to do some hard negotiating with one or more of the original properties. Sometimes, you can actually use *all* your original property choices by holding some functions in each to reduce your overall cost.

Food and beverage costs can be reduced by (1) changing menus or (2) going out of the property for one or more catered food functions. Sometimes food costs can be reduced by working directly with the chef to create menus that reduce food costs. However, negotiation takes place long after you have projected your budget, so it is not wise to anticipate what you might secure through negotiation.

Entertainment is another area that can be reduced rather simply by (1) changing the type of entertainment or the performers, (2) if it is at a banquet, charging a fee for the banquet that includes entertainment, or (3) if it is a form of recreation, having the attendees pay some of the charges—for instance, for golf, let them pay the green's fee while you provide the cart, or vice versa.

Of course, by looking at the total pie you may discover that where you are over budget for certain slices, you will be under for others, and thus the total budget is not affected. This is great, but it doesn't happen very often.

By now you should understand how to reduce individual costs. It depends on your creativity.

Getting Budget Approval

Budget approval is frequently the most difficult aspect of budget projection. There can be no firm guidelines because so much depends on your organization and the type of meeting. However, there is one guideline that applies here as it does to all meeting planning. *Do your homework.*

Summary of Budget Projection

There are five steps in budget development:

1. Project a guide pie budget.
2. Research costs.
3. Compare the researched costs with the guide budget.
4. Modify the guide budget or researched costs as needed.
5. Secure approval of the final budget.

Controlling the Meeting Budget

Financial management is essential to effective *meeting management.* When researching for the guide budget was discussed, several terms were used with which you may or may not be familiar. Therefore, this section begins with definitions of the terms *direct* and *indirect costs* and *fixed, variable,* and *semi-variable costs.* Then, the budget-management tools of spreadsheets, cash-flow charts, income and expense statements, and charts of account are covered, with examples.

The discussion that follows is designed to serve as a guide and should permit you to manage your budgets effectively. However, if you don't have a basic knowledge of accounting, you should probably try to get this knowledge as soon as possible.

Definitions of Financial Terms

Direct Costs. Direct costs can be specifically and directly identified with a particular meeting item. These are costs for space, food and beverage, promotion, rentals, speakers, and so on. Although these costs may vary, the critical distinction lies in the costs' *direct association* with the item or unit involved.

Indirect Costs. As the term implies, indirect costs cannot be identified with any particular activity or event. Typical indirect costs are those expenses associated with the corporate chief executive officer, the association's executive secretary, or the controller's department.

One indirect cost of which organizations are frequently not aware—and, as a result, ignore—is the cost of salaries or wages of attendees at a meeting. When a person attends a meeting, that person is usually not performing the duties for which he or she is paid. The result is the need to hire additional personnel to perform those duties or the expectation the person will put in makeup time. In either case, it is costly to the organization or the individual attendee and is an expense that cannot be related directly to any one meeting expense item.

The usual practice in business budgeting is to allocate indirect costs to one or more budget items based on the *percentage* the budget item consumes of the *total direct costs* of the meeting.

Fixed Costs. Fixed costs remain the same regardless of the level of activity. Fixed costs may increase because of inflation or decrease because of deflation, but they do not vary depending on the *level of activity.*

There are few truly fixed costs in meetings. A cost such as wages paid for on-site facilitation assistance may be fixed for one meeting and may change for the next meeting. Also, the longer the planning period, the greater the chance a cost will not be fixed.

Variable Costs. Costs that vary with each unit or activity are called variable costs. Gratuities are an example of variable costs, since they will vary with the part of the country in which the meeting is held and the consumption of the service on which gratuities are paid.

Semivariable Costs. Some costs may vary with the amount of an activity but not in a direct relationship to it. They are called semivariable costs. For example, it might be assumed that transportation costs for 40 people from a point of origin would be four times that for 10 people. However, group fares could make the cost only two or three times that for 10 people. The costs vary but are not directly related to the amount of activity (number of people).

Total Cost Matrix. The total cost of a meeting is always made up of variable, semivariable, or fixed costs and may be a combination of the three. This combination is called the total cost matrix.

Cost Centers. Cost centers are easily defined. Our pie budget identified cost centers as the "slices" of the pie. The cost center simply identifies a unit for which money must be allocated. It is possible to include third-, fourth-, and fifth-level objective expenses as cost centers depending upon your own preference or the organization's accounting system.

Now that some of the most basic terms in budget management have been defined, it is time to turn to the tools of budget management and control.

Many organizations have a computerized system for budget control that contains many of the tools we are about to discuss. The computerized system is far less time-consuming than a manual system and permits rapid cross analysis, which the manual system does not.

It is a good idea for the meeting manager to purchase a small personal computer to assist with financial management, since the details available are very important to successful financial management. A personal computer can also be tied in to the mainframe of the organization so that details can be quickly called up for analysis when the need arises.

However, whether the organization has a computerized system, whether you have a personal computer, or whether you and the organization use a manual system, knowledge of the following basic tools and their uses should be a part of your meeting management background.

Chart of Accounts

Organizing for financial management should begin with a chart of accounts. This chart is basically a numbering system for each item, whether income or expense, a management needs or wishes to track during the course of the meeting. The chart is divided into the two categories of income and expenses. A four-digit numbering system is used here because it provides for as much detail as may be needed. You arbitrarily select a base number or you use the base number of the organization's system. Since we look at income first, a range of numbers beginning with the base should be decided. For instance, let us say that the first digit stands for *meetings* and is a 3. The second number indicates the *income* of the meeting and is a 1. The third and fourth digits can represent the line item (for instance, registration fees) and is 10. Then all numbers in the range of 3000 to 3999 can be used to represent budget line items pertaining to income.

If we permit the first digit to stand for meetings and the second for type of meeting, then the last two digits, from 00 to 99, can represent the various sources of income.

Obviously either you or the organization makes a decision on the numbering system. However, whatever approach you use for the income category, the expense category will use a similar approach with its own range. The expense range may begin with the next consecutive set of digits following the income range, or you may wish to place a gap between numbers in the event that, in the future, you will need more digits for income. For instance, if we used an income range of 3000 to 3999, we could begin the expense range at 4000. Or, if we used 31 for meetings and income and 00 to 99 for income items, we could begin expenses at 3200.

Any narrative description can be confusing, so an example of a chart of accounts follows.

EXAMPLE CHART OF ACCOUNTS

Income	
3110	Registration fees
3111	Members
3112	Companions
3113	Other nonmembers
3114	One-day
3115	Associated group members
3130	Exhibit revenue
3131	10 × 10 booths
3132	8 × 10 booths
3133	8 × 8 booths
3140	Social functions
3141	Opening banquet
3142	Awards banquet
3143	First-night dance
3144	Final banquet, dance
3160	Investment income
Expenses	
3205	Planning expenses
3206	Personnel
3207	Secretarial
3208	Computer time
3215	Program expenses
3216	Speaker honoraria
3217	Speaker travel

3218	Speaker lodging
3219	Speaker meals
3225	Program design and printing
3226	Program art
3230	Program audiovisual
3240	Exhibits
3241	Space rental
3242	Decorator/drayage
3243	Security
3244	Promotion/contract
3250	Registration
3251	Badges/forms
3252	Personnel
3253	Promotional items
3254	Binders

We could continue this cart with administrative costs, social function costs, and so on. The line items for both income and expenses usually come from a checklist or from your objective tree.

Statement of Income and Expenses

A statement of expenses provides a comparison of financial transactions over a period of time. It may cover one month, many months, or even several years. A system used by many is to provide quarterly statements. The statement usually has three categories: income, expenses, and income versus expenses (designed to show a positive or negative balance). Below is an example statement. It is helpful to retain line item numbers, but there is no requirement that this be done.

Example Income and Expense Statement

January 1, 19— to April 1, 19—

	Actual Year-to-Date	Budget Year-to-Date
Income		
3110 Registration fees	$10,700	$11,400
3130 Exhibit revenue	11,100	9,500
3140 Social functions	850	1,400
3160 Investment income	925	700
Total Income	$23,575	$23,000
Expenses		
3205 Planning expenses	$ 1,433	$ 1,100
3215 Program expenses	4,250	4,500
3240 Exhibits	12,000	12,000
3250 Registration	1,100	1,150
Total Expenses	$18,783	$18,750
Income versus Expense	$ 4,792	$ 4,250

Meeting Balance Sheet

A balance sheet, as differentiated from a statement of income and expense, is usually developed each month and shows the financial condition of your meeting by listing assets, liabilities, and net worth. With computerized management, you can print out a balance sheet each day if you wish, although this is not essential if good accounting methods are used. Let's look at a balance sheet to clarify what it is and the format used.

Example Balance Sheet

BALANCE SHEET FOR MEETING AGZ

April 30, 19—		
Assets		
Cash in bank (checking account)	$ 31,000	
Investments		
Certificate of deposit (6-month)	10,000	
Money market account	3,000	
Prepaid expenses	3,400	
Petty cash	175	
Accounts receivable	4,356	
Total assets	$ 51,931	$ 51,931
Liabilities and equity		
Liabilities		
Accounts payable	$ 58,475	
Total liabilities	$ 58,475	$ 58,475
Equity		
Excess income over expense	$ (6,544)*	$ (6,544)
Total equity		
Total liabilities and equity		$ 51,931

*Parentheses indicate a *minus*, or *negative*, balance.

You can see that assets and liabilities/equity balance, which is, of course, what a balance sheet is all about. We do have a management problem that shows up in the example. If the meeting is months away, the huge sum of $31,000 in the checking account is poor management. That money could be invested in short-term investments that have liquidity—meaning that in an emergency they can be withdrawn and used. Investing in a short-term CD is wise and so is a money market account—but why lose the interest on $31,000?

Given that you may not have some basic accounting background, let us take another look at the balance sheet. You will notice prepaid expenses, which indicate money that has been paid out (possibly for exhibit space rental to the hotel or convention center). Since the meeting is several months away, it will not be considered an expense until the time of the meeting. There are also other problems shown by this balance sheet.

As the responsible manager, you should be very concerned with this example. There is a deficit of $6,544. You need to take immediate action. Place the excess cash in the checking account into a liquid investment that pays excellent interest. Call your staff together, indicate the problem and your intention to make certain the overspending is not repeated. Finally, turn to your objective tree to discover the person responsible for the deficit and then have a private discussion with him or her. Indicate the seriousness of the problem and your intention to closely monitor the person's future expenditures. Make it clear that continued overexpenditure will result in his or her termination. You will then have made constructive management use of your balance sheet.

From this balance sheet you can get a very good idea of the need for effective financial management—and, in this case, personnel management.

Budget Spreadsheet

The last of the financial management or control tools is the budget spreadsheet. There are two terms in the spreadsheet that need definition.

Cash Flow. The simplest definition of *cash flow* is that it is the cumulative profit. We keep adding how much the income is over the expense each month to find out whether our total profit is positive or negative. You can usually assume that in the first months, your cash flow will be negative. However, with effective management of a well-projected budget, you should reach a break-even point.

Break-Even Point. This is simply the point where your income equals your expenses for the meeting and you are on your way to a successfully managed meeting on a financial basis.

Following is an example using the line item number. Many people do not use this technique, but the numbers can serve as quick reference points among the various financial management tools.

The example is based on a six-month period. This is the minimum time; a period of one-year or longer is preferable. This example can easily be adapted to a computerized spreadsheet, which saves time.

Example Spreadsheet

Income	JAN	FEB	MAR	APRIL	MAY	JUNE	TOTAL
3110 Registration	—	$ 500	$1,500	$ 2,000	$ 2,500	$14,500	$21,000
3130 Exhibit revenue	—	—	$3,200	$11,300	$14,800	$ 9,800	$39,100
3140 Social functions	—	—	—	$ 500	$ 1,150	$13,400	$15,050
3160 Investment income	—	$ —	$ —	$ 1,400	$ 1,200	$ —	$ 2,600
Total Income	00000	$ 500	$4,700	$15,200	$19,650	$37,700	$77,750
Expenses							
3205 Planning expenses	$400	$ 800	$ 450	$12,300	$12,300	$18,350	$44,600
3215 Program	—	$ 750	$1,400	$ 400	$ 300	$ 4,330	$ 7,180
3240 Exhibits	$ —	$ —	$1,000	$ —	$ 800	$ 8,000	$ 9,800
3250 Registration	$ —	$ —	$ —	$ —	$ 1,200	$ 4,200	$ 5,400
Total Expense	$400	$ 1,550	$2,850	$12,700	$14,600	$34,880	$66,980
Income over Expense	($400)	($1,050)	$1,850	$ 2,500	$ 5,050	$ 2,820	$10,770
Cumulative Cash Flow	($400)	($1,450)	$ 400	$ 2,900	$ 7,950	$10,770	
			Break-even Point				

As you can see, the spreadsheet provides a clear understanding about the financial situation of the meeting each month, allowing monitoring of projected budget expenses and income. Obviously, this meeting manager was effective both in projecting the budget and in managing the finances.

Of course, you realize that the spreadsheet you would have for an actual meeting would have many more line items than the one shown. These line items come directly from your objective tree, which, of course, is developed from a checklist.

The more you use financial management (control) tools, the more effective you should be as a manager. Computerized systems can save you much time and time is money, to quote an old adage. This is easy to see with finances. The time you and/or your staff spend is a major cost in terms of wages or salaries; if a computer financial package is used, it usually pays for itself over the course of two or three meetings.

Summary

Budget projecting in a systematic manner establishes a solid basis for later control and management of that budget. We guided you through one system (the pie) for systematically projecting a budget that is dependent on travel costs. We then gave you some guidelines for researching the actual costs to be used in the final budget, including securing appropriate approvals. We defined a group of common financial terms and defined these terms. Finally, we presented and gave examples of four financial management tools: chart of accounts, income and expense statements, balance sheets, and spreadsheets.

You have now moved through the third phase, budgeting. (An overview of the phases was presented in Chapter 2.) Next comes Phase IV, development of a meeting plan. However, as a last step before going into the meeting plan, think back to Chapter 4, where you wrote those objectives and left a blank for *cost* in each objective. Now that you have completed Phase III, you should be able to go back to each of those objectives and fill in the costs for each, since each objective became a line item in your budget.

WHAT YOU SHOULD HAVE LEARNED FROM THIS CHAPTER

1. A process for budget projection, research, and control.
2. How to use travel as a basis for projecting a guide pie budget.
3. How to compute "other" meeting costs based on percentage ranges.
4. Approaches to determining actual costs of pie slices through research.
5. Definitions of basic financial management terms for controlling your budget.
6. The four tools for effective financial management:
   - What a chart of accounts is and how it might be prepared.
   - What a statement of income and expenses is and how it might be prepared.
   - What a meeting balance sheet is and how it might be prepared.
   - What a spreadsheet is and how it might be prepared for an individual meeting.
7. How cash flow and the break-even point are determined through use of a spreadsheet.

REVIEW QUESTIONS

1. What is a preliminary budget?
2. How are percentage ranges determined after you have had experience?
3. If you change your percentage of travel allocation from 38 to 43% for a fixed travel cost, will your total budget increase or decrease?
4. Since planning and budgeting are not included in the list of percentage ranges, how can you provide a budget allocation when preparing your pie budget?
5. What are the best sources of preliminary information on hotel and food and beverage costs?
6. How would you project liquor costs for a one-hour cocktail party for a mixed group of 200?
7. You project a meeting budget of $88,000 by using your pie budget. However, when you research costs you find that actual costs will total $95,400. What would you do to make actual costs match projected costs?
8. Look at the checklist in Appendix D. List what you believe would be *direct* costs. List what you believe would be *indirect* costs.
9. Again referring to the checklist, to which items would you assign line item numbers for your chart of accounts?
10. What is the difference between a *balance sheet* and a *statement of income and expenses?* What is the difference between a *statement of income and expenses* and a *spreadsheet?*

APPLICATION EXERCISE

We projected travel costs for Corporate Meeting 2 in Appendix C with Mazatlan as a destination. Now, you project travel costs for Nassau and San Jose. The corporation has given you a total budget of $134,000. Which destination would you select based upon travel equalling 50% of the budget? After completing this, determine which destination you would select if travel were 35% and if travel were 55%. (Assume that all other factors, including other costs, would be equal at each destination.)

Chapter 6

Models for Developing Meeting Plans

Three models for developing meeting plans will be discussed in this chapter: checklist, Gantt, and PERT. The first two are common in the meeting field at present; however, there is a growing trend to use PERT because of its greater sophistication and possibility for cross control.

You need to be aware of the difference between a *plan* for developing a meeting plan and the *plan itself*. The plan contains every detail of what you intend to do. It is variously referred to as a "cookbook," a "bible," and "the baby." Planners frequently give the selected hotel a copy to aid in mutual understanding (communication). They also make copies for their staff and for key individuals in the organization for whom they are planning the meeting.

A Meeting Plan

As a minimum, the following items should be included:

Arrival and departure times (yourself, your staff, VIPs, attendees)

Meeting pattern

Program, including schedule, participants, meeting space, and equipment needed

Registration procedure, setup, and equipment

Food and beverage detail including menus and cost and time for guarantees

Accounting, checking, charges, and billing procedure

Storage for equipment shipped

Letters of agreement

Individual staff responsibilities

Sleeping room blocks and preassigned occupants if used

Exhibit space and arrangements
Ground transportation
Destination management company, if used, and its responsibility
Meeting rooms to be used, with function sheets
Recreation facilities, charges, equipment
Postmeeting evaluation and forms
VIP list with titles and addresses

Copies of meeting correspondence should be kept in the in-house meeting plan but not in the copies given to the hotels.

Now that we have a mutual understanding of the term meeting plan, we can look at how we go about achieving that plan, that is, models for planning.

Checklist

The checklist model involves creating a checklist of all details needed for implementing a meeting successfully. If you are a beginner or relatively inexperienced, you might want to turn to the All-purpose Checklist in Appendix D. You will notice there are hundreds of items, each with a box beside it to check off when the item is accomplished.

General practice is to arrange the items in chronological order—the order in which you anticipate needing to accomplish or perform these items. Here is a good place to use your objective tree, since items are usually accomplished in reverse order of the levels. (The lowest level of objectives is first; you then work your way to the crown, or primary level.) As you gain experience you will probably develop a procedure that works most effectively for you.

Another advantage of using the objective tree is that you have established costs for each item during the budgeting phase of your planning. Thus, you not only take care of the *item* to be accomplished but also have a guide as to the cost limits for that item. By incorporating the costs in your checklist, you establish a basis for your budget-control system.

The checklist model appears to be the easiest. However, you need to be aware that it has some weaknesses: (1) There is no provision for predicting *times* for accomplishment of tasks, (2) there is no provision for anticipating barriers or problems and their possible solutions, (3) there is no provision for decisions on alternatives to approaches to task accomplishment, and (4) there are no interrelationships shown among the elements of a task or among the tasks.

Because of these weaknesses, many planners prefer a more sophisticated model called the *Gantt Model.*

The Gantt Model

The basic Gantt model was developed by H. L. Gantt when he was working on production control. He used what he called a "Gantt Milestone Chart." This is basically a chart depicting work to be done. More importantly for the planner, it denotes relationships between and among all phases of the work. The following figure illustrates one of these milestone charts:

1 2 Task X

3 4 5 Task Y

6 7 Task Z

You can see that milestone 2 cannot be started until milestone 1 is completed, and milestone 5 cannot be started until both milestones 3 and 4 have been completed.

There are other versions of the Gantt chart that have evolved from it. One of these versions is illustrated in the following figure.

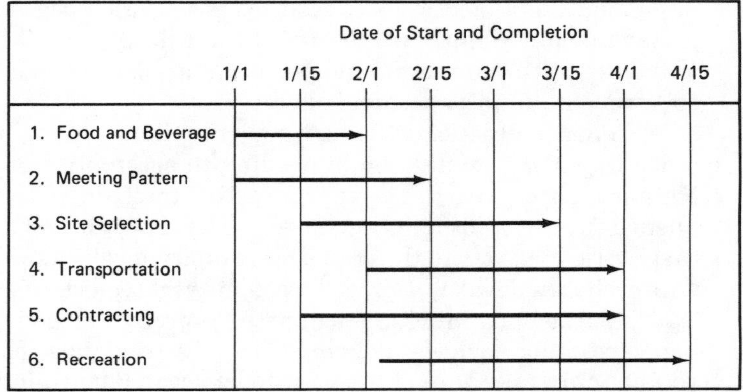

Notice that, again, you can see starting and completion times and some degree of relationship among the tasks. (The arrowhead indicates anticipated completion date.) However, in this illustration, it must be assumed work on most tasks begins on different dates, but must tasks 1 and 2 be completed before task 3, site selection, can take place? Yes. You know from previous chapters that we must have both the meeting pattern and our food and beverage projections completed before we can select a site. How can we begin to arrange transportation before we have selected a site? And, would not task 6, recreation, be almost completed before we could begin site selection, since recreation is a part of the meeting pattern? Yet, according to the chart, site selection needs to be completed before recreation is completed. Why not rearrange the starting and completion times for the tasks? Go ahead, try it; you'll run into more problems. The interrelationships of progress on a task in comparison to completion dates on other tasks is one of the problems faced when using the Gantt model.

Another of the problems you will also face with the Gantt chart, until you have had experience (and even then you will not be entirely accurate) is anticipating the time necessary to complete each task.

Also, although the modified Gantt chart is a great improvement on the checklist, it does not give us a clear picture of task interrelationships. (If you turn to Appendix F, you will see a blank Gantt form and an excellent completed Gantt chart developed for planning an association meeting, seminar, or workshop. This should give you an idea of what an operational Gantt chart looks like.)

Because of the weaknesses in Gantt models, modification of Gantt charts was begun. Most authorities agree that the advanced ideas of Gantt served as the basis for development of PERT, discussed next.

Program Evaluation Review Technique (PERT)

In 1957, when Morgan R. Walker of the C. I. du Pont de Nemours & Co. and James E. Kelly, Jr., of Remington Rand, introduced the network methods of depicting a project plan and of supply-time estimates for the completion of each job segment, it became possible to identify the job elements critical for the completion of an overall project.

This method became known as the *critical path method* (CPM) and is the civilian counterpart of PERT. This book uses the term PERT because (1) It is more commonly used among laypeople, and (2) it is possible to have a PERT network in a microcomputer, whereas a CPM generally requires a mainframe—at least at the time of this writing. (You may even hear this method referred to by the unsophisticated term bubble chart.)

Willard Frazer of the Special Projects Office of the Navy Bureau of Ordinance, with representatives of the consulting firm of Booz, Allen & Hamilton, began the development of a network system for managing the Fleet Ballistic Missile (FBM) program. Their work was eventually named Program Evaluation Review Technique and has become the technique commonly used today, along with its civilian counterpart, CPM, as a major planning tool by U.S. corporations.

Basically, PERT is concerned with the formulation and development of a *sequential* network consisting of the total activities required for implementing the final objective of a meeting. Each activity is analyzed so that a realistic estimate of the time required for completion of each activity and the total meeting plan can be made.

PERT is concerned with *three* concepts:

1. *Events.* An event is a specific accomplishment that occurs at a recognizable point in time. *Events take no time in themselves.* They mark the *beginning* and/or *end* of an activity.
2. *Activities.* An activity is the work required to complete a specific *event.* Activities require *time, money,* and *resources.*
3. *Time.* A selected unit to indicate the *duration* of an activity and the cumulative durations of related activities necessary to accomplish the target event or objective. Normally, *weeks* or *days* are used as the units of time.

An example will help make this less confusing: A *closed door* may be considered an *event. Closing the door* is an activity. When you touch the door to close it, you start an *activity.* The seconds that pass while the door is swinging closed may be considered time for completion of this activity to accomplish an event. This example represents one unit of a total PERT. Shown in picture form, PERT looks like this:

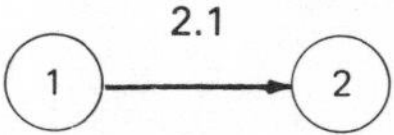

Circle, or bubble, 1 represents you touching the door to close it (an *event*), and the line with the arrowhead represents the *activity* of the door closing. The number above the arrow represents the *time* for the door to swing closed. And, circle 2 represents the closed door (another *event*). (Here *seconds* are used for time, but weeks or days are normally used.)

The next figure illustrates simple PERT networks using proper PERT terminology.

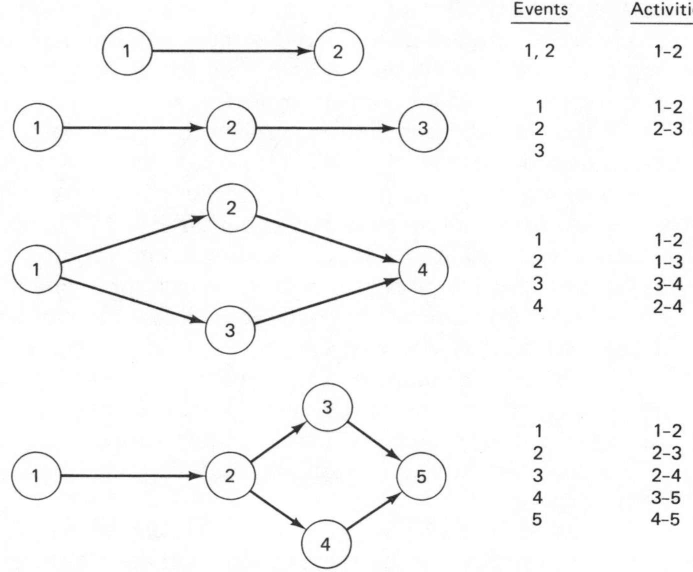

Note: Between any two events, there can be only one activity.

Let us now go back to our objective tree. Each *objective* represents an *event*. The *work* necessary to accomplish an objective is an *activity*. *One* second-level and *three* third-level objectives are used in a simple PERT table below to develop a simple PERT network.

Event	Event Number
Decision to hold event	1
Administration	2
Space	3
Food and beverage	4
Program	5
Meeting held	6

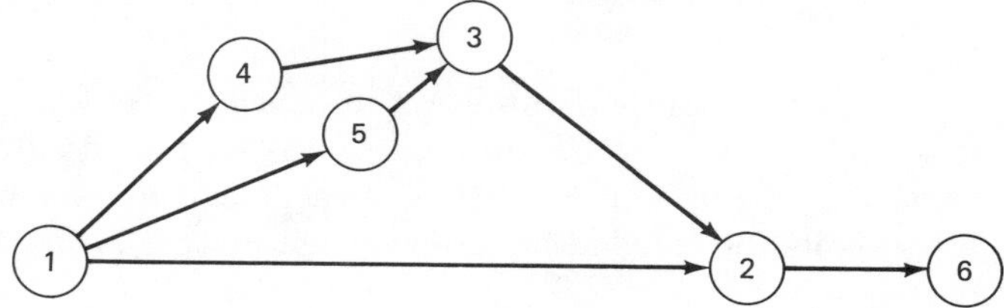

Arrows indicate the *activities* necessary to complete each event. A quick observation shows events 3, 4, and 5 must be completed before event 2, and events 1, 2, 3, 4, and 5 must occur before event 6. The network also shows us that events 4 and 5 must be completed *before* event 3.

One very important note: When drawing a network, no arrow line may cross another arrow line.

Before we can completely construct a PERT network, we have two more tasks: (1) Decide on and list the activities necessary to accomplish each event and (2) calculate the time required to complete these activities.

Step 1: List Activities

As we look at our simple network, we discover that the *space* event cannot be completed until we have completed food and beverage and program requirements. This gives us a *clue* from which to create an activity list. *Go back to the objective tree as a starting point.*

Start *at the bottom* of the objective tree with the lowest-level objectives. Which of these must be completed *first?* Now, go to the next-highest-level objectives. Which of these must be completed first? Continue in this manner. *Now cross-check. Must any of the objectives at the same level be completed before another objective at that level?* From our example, we know both food and beverage and program must be completed *before space.* Yet, they are at the same *level* of importance to the meeting. With this preliminary analysis, we are ready to create an example activity list.

SIMPLE ACTIVITY LIST

Activity	Designation	Beginning Event	Ending Event
Decide on number of food and beverage activities	1–4a	1	4a
Decide on food and beverage serving setup	1–4b	1	4b
Decide on menus	1–4c	1	4c
Decide on agenda	1–5a	1	5a
Decide on meeting pattern	1–5b	1	5b

Note: the lowercase letters (a, b, c) refer to lower-level objectives under food and beverage and under program.

Now that we know our activity list, we are ready to construct a new PERT network. Completion of each unit of work (activity) now becomes and event. These are indicated as lower-level objectives with lowercase letters.

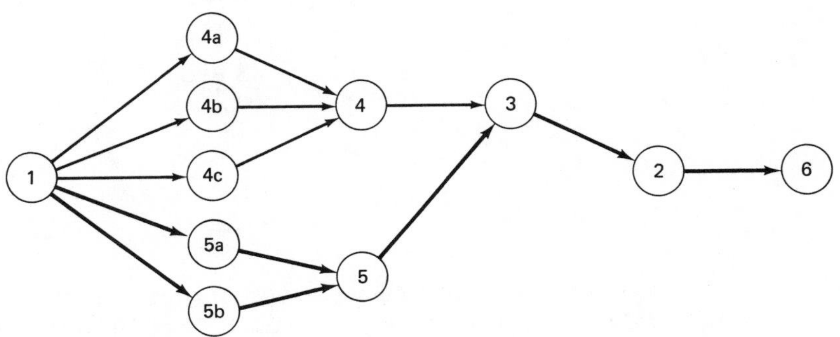

Step 2: Calculate the Time Required for Each Activity

It was said earlier, in discussing the Gantt model, that *time for activities* is uncertain even when you have experience. Because of the uncertain nature of the activities involved, PERT usually requires three *time estimates* for each activity. If the time could be estimated accurately, one time estimate would be sufficient. Those of you who have been involved with meetings realize the virtual impossibility of making one universally accurate time estimate of an activity involved in a meeting. Therefore, the meeting professional utilizes the customary practice of *three* estimates. The three estimates (usually in calendar weeks, although days may be used) are as follows:

Optimistic Time. This is the least amount of time an activity can take. You assume everything works perfectly the first time. Statistically this time is accomplished one out of a hundred times.

Most Likely Time. If only one time estimate is required, this is it. It is the expected time if the activity were to be repeated many times under identical conditions and if many qualified persons were asked to give a time estimate.

Pessimistic Time. The maximum amount of time an activity can take. It is what would happen if Murphy's Law strikes. It usually includes the possibility of an initial failure followed by a fresh start.

By using the optimistic, most likely, and pessimistic times we can calculate an *expected time* (te). This expected time is obtained statistically by the equation

$$\text{te} = \frac{a + 4m + b}{6}$$

where:

a = optimistic time
m = most likely time
b = pessimistic time

Let us use the accomplishment of activity 1–4a from our activity list as an example:

a (optimistic time) = 5 days
m (most likely time) = 12 days
b (pessimistic time) = 30 days

Using the given equation yields

$$\begin{aligned}\text{te} &= \frac{5 + (4)12 + 30}{6} \\ &= \frac{5 + 48 + 30}{6} \\ &= \frac{83}{6} \\ &= 13.8 \text{ days}\end{aligned}$$

Once we have completed our expected time, we can calculate the *earliest expected date* (TE). The earliest expected date of an *event* is the earliest calendar date on which an event can be expected to take place. Dates are predicted for *events,* times for *activities*. The value TE is calculated by adding all activity times.

We must now develop our activity-date time table.

Activity	*a*	*m*	*b*	t_e	TE*
1–4a	5	12	30	13.8	1/14
1–4b	6	13	31	14.8	1/15
1–4c	30	21	60	29.0	1/29
1–5a	40	28	70	37.0	2/6
1–5b	30	25	90	36.7	2/6

*Assume that 1/1 is the starting date.

Let's interpret what our activity-date table shows us. We know that the meeting manager for food and beverage functions cannot *begin* to consolidate the information until January 29. We know that we must provide time for the food and beverage manager to consolidate this information, so we can now calculate the *te* for this consolidation on the activity arrows 4a–4, 4b–4, and 4c–4.

You, as the meeting professional, have also discovered you cannot expect to determine your space requirements (event 3) until sometime *after* February 6, when the meeting pattern and agenda are completed. This in turn will affect events such as destination and site selection and contracting.

Return now to the PERT network for the food and beverage and meeting agenda–meeting pattern. You will note a darker arrow running from 1 to 5a and 5b to 5 to 3 to 2 to 6. This is the *critical path* between event 1 and event 6. What do we mean by critical path? *The critical path is the path that will take the most time to complete and is critical to the event accomplishment or the meeting*). By looking at the dark line (critical path) you realize you *may* have to allocate additional resources (hours and/or money) to the activities on the path so they may be completed on time. Now you see how a PERT has additional value as a management tool.

As a final illustration of PERT networks and the critical path, a ten-objective (event) network and critical path is shown next.

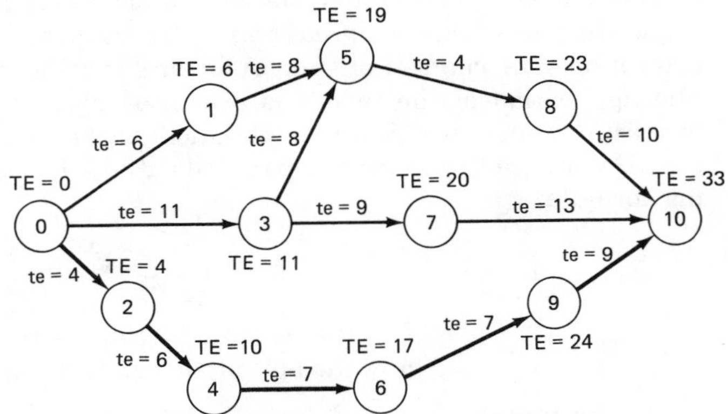

The critical path has a TE of 33 weeks, whereas the other paths have TEs of 26 weeks and 21 weeks.

Step 3: Determine Slack Time

Slack time exists in network system because of multiple junctions that arise when two or more activities contribute to a third. The slack for an event is a measurement of the *excess time* available.

Suppose the preceding diagram represented a meeting plan for a meeting. You discover the hotel you selected has open dates 31 weeks from your time of start but not 33 weeks. Computation of your slack time will tell you if you can possibly meet the deadline.

Slack time is calculated as the *difference* between the *latest allowable date* (TL) and the *earliest expected date* (TE) that the activity can be completed. In the preceding network the TE is 33.

The critical path has no positive slack, since it is already the most time-consuming path in the network. (Slack may be positive, negative, or zero and is thus a characteristic of all network paths.)

We trace slack time for the paths other than the critical path.

The TL is 30 weeks because of the hotel availability of 31 weeks and you need to arrive at the site one week before the meeting (event 10). You need to find three weeks of slack time.

Path 0 through events 1, 5, and 8 could be completed in 18 weeks (33 − 18 = 15 weeks slack time).

Path 0 through events 3, 5, and 8 could be completed in 23 weeks (33 − 23 = 10 weeks slack time).

Path 0 through events 3 and 7 could be completed in 20 weeks (33 − 20 = 13 weeks slack time).

We thus have 38 weeks total slack time (15 + 10 + 13).

As a meeting professional, you know you can reallocate labor and financial resources from the paths with slack time to the critical path. With a total slack time of 38 weeks, you should be able to expedite activities along the critical path by reallocation of resources and meet the target date of 31 days. Note that in most cases you will not have as much slack time.

Step 4: Determine Probability and Deviations

A feature of PERT that makes it different from other management systems is the use of probability theory as a tool to predict the probable outcome of specific plans. This is a great help to the meeting manager because you can determine your chances of success for any specific event or for the meeting. The application of the theory is presented here in simplified form for the benefit of readers who have no statistical background.

Determine the *variance* associated with each activity by using the following formula:

$$\sigma^2 = \left(\frac{b - a}{6}\right)^2$$

b = the pessimistic time estimate
a = the optimistic time estimate

Now, find the *standard deviation* for any event in your network by adding all activity variances on the longest path (in terms of time) of the network to the event in question (probably the holding of the meeting). Extract the square root of the sum. (You can use a calculator with the square root key.) Use this formula for finding event standard deviation:

$$\sigma_{Te} = \sqrt{\Sigma\sigma^2}_{te}$$

The probability of meeting any date is derived by using the standardized random variable z and normal probability tables.

$$z = \frac{Ts - TE}{\sigma TE}$$

Ts equals the scheduled date, TE equals the earliest expected date, and σt is the standard deviation (determined before) for the event in question.

Now, go to almost any collection of statistical tables and you will find z tables, or normal probability tables. Look up the z you determined. As a guide, a z value of 1.196 has a probability of 0.85 in a normal curve table.

There are no firm ground rules for interpreting probability data. However, there are guides: 50% probability for event completion on schedule is considered ideal. If you get a probability of 84% or higher, you are in serious trouble. Also, if you get a probability of less than 15%, you are in trouble. You will find that some PERT experts consider the 15 to 84% range much too broad a deviation and prefer 25 to 75%. In a social science such as meeting management, you are much better to use the broader range. (*Remember:* PERT was developed for construction and production and has been modified for management, so the broader range is preferable.)

What do you do if you find some undesirable probability and slack conditions? (It is not unusual, since we all seem to want to set up an "ideal" project plan, which leads to dreams and thus poor probability and slack conditions.) Fortunately, there are procedures we can use to overcome the problems of our dream plans.

1. *Remove planned constraints.* Planned constraints are those activity/event relationships that we have set up as desirable but not absolutely necessary (the champagne brunch, for example). Remove the least significant activity or event.
2. *Make some activities parallel.* Look at your bubble network. If you have some activities in a sequential order, you can, with some management risk, set them up as parallel. Your decision will depend upon the resources available to you and the amount of risk you want to take.
3. *Eliminate activities.* You may have planned some activities that, while nice, are possibly more time-consuming than is desirable. If they are not absolutely essential, eliminate them.
4. *Reallocate resources.* Remember, the addition of resources to activities along your critical path will normally result in reduction of activity time along the path. If you use this, decide if the time savings will justify the cost.
5. *Redefine activities.* Many times your original plans will contain some activities where you have either intentionally or unintentionally incorporated great amounts of work. You can, in this case, redefine the activity and eliminate all but the most critical amount of work.

Warning: Never shorten time estimates just to make them work.

Following is a PERT for a corporate meeting. The first two pages present objectives from the objective tree with the *indentation* indicating the *level* of objective. Pages 71 and 72 consolidate events, activities, responsible party, and time estimates. The last column on these two pages illustrates possible deviations from the time estimates. Page 73 is a photoreduction of the PERT network for the meeting.*

When you complete reading the PERT illustration, go to the end-of-the chapter summary, review questions, and application exercise.

Level:	I	II	III	IV	V	VI
1.		Decision to hold meeting				
2.		Primary objective stated				
3.		Preliminary meeting outlined				
4.					Group demographics researched	
5.					Training needs researched	
6.				Group analysis complete		
7.			Preliminary program established			
8.				Food and beverage estimated		
9.				Entertainment estimated		
10.				Housing costs estimated		
11.			Site feasibility conducted			
12.				Tentative itinaries researched		
13.			Transportation cost estimated			
14.		Alternative budgets estimated				
15.		Site selected				
16.		Final budget approved				
17.		Property contracted				
18.				Group rates negotiated		
19.				Ground transportation planned		
20.			Travel reservations made			
21.		Meeting pattern established				
22.				Speakers researched		
23.				Learning materials designed		
24.					Graphics layout complete	
25.					Printing complete	
26.				Audiovisual equipment selected		
27.			Training sessions programmed			
27a.				Speakers scheduled		
28.				Recreation and entertainment planned		
29.				Dining accommodations planned		
30.				Sleeping accommodations planned		
31.				Registration, entertainment, welcome planned		
32.				Meeting room needs planned		
33.			Housing needs determined			
34.					Menus planned	
35.					Room setups planned	
36.			Event sheets (orders) completed			
37.		Final agenda approved				
38.		Contracts and purchase orders written				
39.		Detail tasks completed				
40.	Meeting conducted					
41.				Equipment returned		
42.			Invoices received			
43.			Invoices paid			
44.		Postmeeting evaluation conducted				

*This PERT was developed by Judith K. Giles, a meeting professional and former student. Ms. Giles has granted permission to use the material in this book for illustrative purposes.

Event	Activities	Responsibility	a	m	b	te	σ^2
1–2	Draft primary objective	Management	0.00	.5	1	.5	.167
2–3	Form objective tree	"	.125	.5	1	.521	.128
3–4	Study personnel, company files	Emp. rel.	3.	10	14	9.5	20.176
4–5	Determine effective learning form.	Trainers	1.	3	7	3.33	6.
5–6	Report findings	Trainers	.125	.5	1	.521	.128
6–7	Plan program content	Trainers	.5	1	2	1.083	.375
3–8	Research costs	Food and beverage	.5	2	3	1.917	1.042
3–9	Research costs	Hospitality	.5	1	2	1.083	.375
3–10	Research costs	Housing	1.0	2	4	2.167	1.5
3–12	Research costs	Travel	1.0	1.5	4	1.833	1.5
12–13	Calculate avg. fares	Travel	.125	.5	1	.521	.128
13–11	Report to site team	Travel	0.	.13	1	.25	.167
3–11	Compile information	Management	2.0	7.0	14	7.33	24.0
8–11	Report to site team	Food and beverage	.5	1.5	2	1.4	.375
9–11	Report to site team	Hospitality	.5	1.5	2	1.4	.375
10–11	Report to site team	Housing	.5	1.5	2	1.4	.375
7–14	Report program content/form	Trainers	.5	1.5	2	1.4	.375
11–14	Report estimated costs	Site team					
14–15	Review & select site	Management	.125	.5	1	.521	1.28
15–16	Sign-off, notify depts.	Management	0.0	.13	1	.25	.167
16–17	Sign contract w/ hotel	Management	.125	1.5	4	1.687	2.5
17–21	Monitor planning	Management	1	2	3	2.0	.666
7–22	Research speakers	Training	3	5	10	5.5	8.166
22–23	Write copy, design learn. mater.	Training	5	14	21	13.66	42.66
23–24	Typeset, pasteup	Graphics	3	7	14	7.5	20.16
24–26	Select equipment needed (A/V, etc.)	Trainers	.125	.5	2	.69	.586
26–27	Compile program	Trainers	1	2	3	2	.666
13–18	Negotiate transportation	Travel	2	7	10	6.66	10.666
18–19	Negotiate ground transp.	Travel	1	2	5	2.33	2.666
19–20	Make reservations	Travel	.125	.25	1	.354	.128
20–21	Report arrangements	Travel	.125	.25	1	.354	.128
21–27	Adjust training to pattern	Training/management	0	.5	1	.5	.166

(continued)

Event	Activities	Responsibility	a	m	b	te	σ^2
21–30	Room reservations	Housing	1	2	4	2.166	1.5
21–28	Plan entertainment	Hospitality	1	3	5	3	2.666
21–37	Monitor planning	Management					
27–27a	Speakers: confirm dates, topics, etc.	Trainers	1	2	5	2.333	2.666
27–32	Select meeting rooms	Training	.125	.5	1	.854	.128
28–29	# people/facilities/# meals/needs	Food and beverage	1	3	5	3	2.666
30–31	Registration, information, welcome	Hospitality	1	3	5	3	2.666
	Report needs to housing:						
27a–33	Guest speakers	Training	0	.25	1	.333	.166
32–33	Meeting rooms	Training	.125	.5	1	.845	.128
31–33	Registration	Hospitality	0	.125	4	.75	2.666
29–33	Dining	Food and beverage	.125	.5	1	.521	.128
33–34	Menu details	Food and beverage/chef	.25	1	2	1.042	.510
34–35	Draft floor plans	Housing	1	2	4	2.166	1.5
35–36	Draft event sheets	Housing	1	3	10	3.833	13.5
	Floor plans—meetings	Training					
	Floor plans—meals	Food and beverage					
	Menu, gratuities	Food and beverage					
	Equipment, A/V setups	Trainers					
	Timing, pattern	Trainers					
	Registration, entertainment	Hospitality					
36–37	Adjust details, deliver sheets to management	Housing	.125	.5	1	.521	.128
37–38	Issue needed contracts, P.O.'s; check event sheets/hotel cont.	Management	1	5	10	5.166	13.5
38–39	Execute all tasks	All dep.	7	14	30	15.5	88.166
39–40	Arrive, setup, *conduct meeting* clean up, pack, depart	All deps./staff	4	5	6	5	.666
40–44	Collect evaluation, analyze info.	Management/housing/ training	3	5	10	5.5	3.5
38–42	Certify invoices against contracts and budget	Management	1	30	60	30.166	580.166
42–43	Cut checks, mail	Management	1	30	60	30.166	580.166
43–44	Compare expenses to budget, analyze variances, report results	Management	1	3	5	3	2.666

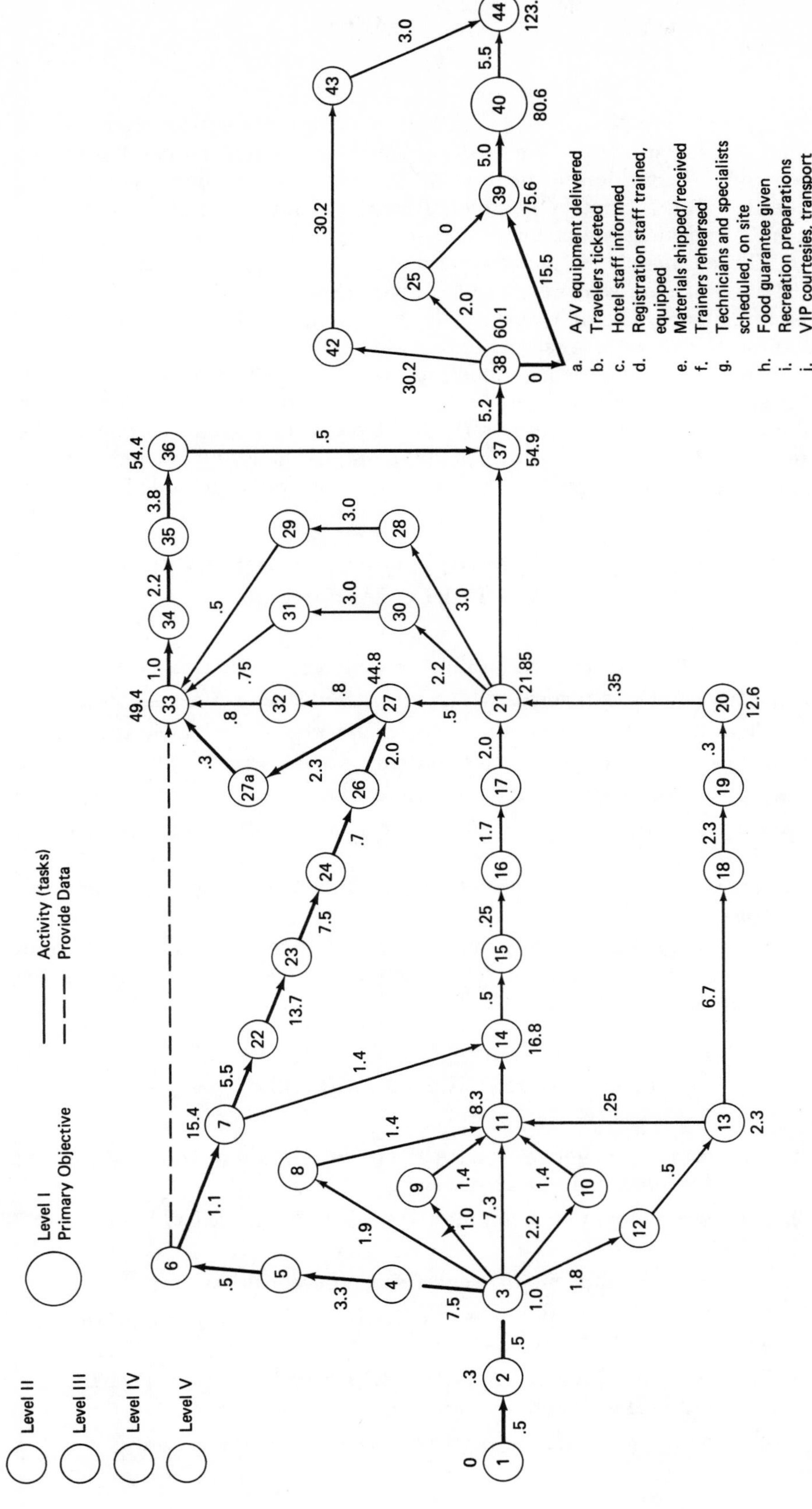
Level I
Primary Objective
Level II
Level III
Level IV
Level V
Activity (tasks)
Provide Data
a. A/V equipment delivered
b. Travelers ticketed
c. Hotel staff informed
d. Registration staff trained, equipped
e. Materials shipped/received
f. Trainers rehearsed
g. Technicians and specialists scheduled, on site
h. Food guarantee given
i. Recreation preparations
j. VIP courtesies, transport

Summary

We differentiated between a plan for developing a meeting plan and the plan itself. A brief summary of a meeting plan was given. A more detailed explanation with illustration forms appears at the end of the next chapter, since the meeting plan cannot be completed until we have a program complete with agenda and meeting pattern.

Three models for planning a meeting were given: checklist, Gantt, and PERT/CPM. You were referred to appendices for examples of both the checklist and an operational Gantt model. An example PERT was shown that incorporated the procedure (steps) for development of a PERT.

You, as a professional meeting manager, should select one of the three models depending upon your degree of sophistication and experience as a planner. You may find that you will progress through all three and then use the PERT for all meetings except small one-day meetings, which already have general plans developed and to which specifics must be added.

WHAT YOU SHOULD HAVE LEARNED FROM THIS CHAPTER

1. The difference between a plan to plan and a meeting plan.
2. The general categories which are included in a Meeting Plan.
3. The strengths and weaknesses of a checklist model, a Gantt, and a PERT.
4. How to develop your own Gantt for a meeting.
5. How to develop a PERT for a small meeting.
6. How to compute *estimated time* for each activity you list in your Gantt or PERT.
7. How to compute the probability of completing a given activity by your projected target date.
8. The five management techniques to use if your probability of completing necessary activities indicates accomplishment is extremely difficult or impossible.

REVIEW QUESTIONS

1. What are five major categories you believe would be the most important to consider when using a checklist?
2. Is it possible to predict completion times for a checklist? For a Gantt? For a PERT?
3. What are the four major weaknesses of a checklist?
4. What are three weaknesses of a Gantt model? Do you believe any of the weaknesses can be avoided? If so, how?
5. What are the three concepts with which PERT is concerned? Name each concept, define it, and give an example.
6. How many activities can there be between any two events?

7. How would you use your objective tree in developing an activity list for a PERT?
8. If optimistic time = 12 days, pessimistic time = 45 days, and most likely time = 21 days, what is the te?
9. What, in your own words, does earliest expected date (TE) mean?
10. How is *slack* time computed? How is it used? What are the implications of slack time for meeting management?

APPLICATION EXERCISE

You are to plan a one-day meeting at a local hotel. No transportation is needed because attendees are local. You will need: two nutrition breaks, one luncheon, two general sessions (one morning and one afternoon), two concurrent workshops during the morning and the afternoon, registration and fee collection, printed handout material, name badges, a featured speaker, and two workshop leaders. The purpose of the meeting is enlightenment. Create a PERT including all time estimates and slack time. How much time would you need to plan and produce this meeting?

Chapter 7

Programming: Agenda and Meeting Pattern

This chapter on programming, Phase V of the meeting process, is based on how a basic knowledge of communication theory is fundamental to the development of effective agendas and meeting patterns. Therefore, the basics of communication theory are discussed before agendas and meeting patterns.

Communication is fundamental to the interaction that produces an effective meeting. George Bernard Shaw said "The greatest problem with communication is the assumption it has happened." Communication is made up of *transactions*. A transaction is one person transmitting and another receiving and feeding back—a loop. We can visualize a transaction like this:

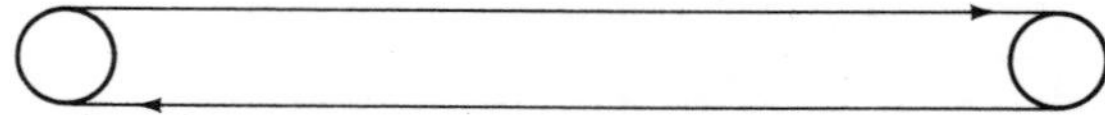

Here we have *two people* and *one* loop. If we had three people, the possibilities would look like this:

Three Potential Transactional Loops

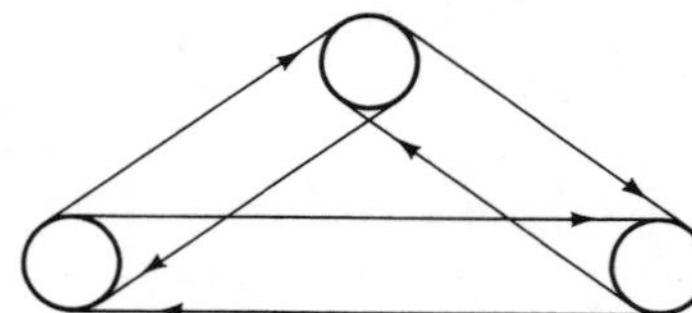

However, notice what happens if we have *six* people:

Fifteen Potential Transactional Loops

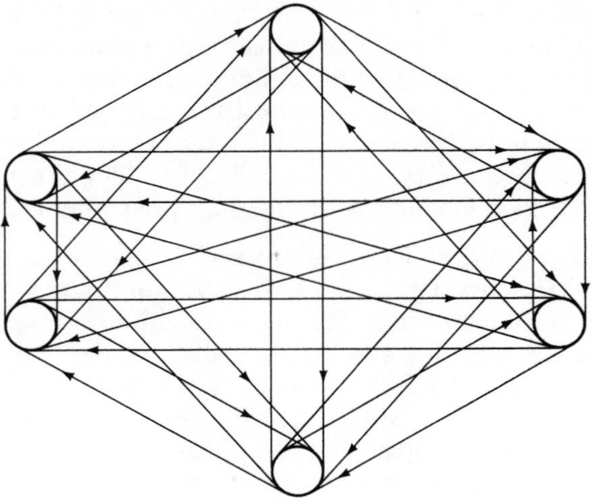

As you can see, as more people are added, the number of transactional loops increases rapidly. We could not possibly diagram all situations, so we use an equation:

$$TL = \frac{NP}{2} \times (NP - 1)$$

where

TL = transactional loops
NP = number of people

Let's quickly apply this equation to different group sizes before moving to room setups.

A group of 12:

$$TL = \frac{12}{2} \times (11) = 66$$

A group of 20:

$$TL = \frac{20}{2} \times (19) = 190$$

A group of 100:

$$TL = \frac{100}{2} \times (99) = 4950$$

A group of 1000:

$$TL = \frac{1000}{2} \times (999) = 499{,}500$$

Notice that throughout the discussion, we refer to "potential" transactional loops. There are many barriers to transactions that prevent all transactions from occurring. However, these are not our concern. Rather, our concern is primarily with room setups for meetings, which represent physical barriers we can strive to overcome. These physical barriers may be grouped into categories: numbers, distance, objects, and positioning.

1. *Numbers.* The equation for potential transactional loops illustrates the impact of the number of people. Potential transactions increase very rapidly when the number of people is increased. Assume all 4950 loops *oper-*

ated in our group of 100. A Tower of Babel would result. (Have you *heard* of a cocktail party of just 40 or 50 people?)

Therefore, when we desire interaction, we must keep the group as small as possible and yet provide for "mind sharing." The *ideal* group is from 6 to 12 people. Practical considerations usually make this impossible. You will find 20 to 30 people *can* function if the proper format and leadership are provided. Beyond 30, our hopes for interaction are reduced and our efforts as program planners must increase. All too often we get a few people participating, while the rest become the "silent majority." The size of this silent majority will depend upon our efforts as meeting programmers.

2. *Distance.* There is a direct proportional reduction in interaction for each 2 feet beyond an individual *personal space.* (This personal space differs based on our culture. For instance, Middle Eastern cultures allow approximately 6 inches around their bodies, whereas in the United States our distance is approximately 2 feet. This is one of the problems in intercultural communication. A Middle Easterner will attempt to get close to you, making you step back because you are uncomfortable; when you step back you make the Middle Easterner uncomfortable.)

Let us apply distance as a barrier in room setups. The conference setup is an excellent example. Four conference configurations are:

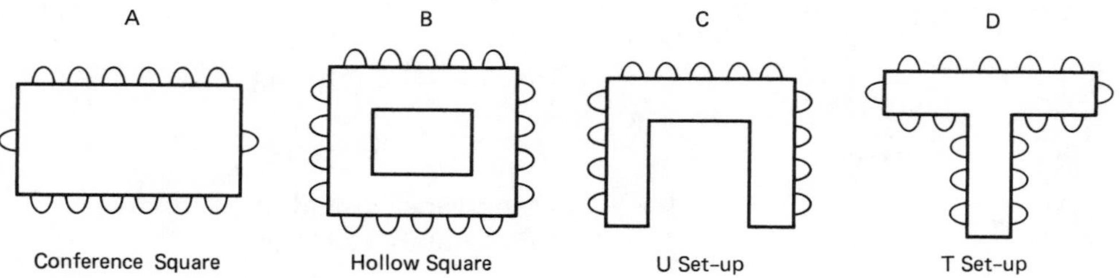

Setup A illustrates the problem of distance. All of us have experienced sitting at the end of a table and attempting to communicate with the person at the opposite end. We also know it is easier to talk with the people beside us or directly across the table. The wider and longer the table, the greater the difficulty.

Setup B, in addition to illustrating distance, shows the problem of empty space between physical objects—the tables. In addition to being wasted space, the hollow area creates a *void,* which humans tend not to attempt to cross.

Setup C presents a dilemma. If we place people on both sides of the legs of the "U", the people on the inside have their backs to each other, reducing communication. Those near the cross bar of the U are barriers to the people at the feet of the U.

Setup D presents still another problem—sight lines. People at the end of the leg of the T have difficulty in seeing those people at the ends of the bar of the T because of heads and bodies. As in setup C, we don't communicate very much with people we can't see.

A simple O shape would appear to be ideal. There are two problems, however. The normal hotel has only 5-foot or 6-foot round tables, which will limit your participants to the preferred 6 or 8 because 10 or 12 people at a 5-foot or 6-foot round table forces individuals to violate others' personal spaces.

The second problem with the O-shaped table is that if we try to get a larger round table, we begin to increase distance and reduce communication, as was indicated for the conference setups. A famous example of this was the use of an oval-shaped table during the Vietnam peace negotiations to eliminate "power" positions at the head and foot of the table. The number of people required a large oval, and distance became a factor adding to the already existing communication problems.

A possible solution would be the use of armchairs arranged in a circle, but most hotels do not have this capacity. Armchairs are almost impossible to stack for storage, and in a hotel, storage space is nonincome producing. The use of armchairs leads us to the next category—objects.

3. *Objects* produce a drastic impact on communication. Two people may start to communicate around a pillar but immediately work their way into a face-to-face situation. Management "power theory" talks about placing a desk between the power figure and a subordinate.

A reticent person appreciates the security offered by an intervening object, yet if you wish to draw that person into the interaction, you must eliminate the physical as well as the psychological barrier.

Most standard room setups produce objects as barriers. The only one that does not is when people are placed in a circle on open chairs. However, if no writing arm is on the chair, writing is difficult, as is handling of papers and books.

4. *Positioning* is our last category. The greatest interaction is produced in face-to-face situations.

The four conference setups discussed earlier allow for at least some face-to-face situations. On the other hand, the usual hotel theater setup, technically called American Theater Seating, minimizes face-to-face interaction. American seating looks like this:

OOOOOOOOOOO OOOOOOOOOOO OOOOOOOOOOO
OOOOOOOOOOO OOOOOOOOOOO OOOOOOOOOOO
OOOOOOOOOOO OOOOOOOOOOO OOOOOOOOOOO

Continental, or European, Theater Seating can improve on interaction by producing at least *quartering* face-to-face situations rather than one-half. The difference is this:

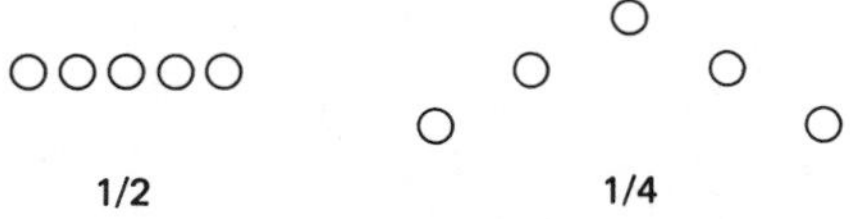

The people in the $\frac{1}{4}$ position are partially turned to each other.

Continental seating looks like this:

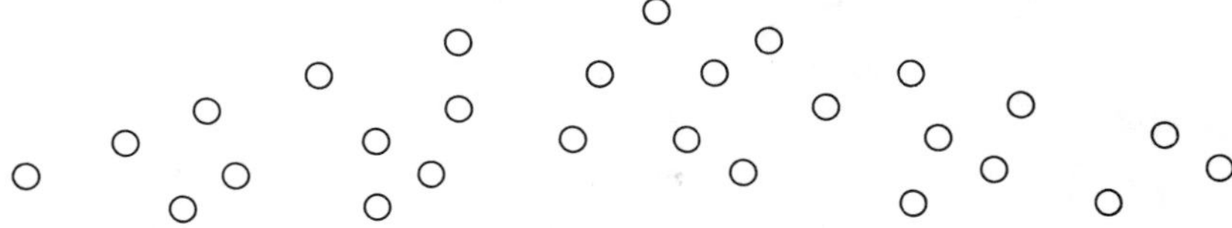

Hotels are not normally familiar with this setup, and their first reaction will be that wider space between rows reduces the number of people you can get in a room. However, if you draw American and continental seating to scale you will discover the *aisle space* in American seating equalizes the space between the rows, and room capacity will remain approximately the same.

Also, continental seating offsets the chairs so the heads of people in the front do not break sight lines of people behind, as happens in American seating.

The last setup to be discussed is the schoolroom:

This setup presents a different approach to the handling of distance, objects, and positioning. As shown, the setup represents poor positioning—single transactional loops are isolated—and barrier objects (the heads of the people in front) are introduced, thus breaking sight lines.

A compromise can be developed that minimizes barriers from objects and positioning. For the preceding setup, we use a concept called a *herringbone*. It looks like this:

You notice immediately that the herringbone application produces the advantages of continental seating by offsetting the positions of people for improved sight lines and by producing the $\frac{1}{4}$-facing position. However, objects (tables) still remain.

This section on communication in room setups has shown the following:

1. The meeting professional must always have the communication effectiveness of the room in mind.
2. The degree of interaction desired will determine the room setups.
3. There is no perfect room setup. You must always balance the barriers in terms of the practical, the importance of each barrier, and the maximizing of transactional loops.

You now have a basic knowledge of communication theory related to meeting management. We next turn our attention to developing an agenda.

Developing Agendas

An agenda consists of those *content* activities that make up a specific program designed to accomplish the meeting's purpose. All purposes (except maybe enjoyment) require some information or enlightenment as a basis.

Most room setups permit some transmission of information. Normally, the room setups most helpful for imparting information are theater, the U shape, and the classroom. Conference setups work best for interaction and problem solving.

Usually the meetings we plan and conduct are for adults. Therefore, I will touch briefly on what is called *adult learning theory* and then apply it and general factors to development of the agenda.

1. The adult factor

a. *Adults vote with their feet.* Long lectures, periods of interminable sitting, and the absence of practice opportunities reduce adult learning and increase nonparticipation and noninteraction.

b. *Adults have a background of firsthand experience.* As a result, adults know—or think they know—a good deal about what you're trying to teach them. An effective program builds on participant experience.

c. *Adults have a great many preoccupations outside the particular learning situation.* A content session should maximize learning and minimize wasted time.

d. *Adults have real decisions to make and real problems to solve.* Be sure your content sessions cover information and skills relevant to current problems and decisions. Avoid wandering.

e. *Adults have set habits and strong tastes.* Provide coffee in the morning and smoking and nonsmoking sections of the meeting room. Make certain your speakers know whether the group accepts or is offended by profanity.

f. *Adults have some amount of pride.* Adults prefer to be self-directed. Make your meetings foster responsibility, not obedience. A meeting is not an elementary classroom.

g. *Adults have developed a reflex to authority.* Meetings that tend to derive justification from authority are resisted or rejected. (Don't let them get the impression "the boss" says they must attend and this is good for them.) If it is necessary to use authority, make certain participants feel their suggestions and ideas have been incorporated.

h. *Adults have strong feelings about learning situations.* Make certain your meetings provide chances for successful experiences and give attendees positive reinforcement.

i. *Adults have established emotional frameworks consisting of values, attitudes, and behaviors.* Effective meetings are a blending of many kinds of behaviors. Effective meetings should attempt to meet the needs of participants in ways helpful to the entire group.

j. *Adults react equally well to visual as well as audio stimuli.* Effective meetings blend visual with audio experiences.

It may appear to you that we are going back to Chapter 3 and the phrase, know your group. We are—because a successful program and agenda must be based on this concept.

The foregoing considerations indicate agendas of meetings (1) should be adapted to the needs of the group, (2) should be "real" to the participants, (3) should provide a combination of hands-on, audio, and visual experiences, (4) should build upon the group members' previous experience, (5) should provide short (90-minute to 2-hour sessions), and (6) should incorporate as many group suggestions as possible.

2. General factors affecting agenda development
   a. People are more physically and psychologically alert between 9:30 A.M. and 12 noon and between 2:00 P.M. and 5:00 P.M.
   b. The physical endurance and attention spans of people do not exceed 1 hour 50 minutes to 2 hours.

With the two factors affecting agenda development and the concept of knowing your group in mind, we are ready to address the development of an agenda.

The Steps of Agenda Development

Prepare Objectives

The objectives for programming are different from those for meetings in the sense that they are directed toward the performance of certain received content, whereas meeting objectives are oriented toward managing or planning performance.

Some of the material in this section is based on the ideas of Robert F. Mager in his book, *Preparing Instructional Objectives*. Here, his ideas are directed toward the program content of meetings, but you should make every effort to secure Dr. Mager's book so that you have more of the general theory behind the applications discussed here.

Dr. Mager, when considering the characteristics of program objectives, says [1]:

> The format includes three characteristics that help make an objective communicate an intent: These characteristics answer three questions: (1) What should the learner be able to do? (2) Under what conditions do you want the learner to be able to do it? and (3) How well must it be done? The characteristics are these:
> 1. Performance. An objective says what a learner is expected to be able to *do;* the objective sometimes describes the product or result of the doing.
> 2. Conditions. An objective always describes the important conditions (if any) under which the performance is to occur.
> 3. Criterion. Wherever possible, an objective describes the criterion of acceptable performance by describing how well the learner must perform in order to be considered acceptable.

Now let us apply these characteristics to our meeting program. Program objectives, like other objectives, contain the word *to* followed by an action verb.

Example:

To write an abstract of the company's new affirmative action plan for presentation to company department managers.

Example:

To write a paragraph indicating the difference of each publication from other publications in the field, given a list of six new company publications.

Example:

To merge, sort, and subject search with a maximum of two errors and without assistance, given an opportunity for hands-on use of a new word-processing system.

You will notice that the examples include Mager's characteristics of performance, condition, and criterion.

Now that you understand how program objectives may differ from planning and management objectives, we turn our attention to structuring the agenda.

Structure the Agenda

1. Make a list of your objectives.
2. Determine if the objectives may be most effectively addressed through a general session or small-group (breakout) sessions.
3. Determine the time of day (given the psychological characteristics of attendees) that would be the best time to schedule the session.
4. Determine what presentation method (format) would best accomplish the objective.
5. Determine what presentation resources (such as speakers, trainers, or group leaders) you will need.
6. Schedule your sessions for the most effective psychological times and physical length.*

Suggestions for Preparing Your Agenda

1. Submit a questionnaire (if possible) or conduct spot interviews with potential attendees to get their ideas.
2. Provide a variety of session approaches, from visually augmented lectures to hands-on problem solving.
3. Since you have the entire meeting time from which to choose, place your most difficult material and/or lecture-type material between 9:30 A.M. and noon and/or between 2 P.M. and 5 P.M.
4. Place hands-on experience at the *start* (9:30 A.M. or 2 P.M.) of the best time, or, if you *must* present difficult lecture material, do so at the start of this time and follow it with a hands-on experience session, where the lecture material is put to use.
5. Provide a variety of approaches (formats) during each day of the meeting.
6. Supply speakers with suggested communication approaches such as visually augmented lectures and hands-on problem solving.
7. The success suggestion: Provide for as much meaningful and realistic interaction as possible.

*Do not worry about other events of the meeting, since the program is the core and the element most necessary for the accomplishment of your primary objective.

8. Decide your room setup based on the material to be covered and the techniques to be used in communicating.
9. Schedule sessions for a minimum of 90 minutes and a maximum of 2 hours.

The Steps of Meeting Pattern Development

Once you have established the approach and the times for your agenda, you begin to look at your meeting pattern.

1. *Determine arrival and departure times.* If you are in a position to control the travel for your attendees, there are some factors to consider.
   a. They should depart from their points of origin at a *reasonable* hour. If they have to depart between 3 and 5 A.M., they will need to arise two hours before departure depending on where they live in relation to the departure point. Add to this a two- to five-hour flight and you have a fatigued attendee upon arrival. *Be careful* of time-zone changes.
   b. Provide for prompt courteous check-in upon arrival, regardless of time.
2. *Provide for free time after arrival.* An attendee who has been traveling usually needs to relax and change clothing.
3. *Provide a problem-free meeting registration.*
4. *Provide a casual first event.*
5. *Provide time for breakfast each morning, whether it be for a scheduled group breakfast or on their own.*
6. *Provide a 90-minute minimum for lunch.*
7. *Refreshments in the meeting room in the morning, which, although distracting, permit attendee utilization of break time for nature or conversation needs.*
8. Note traffic flow to restrooms. Provide an adequate break time. Remember, the statistical average turn-around time in restrooms is 5 minutes for women and 3 minutes for men. Air hand-driers extend those times by 30 seconds.
9. *Provide time for movement between sessions.* If there is a change of floors, the time must be extended.
10. *Provide free time or group relaxation after the presentation of difficult material.* This permits attendees to discuss the material or problems informally if they wish.
11. *Plan evening or sports activities with the next day's agenda sessions in mind.* Don't tire the attendees the night before an important presentation.
12. *Schedule departure times in such a way the attendee has time to pack before or after the final session without being rushed.* Be aware of hotel checkout times.
13. *Schedule an exciting last session to discourage early departure by attendees.*
14. *Schedule extra cashiers to expedite departure if you have a large group.* Also, schedule extra bellpersons.

15. *Make certain you schedule adequate ground transportation and that it arrives on time for arrival, departure, and special events.*
16. *Once you have completed both your agenda and meeting pattern, lay out all events on a large sheet of paper, using one sheet for each day. Double-check for conflicts.*
17. *When all events fit in a chronological sequence, number each event consecutively, from check-in and registration to checkout. Note:* If you provide meeting registration during more than one time block, list each registration and assign it an event number in the order in which it occurs. Event numbers are very important. They provide you and the hotel with a quick reference.
18. *Type or enter in a computer your chronological list of events because this is your meeting pattern.*

The meeting pattern you have developed will be used later in your selection of a hotel and in negotiations with that hotel. You should have multiple copies of the pattern for use by you, your staff, and appropriate people in your destination hotel.

Summary

This chapter has emphasized three important aspects of Phase V of meeting planning and management: communication theory, agenda development, and creation of a meeting pattern that includes not only your agenda but also each event planned for the meeting, from arrival to departure. The entire meeting program is based upon communication theory and includes the agenda and meeting pattern.

WHAT YOU SHOULD HAVE LEARNED FROM THIS CHAPTER

1. The use of transactional loops as a basis for communication.
2. The equation for determining the number of transactional loops.
3. The importance of transactional loops as a guide in determining room setups and the agenda.
4. The effectiveness of some room setups over others in furthering communication and interaction.
5. Three characteristics of program objectives: performance, condition, and criterion.
6. How program objectives determine the type of session (general or breakout) and the communication approach.
7. The two major steps to follow in developing an agenda.
8. The adult factors and general factors to be recognized and applied in agenda development.
9. How to develop a meeting pattern *after* the agenda is developed and scheduled.
10. The 18 steps to be followed in developing a meeting pattern.

11. The need for understanding and development of communication interaction, agenda, and meeting pattern in developing a meeting.

REVIEW QUESTIONS

1. You are planning a meeting for 350 people. How many potential transactional loops are there?
2. You are planning an agenda that requires a general session and four break-out sessions. Two of the break-out sessions will involve hands-on activities and use of audiovisuals. What kind of room setup would you use for the general session, and why? For the two hands-on sessions, and why?
3. What do you consider to be the five most important factors in adult learning as related to meetings? Why?
4. What would be four program objectives for corporate meeting 1? Make sure they meet the three characteristics. (You are free to be creative in terms of an agenda.)
5. What are the advantages and disadvantages of using American seating for a large group?
6. What are the advantages and disadvantages of using continental seating for a large group?
7. Why should an agenda be developed before the meeting pattern?
8. Would it be possible to schedule an opening session for the Great Corporation meeting at 9:00 A.M. on the first day of the meeting? If so, how would you accomplish it? If not, why not?

APPLICATION EXERCISE

Turn to the description of the Great Corporation meeting (Appendix C). Notice the purposes, number of sessions, the kind of equipment, and the exhibits.

1. Prepare a set of program objectives for the agenda.
2. Develop a meeting pattern after you have completed the agenda.

You are free to create additional information you believe you need, but you may not change the basic information given.

References

1. Robert F. Mager, *Preparing Instructional Objectives,* 2d ed., D. S. Lake Publications, Belmont, Calif., 1984, p. 21.

Chapter 8

Determining Space, Destination, and Site

Space, destination, and site create the atmosphere and ambience in which the communication and interaction of the meeting take place.

Determining Space

After completing the meeting agenda and pattern, we have a good idea about the number of meeting rooms we well need. However, we still need to know the number and type of sleeping rooms and the size of the meeting rooms.

Sleeping rooms are determined, in large part, by the organization's policies. If your organization is an association or if you are planning an independent seminar or workshop, the chances are that you will rely upon *attendee* decisions. For instance, since the attendee pays for the sleeping room, the individual will decide whether he or she wishes single, double, or multiple (where several people may share a two-bedroom suite to reduce individual cost) occupancy. In the case of attendee decision, you will need to have a *room block* (reserved group of rooms) with the most rooms being singles, the second-most being doubles, and the third, suites. To make the decision, decide on the number of potential attendees. Reserve about 50% singles, 40% doubles, and 10% a mixture of one and two-bedroom suites. This will give you the number of sleeping rooms you will need.

On the other hand, if you are planning a corporation meeting, then determine company policy on single or double occupancy. This, when combined with your number of potential attendees, will give the number of sleeping rooms needed. Also, company policy will determine whether VIPs need suites or single occupancy. You will reserve a block of rooms based on this information.

As a final note on sleeping rooms, when you make your room block reservation, secure agreement to add to or reduce the size of the block at set dates before the meeting. Normally, the hotel will require that you not change the room block any later than 30 days before the meeting, but this cutoff date is subject to negotiation.

Size of Meeting Rooms

There are at least two methods for determining meeting room size: using the square footage approach or using instruments such as the *Comfort Calculator* or *Perfect Fit*. (Both the *Comfort Calculator* and *Perfect Fit* are available through Meeting Planners International.)

The *Comfort Calculator* is an instrument that has been developed over several years and is designed to give the planner an index of space needed for various room setups based on the number of people. However, the *Comfort Calculator* seems to be designed to get the most possible people in a meeting room without a real regard for "creature comfort." It is an aid to hotels, who can legitimately say they have rooms that fit your needs and cite the *Comfort Calculator.*

The *Perfect Fit* is a scaled floor-space-layout package. It comes complete with ¼-inch graph paper and scale cutouts of tables, chairs, and the like so you can lay out the room and have a visual impression of how it will look. However, some people have trouble visualizing what the actual room will look like from this kind of pasteup.

Square footage approaches are best represented by a system developed by Fred Handy, former meeting manager for the Geological Society of America, which is presently known as the RMAMPI (Rocky Mountain Association of Meeting Planners International) standard. The square footages shown in the following table are based on actual measurements of the human being and the physical objects in the meeting room, such as tables and chairs. For instance, with theater seating, the normal hotel chair is either 19 inches or 21 inches wide. From front to back, it is usually close to 21 inches. Then we need to look at "elbow room." If we draw a square 3 feet by 3 feet, the average person can occupy the space comfortably while sitting. Thus, we can calculate *9 square feet per person* for theater seating. When we use tables, as in classrooms, conferences, and banquets, there has to be an allowance for "scoot" space (that space needed to move the chair back in order to be seated or to stand up). The scoot space plus the size of the object (table or chair) determine the per-person space to be provided.

PER-PERSON SQUARE FOOTAGE CALCULATIONS

Setup	Square Feet Per Person
Theater	9–10
Reception (standing)	8½–9½
Conference	23–25
School room	15–17
Banquet (rounds)	11½–12

Based on the form of space calculation you decide to use, go back to your meeting agenda and meeting pattern. Take each session and the setup you have decided to use for most effective communication and interaction. Project how many people will be in the session (see Planning Checklist, Appendix D), and then calculate the room's size. Note that you must provide for access to fire exits and traffic flow. (Don't forget your registration area and meeting headquarters room.)

Now, make a list of each session and the size of room you need. This will give you the amount of meeting space needed. The list of both meeting space and number of sleeping rooms will be needed when you approach a hotel.

Determining Destination

There is a process of determining a destination that you would be well advised to follow.

First, determine the organization's policies. Sometimes you will find the organization has definite ideas and may have even predetermined destinations well in advance. Some organizations like to move their meetings to different geographical areas, including international destinations. If you have a large meeting (500 or more), you will need to determine destinations at least 5 years in the future. If you will be using a convention center you will need to determine and tentatively book the center as far as 10 to 20 years in advance because most centers have meetings booked that far in advance.

Second, use your budget projection to determine destination feasibility. (Assuming destinations have not been predetermined.) We have already gone through the process of budget projections (Chapter 5), where travel was the basic factor in determining destination.

Third, conduct needed research on the destination. There are three forms of this research: (1) reviewing written materials published by *Successful Meetings, Meetings & Conventions, Meeting News,* the *Hotel/Motel Redbook, Hotel/Travel Index,* and *Official Meeting Facilities Guide,* (2) contacting the convention bureau(s) in potential destination cities indicating your needs (the service provided by convention bureaus is covered in Chapter 12), and (3) visiting the destinations, if practical.

Fourth, compile all your data, make a decision, and secure needed approvals of your decision.

Following is an example destination consolidation–analysis table.

DESTINATION CONSOLIDATION–ANALYSIS

Item	Destination 1	Destination 2	Destination 3
1. Budget			
Travel cost			
Air			
Ground			
2. Accessibility			
3. Organization policy			
4. Climate			
5. Research data			

The use of a table similar to this one will be very helpful to you in securing approval of your decision.

Determining the Site

Site selection is probably the most difficult single process to be covered in this chapter. Again, it needs to be approached systematically. Here are three "do nots."

1. Do not be initially swayed by the status or image of the hotel.
2. Do not be swayed by the decor of the hotel to the point you ignore other vital factors.
3. Do not accept free gifts from the hotel except as indicated in this chapter.

Now, let us go into a system of site selection.

1. Review the data you have collected for destination selection. Look at the publications again. Look at the listing of hotels at the destination. Look specifically at details such as number of rooms, types of meeting-support facilities and services, and the general room costs. (Remember room costs are subject to negotiation.)

2. Call or write other meeting professionals you know who may have held meetings at the destination.

3. Prepare a proposal and submit it to three properties at the destination that seem to *best* fit your meeting needs. *Write (don't call) the three selected properties.*

Include in your letter and proposal:

- **a.** Name and type of your organization
- **b.** Approximate dates of your meeting
- **c.** Length of your meeting (days/nights)
- **d.** Number of sleeping rooms of each type you will need (or compute "room nights"—the total number of rooms times the number of nights)
- **e.** The number of food and beverage functions
- **f.** Required number and size of meeting rooms
- **g.** Support services needed

4. Request a written proposal from each hotel. If they are interested in your meeting and have your approximate dates available, ask them to submit a proposal containing the following:

1. How their property *specifically* meets *your* meeting needs.
2. Scale or dimensional diagrams of their space that you might utilize
3. Any special facilities or services they might suggest to you
4. Their proposed group and meeting-space rates

Some hotels will call you rather than write. (Ask them to write, since you want a proposal in writing to use in making a decision.) Some will send you a hotel brochure and a cover letter saying in effect they want your business. (These will frequently be form letters with no specific information relevant to your meeting.) Other hotels will specifically answer your requests and show a real concern for having their property host your meeting.

In the hotel business, as in the meeting industry, there are professionals and nonprofessionals. You may be assured those responding specifically to your request (in writing) are more professional than those who do not. This degree of professionalism will probably also be shown in the handling of your meeting. If you receive any contact other than a written proposal, drop consideration of that property, look for another property at that destination, and send them a request for a proposal.

5. Evaluate, systematically, the proposal received. The evaluation system you use should compare your meeting objectives, the budget items, the meeting pattern, and other requirements with each of the proposals individually. (This can be done by computer if you have the necessary software; see Chapter 14.)

6. Arrange for personal site visits to the three properties selected. Never select a sight you have not personally inspected for the meeting under consideration.

a. Write a letter to each of the three properties indicating your date of inspection, approximate time for which you would like an appointment, and, if appropriate, request complimentary accommodations at the top-ranking property.

b. Write to the district sales manager of an airline serving the destination asking for a complimentary flight for a site inspection trip. You must include:

Details about the organization, the meeting, number of attendees, dates, approximate number of attendees who would be using the airline and from which points of origin, and an intent to route all possible attendees on that airline, and, the dates you would prefer for your inspection trip.

7. Prepare for and organize your site inspection. You need to prepare your own site inspection checklist. An example, for continental U.S. properties, is shown in Appendix F. An addendum for international and off-shore properties is Appendix G. Incorporate into your site inspection list any special considerations, such as recreation requirements.

Many meeting-site evaluators like to set up an appointment around 9:00 A.M. to 10:00 A.M. If it is an out-of-town property, arrive the night before, without telling the property. Collect the site-inspection checklist and then observe the hotel as a *guest* rather than with the usual VIP treatment once the interview begins.

8. Conduct a preinterview inspection.

a. Upon arriving, enter the hotel as would a regular guest. Observe the door- and bellpersons. Are they efficient and courteous? Do they make you feel welcome? How many stations are there at the registration desk? Would the number of stations be adequate for your group arrivals? How efficient and courteous are they? (Remember, you are just another guest, if you have arrived early. You are not "flagged" as a VIP so you can see how your attendees will be handled.) Is there a function board listing events and meetings in the hotel? Is there a manager on duty in the lobby or in a special office off the lobby? Is there a registration or reservations manager on duty? (Remember, a late-night check-in will not necessarily have a reservation or registration manager.) How many cashier positions are there in the event your attendees should check out in a group? Are there advertised procedures for quick checkout?

As you go into your room: (a) Is the bellperson pleasant? (b) Does the bellperson knock before entering the room? When you enter your room: (a) Is there an odor of cleaning fluid or a musty odor? (b) Does the bellperson turn on your lights and in other ways make your room inviting? (c) How does the bellperson indicate he or she is finished and awaiting a tip? (There are professional and unprofessional bellpeople. The pros don't shove out an open hand, and the nonprofessional can embarrass or antagonize your attendees.) Also, before leaving, does the bellperson conduct a thorough inspection of your room, noting any dust, lights or light switches not working, or dripping faucets and indicate engineering or housekeeping will be notified?

After the bellperson leaves, conduct your own check of towels, washcloths, television, heat or air conditioning. If you find problems, call housekeeping and see how quickly they respond. Remember, an attendee in a room with a problem who cannot get the problem solved in a hurry is an unhappy attendee, and your meeting is off on the wrong foot with at least that one person. Do you find dust? (Always run your fingers on top of the door. In a hotel with an effective housekeeping staff, there should be none.) Is there lint under the bed? Is there discolored caulking around the tub or shower? Take off your shoes and walk on the carpet (particularly in beach resorts, you might feel sand under your feet). Make notes on all the problems you see so you can check these items in rooms you will inspect during your formal tour the next day.

b. Relax and organize yourself.
- (i) Unpack, refresh yourself, and prepare to enjoy your self-guided tour of the hotel.
- (ii) Reread your site inspection checklist.
- (iii) Dig out and read the hotel literature in the room: menus, directory or services and phone numbers, list of attractions in the hotel and the area, and so on.

c. Go on a self-guided tour.
- (i) Check the meeting rooms. If there are some in which meetings are in progress, observe the setups. If it is evening, see if the room has been refreshed (normally, the meeting rooms are refreshed early in the morning, but some hotels refresh rooms at the end of the day's schedule).
- (ii) Check the location of the kitchen(s). Are they convenient to the meeting rooms where a food function may be held? Is there serving access to rooms where hot tables can be located?
- (iii) Check the kitchen. Dressed in business attire and with a clipboard and checklist, you will not be disturbed if you don't get in the way. (Do not inspect a kitchen while the staff is preparing for or serving a meal.)
- (iv) Walk through the meeting and restroom area. Could your attendees find their way? Could they move easily from room to room, or would

halls be congested? Are there restrooms adequate in number and facilities, and are they conveniently located to meeting rooms?

(v) Check the signage. Are signs showing directions to meeting rooms well located and easily read? Is there sign provision for visually handicapped in the lobby, the meeting area, and the elevators or escalators? Are the meeting room names (numbers) well marked so they can be seen and read from a distance?

Anything you can check on your self-guided tour will save you time on your formal tour, since you will just need to check against what you have already noted. (You might even have some prepared questions.)

d. Sample the food and beverages. Have your evening meal in a dining room so you can check food quality and service. Eat breakfast in a coffee shop, looking at the menu variety, efficiency of service, and how quickly, without pushing, the coffee shop turns over their tables. (*Turn over* means seat, serve, reset for the next guest.) If you wish, inspect the lounge. Find out what their house brands (served if a customer does not ask for a specific brand) are. Do the bartenders and servers keep an eye peeled to discourage overconsumption by customers? Are bartenders and servers efficient, courteous, and friendly? Will the atmosphere appeal to your attendees?

e. Finally, do your own summary of your inspection in preparation for the formal interview/tour. Use your site inspection checklist and try to rate the property on a scale of 1 to 10. After you have rated the property, rate the personnel you have observed. Did they move briskly—not running and not ambling? Were they courteous? Did they have an "esprit de corps" as if they enjoyed their work and the hotel? The personnel you observed should give you a good impression of the management and how your total meeting will be handled. Now, combine the ratings of the property and of the personnel. A good balance is to allow 40% for the property and 60% for the personnel. Remember, the finest property can be destroyed in effectiveness by the personnel it employs. The hotel business is a *service* business and *employees* provide the service.

9. Conduct a formal interview and tour. *Relax!* Remember, you are the *buyer* and the product (property) must be *sold* to you. You and your meeting represent *income* to the hotel. The burden is on the salesperson.

Set your appointments at about 9 or 10 A.M. Make certain you are working with a *decision maker.* It is recommended that you request the general manager or other senior executive officer be present for the *start* of the interview so you may ask if the person with whom you will be working can make decisions for the property. A good way to test your salesperson and the executive officer is to set up a hypothetical situation and ask if the salesperson can make a decision on it. For example:

> Assume you represent excellent business for the hotel because your group will occupy a large room block, have several food and beverage functions, and your group likes to spend money as individuals in a hotel. You also represent possible *repeat* business.
>
> You want a hospitality function complete with four kinds of hors d'oeuvre, call brand and house liquors, and a major spread of cold hors d'oeuvre. You want the hors d'oeuvre to be served by at least four servers in tuxedos.
>
> Then, ask if the hotel will *host* the function and can the salesperson make such a decision for the hotel.

The executive officer is in a dilemma. The hotel would like to have your business because it represents very good income for the property. If the executive says *yes,* he or she is delegating authority in an area where it is not normally delegated. If he or she says *no,* he or she faces three problems: (1) he or she may be frequently called away from other important duties to make this kind of decision; (2) another responsible person who could make these decisions must be pulled from other responsibilities and assigned to your account; or (3) the hotel will lose your business because you will only deal with a decision maker.

The normal response is to delegate the responsibility to the salesperson present.

This may seem harsh, but if you have had to sit through sessions where everything must be "cleared," you understand the point. Your time is valuable.

After you have assured yourself of the decision maker, go to work. Don't waste your time and the salesperson's with small talk.

- **a.** Go over your meeting needs and your meeting pattern.
- **b.** Ask for a tour focused on *your* meeting needs—not a promotional tour of the property.
- **c.** Ask to come back and talk about specific needs after the tour.

During your tour, you should be concerned with your group and your meeting needs. There are six general areas for you to observe.

Housekeeping. As in your pretour, you are looking for cleanliness and efficiency. Compare what you see with your self-guided tour.

Traffic flow. Check meeting-room location, accessibility, and ease of movement from one to the other as well as to restrooms. In which rooms does the hotel want to put your meeting?

Meeting rooms. There are several things to look for in a meeting room. (1) The *ceiling height* must be at least 10 feet to allow for audiovisual projection. (2) *Dimensions* are important. Rectangular rooms are fine *if* they are wide enough for the length. (A 20-foot by 80-foot room is poor because your audience will feel "compressed" if you use the length of the room for theater-style seating. If you use continental style facing a side wall, you'll get three rows and presenters will be faced with having their backs to a portion of the audience if they look to either side. Also, a projection screen in front can only be seen by the people located in the middle.) (3) Check for *obstacles*. The three most common obstacles are pillars, posts, and chandeliers. All break sight lines and audiovisual projection lines. Chandeliers break sight lines for audiovisual projection if they hang down very far.

(4) Check *decor.* Light in the room is important. Therefore, walls should be light-colored. Blues can be depressing for people in a meeting; shades of red can stimulate but can become irritating; and greens are relaxing but can become too relaxing. Generally, a beige color will produce best results. Wall paper is acceptable if it is not too patterned. Pictures, mirrors, or designs are distracting. Windows are a problem. While admitting light, they will draw attendees eyes to the landscape or any movement outside. They also need blackout curtains for audiovisual presentations. If a room does not have windows, some of your attendees will feel claustrophobia, and you will need to shorten your sessions or

give more breaks and/or activities. Room decor should further communication rather than hinder it. The judgment must be yours in terms of your group, session objectives, and method of presentation.

(5) One of the most important concerns about a meeting room is the *acoustics*. Snapping your fingers in an empty room will tell you something. If you get an echo or metallic sound, the hard surfaces are "bouncing" the sound, and if your attendees are exposed to much bounce, they'll become fatigued. However, human bodies and clothing absorb sound, so the acoustic level will change. The other end of the sound spectrum is the "dead" room. If walls, floors, and ceiling all absorb sound, there is little sound bounce. Add people to absorb more sound, and the room will become depressing over a period of time. The last factor is the so-called soundproof wall between rooms. First of all, there is no such thing in a hotel as a *soundproof* wall or door. There are *sound-treated* walls and doors. The degree of treatment varies. Take a transistor radio with you, place it in one room, and go to the adjoining room. If you can hear it but if it is not distracting, you have good sound treatment. Can your speakers be heard even if there is an audiovisual presentation next door?

(6) Finally, meeting rooms should have light and heat *controls* in accessible positions; sound controls are needed if the room has a built-in public address system. A meeting room should have a phone jack but not a phone.

Sleeping rooms. Let's look at sleeping rooms from a slightly different perspective. Cleanliness is most important, but what about the bathrooms? Are there two sinks? If you have a double-occupancy room and both occupants must shave or apply makeup, two sinks are important. Be sure the rooms do not seem too small and confining.

Provision for handicapped attendees is very important, particularly in the bath. There should be no step up to enter the bath. The door should be wide enough to permit a wheelchair to enter. There should be "grab bars" near the toilet and in the bathtub area. Toilet tissue should be positioned where it is easily accessible—to the *side* of the toilet, not behind it.

As a reminder, check the lighting for shaving or makeup. Check telephone location. Check for the amenities in the bathroom. (Meeting attendees have become spoiled. They need shampoo, hair conditioner, shower caps, complexion and deodorant soaps, shoeshine cloths, ice buckets, bottle openers, facial tissue, and many other items that are expensive to the hotel and cause room rates to increase.)

Kitchens. Be certain you tour the kitchens. Observe how the ovens, stoves, grills, vent hood, dishwashers, and preparation areas are laid out. Do the kitchen personnel move easily without having to dodge each other?

Again, how clean is the kitchen? Some grease will normally be on a vent hood when the kitchen is in use, but there should never be a grease buildup. Floors should be clean and free of grease if the personnel are not preparing a regular meal or a food function. Do the food preparation people have their hair covered? You'll think of other questions, particularly if you have had a seminar or course in kitchen management.

Finally, be concerned with the location of the kitchens. If a kitchen is far from an eating room, you'll encounter carts for keeping food warm until it can be served. This will tell you immediately that any menu you plan must not contain foods that continue to cook when they are removed from the grill, such as steak and eggs.

While on your tour, *meet the chef.* Become friends if possible. At least give the chef your business card and indicate looking forward to working with him or her. You might also ask about the person's training background. Be properly impressed, whatever it is. After all, the chef is king or queen in the kitchen, and the quality of food you get for your group will depend on how you get along with the chef.

Available hotel services. Find out what services the hotel has available. Some will not be listed in the brochure and may not be on your list. They may provide coffee and newspapers to the sleeping rooms each morning. They may have a hotel print shop to produce special stationery, napkins, and matchbook covers for your meeting. One conference center has its own graphics facility and can also develop film and produce slides. Many modern hotels have coaxial cable throughout, including to sleeping rooms, which permits evening instruction via closed-circuit videotape. Also, several hotels now have teleconferencing facilities, and still others, after appropriate security measures, will permit you to access their reservations computer into your room block from your own computer. (This means, within limits, you can handle your own reservations and permit a running check of how your attendees are reserving rooms from your room block.) You should ask to be told about special or additional services the hotel can provide.

10. After your tour, start negotiations. Negotiation is an art that can be learned; you should probably take a seminar in the art.

Following are some suggestions for an approach after your tour. Sit down in the salesperson's office and begin to put together the hotel's charges for your meeting. Sleeping room costs should not be a *major* concern. Give the hotel as much of their markup on sleeping rooms as you can. (The two main profit centers for a hotel are sleeping rooms and beverages. Usually, food is barely a break-even cost center.)

In return for your flexibility on sleeping-room rates, expect the hotel to reciprocate with service at no or reduced cost. It is possible to negotiate beverage costs in return for your flexibility on food costs. An example of additional service that can be costly to you is additional bellpersons for your group arrival and departure, additional front desk clerks for group arrival, and additional cashiers for departure. Many beginners don't even attempt to get prekeying for their groups. (Prekeying is when a room is already assigned and a key awaits upon registration—usually at a separate table or desk away from the formal registration desk.) Also, you can arrange for quick checkout.

You may wish to work directly with the chef in creating your own menus. Recreational facilities and fees are negotiable items. Some hotels want a partial advance payment. The amount and time of this payment are negotiable. Penalties are sometimes assessed for cancellation or change of your meeting. An equal penalty should be assessed to the hotel for nonperformance such as overbooking and moving your people to equal accommodations in another hotel. (You, as the meeting manager, need to include in your contract with the hotel that you will be involved in determining what is an equal accommodation.)

Remember, what you are after is a *bilateral* agreement that will create a "win-win" situation.

Discuss all elements of your possible agreement in this face-to-face situation. *But do not agree at this time to use the property.* Wait until you've studied all sites, have returned home, and have done careful, unhurried, and unpressured evaluation and analysis.

One last note on the site-inspection evaluation and negotiation. Amateur planners frequently develop an attachment or predisposition toward one property. This places them at a disadvantage in negotiation. *Don't be afraid to walk out of a negotiating session.* There are always other properties that, while not your personal favorite, can provide equal and sometimes superior services. Whether or not you are a comparative shopper in your personal life, *be a comparative shopper in your professional life.*

11. After you return home, make a decision. Your first task after returning to your office is to conduct a thorough and objective analysis of *all* your notes and collected information. Compare your data to your meeting needs and objectives. Attempt to complete your analysis, make a decision, and notify *all* properties visited of your decision within 10 days.

When notifying the selected property, indicate your acceptance and that they will be receiving a letter of agreement, or contract, from you. Of course, you will receive a letter of agreement from the hotel. If you would like a preview, read the letter of agreement that appears in the *Convention Liaison Manual.* Take it to an attorney and simply ask if this will provide you and the hotel with equal rights and protection. (If your attorney has a sense of humor, you'll thoroughly enjoy the discussion.)

In any case, the adage of the meeting professional prevails. *Get any and all agreements in writing.*

Summary

This chapter has lead you through the process of determining the amount of space you will need for meeting sessions, sleeping rooms, and special activities. Destination selection was based upon a thorough analysis of your budget, your research, and organization policy. Site determination was treated as a crucial factor that sets the atmosphere for the communication and interaction that will occur in your meeting.

Factors and a method for approaching site selection were discussed in terms of a step-by-step procedure, including your submission of a written proposal and requesting a written response, making arrangements for a site visit, and procedures and criteria to use in conducting the site visit. The chapter concludes with making and communicating your decision and the importance of *getting all agreements in writing.*

WHAT YOU SHOULD HAVE LEARNED FROM THIS CHAPTER

1. How to decide upon your room block of sleeping rooms.
2. How to determine the space needed for each session based upon the type of room setup to be used.

3. How the agenda and meeting pattern affect the decision on the amount of space needed for a session.
4. How to use your budget and organization policy to assist in establishing a basis for further research of possible destinations.
5. How to conduct a destination consolidation analysis.
6. How to use 11 steps in site selection to make a decision on the actual site (hotel or other property) you will use for your meeting.

REVIEW QUESTIONS

1. What is a room block? How do you determine how many single and double rooms and how many suites you will need?
2. What are two methods of determining the amount of space you will need for a meeting room?
3. You plan a session for 30 people. Use the RMAMPI Standard. How many square feet will you need for a conference-style session? How many square feet will you need for a schoolroom-style session?
4. What are six sources to use in selecting a destination and as an indicator of properties to whom you wish to submit a proposal?
5. How would you analyze the material received in proposals from hotels?
6. If a chef indicated to you that he or she had three special entrées you might wish to serve at your meeting and gave you a general indication of how each would be prepared, how would you decide which to select?
7. What would you do if the actual costs you were able to determine through negotiation with three properties at your selected destination exceeded your meeting budget? Remember, you accepted free airfare for site inspection at the destination and thus cannot change destination.
8. What procedure would you suggest if your letter of agreement disagreed with the hotel's letter of agreement?
9. What do you believe is the single most important step in selecting your site? Justify your answer.

APPLICATION EXERCISES

1. Determine the amount of space you would need for Corporate Meeting 3 (Appendix C). (You may add information if needed.) Itemize the space needed by: (1) sleeping rooms, (2) meeting rooms, (3) administrative space, and (4) special events.
2. Write a proposal to submit to the two hotels at one of the destination cities listed for Corporate Meeting 3 (Appendix C).

Chapter 9

Planning Food and Beverage

Chapter 9 separates food from beverage in the planning process because, although both are used for managing the minds and energies of attendees, they involve some different considerations. It is the purpose of this book to give you a basic working knowledge so that you (1) may speak with understanding when dealing with catering or food and beverage managers and with chefs and (2) may approach your use of food and of beverage in a manner that will further the objective(s) of your meeting.

Although the concept of using food and beverage to manage the minds and moods of people is not a new idea, it unfortunately was not a commonly used approach in the meeting profession until recent years. When you have finished reading this chapter, you should continue your study by reading *Managing Your Mind and Mood Through Food* by Dr. Judith Wurtman. (See the bibliography.) This reading will give you greater depth and insight than one chapter can possibly attempt.

Planning Energy and Mind Management Through Food

In planning food at meetings, it is necessary to have a *basic* understanding of different foods because our attendees are much more health conscious now than they used to be and demand the same healthful, low-cholesterol foods when away from home as they eat at home.

Based upon changes in the American diet and in health awareness, we give "dietary guidelines for the future" to be used in planning food functions for American meetings. (Note that diet and health consciousness are not as prevalent in other countries. There is more universal smoking and use of more starchy foods in Central and Latin America than in the United States.) However, if you do meetings for American organizations in other countries, you can still follow these guidelines in planning and negotiating your meals.

Guidelines for the Future

1. Serve decaffeinated coffee only except at the afternoon nutrition break. (Most people cannot tell the difference if they are not told.)
2. If you have difficult material to present at a first morning session, plan breakfasts with juices, fruit, coffee, cereal with milk, toast, bagels, or muffins.
3. Keep "sugary" foods to a minimum, since research shows they have a *calming* not energy-boosting effect.
4. Foods and beverages influence *the brain* to produce substances that stimulate, energize, or calm you.
5. Alcoholic beverages produce a delayed sluggishness. Therefore, "hydraulic" functions should be calculated and scheduled carefully in terms of your agenda.
6. Serve *protein* foods *first;* then follow the protein with carbohydrates.
7. The food selections you provide your attendees will have as much effect on their mental awareness, retention, and sharpness as the methods of presentation you use.

Nutrition Breaks

N. J. "Case" Hanou, writing in the May 1982 *Health Care Conference Planner,* refers to nutrition breaks as "energy breaks." If we are using food functions to influence the mind and energy of our attendees, this is probably a much better choice of words. How can we provide mind-enhancing and energy-enhancing breaks? More importantly, *what* can we plan that will accomplish this purpose?

The Morning Break

Do not provide sweet rolls or Danish. Let's not put them to sleep.

Provide a selection of fruit juices, toast, muffins, and fresh fruit plus decaffeinated coffee and hot tea (decaffeinated if available). (Cut toast into quarters and fresh fruit into pieces for easy handling.)

Allow at least 20 to 30 minutes for your break to provide time for refreshments, restroom, and chatting about the previous session.

Think about a break during a complex or difficult session in the morning, afternoon, or both. Such a break is, of course, for restroom use, but put juice, mineral water, and decaffeinated coffee and tea in the meeting room to encourage attendees to stand up and move. Generally 10 minutes is adequate. The principle is to supply a little energy and stress relief.

The Afternoon Break. Here again, we must think of the mind and energy of the attendee. Think about how you and the people around you felt in the afternoon sessions at meetings you have attended. Bored? Fidgety? Sluggish? Mentally fatigued?

Think about a synergistic solution where two items complement each other. Carbohydrates will calm that fidgetiness. Caffeine will stimulate mental energy.

So, what do we serve?

Option 1: A Selection of

frozen yogurt in cups, trail mix (use dried fruit, coconut, nuts), fresh fruit such as pineapple, melon, strawberries (served in cups). Coffee, tea (caffeinated and caffeine-free), fruit juices, and mineral water.

Option 2: A Selection of

barbecued chicken chunks, smoked oysters, boiled shrimp, crudités (raw vegetables) with yogurt dip, zucchini bread, cranberry bread, and even popcorn and no-salt pretzels, coffee, both caffeinated and caffeine-free tea, fruit juices, mineral water.

With either of these options you must think about ease of eating: plates, dishes, and so on. (If you are being elegant, glass dishware; otherwise plastic is satisfactory.) Remember, a person has a plate and a cup. Both men and women hate to try to balance a plate and cup on the lap when eating and drinking. *Provide a place for them to stand (since they've been sitting) and place the plate and cup on a table.*

Plan the Lunch Menu. We must remember, when planning a lunch menu, that the attendee will be involved in sessions after lunch. A heavy lunch that includes carbohydrates and starch will have a calming effect. Remember, humans are like animals in the sense they become sleepy after eating. Therefore, we need to provide some fuel that will stimulate their mental energies. Here are some menus from the New York Hilton at Rockefeller Center, which were contributed to Dr. Wurtman and may provide ideas. They also indicate the value of dealing with a chef as distinguished from a cook.

Menu 1

1 cup gazpacho Andaluz

$\frac{3}{4}$ cup salad Niçoise, made with chunks of tuna, blanched string beans, and sliced fresh mushroom on a bed of lettuce and garnished with tomato wedges, sliced yellow squash, blanched broccoli buds, and sliced new potato

1 tablespoon Dijon vinaigrette dressing

1 whole-wheat or pumpernickel raisin roll

$1\frac{1}{2}$ cups sliced fresh fruit in season

coffee, tea, or decaffeinated beverage as desired

Menu 2

1 cup cold consommé Madrilène

5 ounces sliced cold breast of chicken on a bed of lettuce

1 cup tortellini salad with pesto dressing, garnished with blanched broccoli and cauliflower buds, sliced fresh zucchini, and cherry tomatoes

1 whole-wheat or pumpernickel raisin roll
1 cup raspberry sorbet
coffee, tea, or decaffeinated beverage as desired

Menu 3

1 cup vegetable beef soup
4 ounces thinly sliced beef with mustard-horseradish sauce
$\frac{3}{4}$ cup oven-roasted potatoes
$\frac{1}{2}$ cup blanched carrots
$\frac{1}{2}$ cup fresh asparagus
1 cup fresh fruit cup

These menus include a blend of protein, carbohydrate, and starch, which will not impair mental alertness. Such menus can give you a starting point when working with a chef and will permit the chef to use his or her own creativity while staying within your guidelines. An all-male group could be served slightly larger portions than those indicated.

Through your promotional material and on-site conference communication, make clear to your attendees that you have prepared food functions designed both to be healthy and to permit them to get more out of the meeting. You might even indicate that your conference evaluation form will be designed to discover any changes they might notice in their mental and physical alertness as compared with previous conferences.

Plan Conference Dinners. Again, conference dinners should be planned in terms of the mind and energy concept—but also with the agenda for the following day clearly in mind.

What about your group? Will they want to party in the evening or are they more concerned with getting all they can from the content of the conference? If they are a partying group, your dinners can provide mental and physical stimulation to counteract, in part, the effects of the alcohol they may consume. If they are a more serious group focused on content, you should think of dinners that calm them and promote stress-relieving sleep.

Meals for both groups should begin with protein and then be followed by carbohydrates. You will notice in the menus for lunch that they began with protein. Protein will stimulate mental alertness. However, at the end of the day, many attendees will have a difficult time coming down off of the mental and physical high-activity level. Carbohydrates will assist this process. Portions of protein foods should be between 5 and 8 ounces. Include carbohydrates and end the meal with high carbohydrate desserts.

Red meats may be served once or twice during the conference but try for milk-fed veal (not grass-fed). Consider turkey, chicken, fish (not shrimp), and *lean pork* for you other entrées. Fat-free soups, plain vegetables (steamed and without butter or sauce), and meats that are grilled or roasted (not fried) will help maintain the calorie and carbohydrate level you are seeking to provide.

Desserts can be a problem. Europeans frequently serve whole fruit and provide a fruit knife. Frozen yogurt, sorbet, and cake without a buttery icing, such as angel food, can top off the meal. (A basket of fresh fruit with a decorated basket will stimulate both favorable comment and consumption of the fruit.) *Stay away from cream pies, cheesecake, puddings, and pastries. They can destroy your best intentions.*

If the guidelines you have received are communicated to a good chef, you will be delighted with the quality of what the chef can produce, so no menus are suggested.

Calorie requirements vary from person to person. However, remember your attendees are *sitting* most of the day and don't burn up many calories. Therefore, as a guideline only, 500 to 700 calories for lunch and 700 to 1000 calories for dinner will be more than adequate for most people. (Remember, they are getting calories at your nutrition/energy breaks, so they will probably not lose much weight.)

A final note on food. Set your caloric limits, establish protein and carbohydrate targets, and then distribute them in terms of your agenda and meeting objectives.

Planning Beverages and Beverage Functions

There are two kinds of beverages with which we must be concerned: alcoholic and nonalcoholic. They can have similar yet entirely different effects, depending on how you use them and the type of nonalcoholic beverage used.

Alcoholic Beverages

It is amazing how many people who use alcoholic beverages know little if anything about the beverage itself. Therefore, following are some brief definitions before a discussion of their use.

Whiskey. Whiskey is a spirit, suitably aged in wood (usually oak), obtained from the distillation of a fermented mash of grain. There are two types of whiskey: (1) straight and (2) blended.

Straight whiskey, by U.S. federal regulation, is whiskey that has been distilled off at a proof not exceeding 160, aged in a new charred white oak barrel for at least two years, and reduced by the addition of water at the time of bottling to not lower than 80 proof. Nothing may be added but water. Straight whiskey may be mixed, provided the mixture is made up of whiskeys of the same distilling period and from the same distillery. The predominant grain used in the mash formula determines the final designation under which the whiskey will be labeled and marketed. If 51% or more of the grain is *corn,* it is straight bourbon. If 51% or more of the grain is *rye,* it is straight rye whiskey, and so on.

Nearly half the American produced whiskey consumed in the United States is *blended* whiskey. Blenders devote their art to mixing carefully selected full-bodied straight whiskeys with grain neutral spirits to produce a lighter, more balanced whole and to produce day in and day out, an identically uniform product. The straight whiskeys give aroma, flavor, and body, whereas the unaged grain spirits give the marriage lightness and smoothness without sacrificing character. The straight whiskey is full-bodied and full-flavored, whereas the blended whiskey is comparatively light-bodied and light in flavor.

Scotch whiskey is obtained primarily from barley, which is preferably grown in Scotland, but recently barley from California, Canada, India, Africa, and other countries has been imported for distilling purposes. There are five main processes in the making of *Scotch:* first, malting; second, mashing; third, fermenting; fourth, distilling; and fifth, maturing and blending.

Irish whiskey is distilled from a fermented mash of the same grains as are used in Scotland—namely, malted barley, unmalted barley, corn, rye, and other small grains. However, malt is not smoke cured, as is the case in Scotland. All Irish whiskey is triple distilled. Most Irish whiskies are seven years old or more before they are shipped. Irish whiskey is a particularly smooth whiskey, but with a great deal of body and a clean, malty flavor.

Gin. There are only two basic styles or types of gin: Dutch—Hollands, Genever, or Schiedam gin—and Dry Gin—English or American gin. In England the making of gin begins with a grain formula made up of 75% corn, 15% barley malt, and 10% other grains. This is mashed, cooked, fermented, and then distilled. After the addition of water and flavoring agents such as juniper berries, orange peel, lemon peel, and coriander seed, the mixture is redistilled. After redistilling, the spirit is 150 to 170 proof and is diluted with distilled water to 80 to 97 proof before bottling.

Rum. Rum is any alcoholic distillate from the fermented juice of sugarcane, sugarcane syrup, sugarcane molasses, or other sugarcane by-products distilled at less than 190 proof, in such a manner that the distillate possesses the taste, aroma, and characteristics generally attributed to rum. There are four main classifications of rum: The first are the very dry, light-bodied rums generally produced in the Spanish-speaking countries. (Puerto Rican rum is an example.) The second are the medium-bodied rums. The third are the rich, full-bodied, pungent rums usually produced in the English-speaking islands and countries. (The best example is Jamaican rum.) The fourth is the light-bodied but pungently aromatic East Indian Batavia arak rum from Java.

Vodka. Vodka has always been distilled from the most plentiful and least expensive material available to the distiller. Vodka is made from potatoes and various grains, principally corn, with some wheat added. Vodka is an alcoholic distillate from a fermented mash. It is distilled to a high proof and is distilled still further in order to remove all flavoring agents. Because of this, vodka has no character, color, or flavor to speak of.

Brandy. Brandy is a spirit, suitably aged in wood, obtained by distilling wine or a fermented mash of fruit.

Cordials and Liqueurs. These are flavored beverages, whose flavor is obtained either by infusion or distillation of a flavoring agent, to which a simple syrup for sweetness is then added. They may be artificially colored. All cordials and liqueurs are sweet.

Finally, there is one last term that needs defining.

Proof. In the United States, a 100-proof spirit is a spirit containing 50% alcohol by volume at a temperature of 60°F. This is an arbitrary measurement. Each degree of proof is equal to *one-half* percent alcohol. Therefore, a 90-proof spirit contains 45% alcohol, and a 150-proof spirit contains 75% alcohol.

Now that you know all you need to know about the nature of the alcoholic beverages a meeting manager might have to encounter, it is time to examine some health factors.

An average alcoholic drink, without soda mixer, contains approximately 100 calories. This may be equated with a tablespoon of salad dressing, sour cream, or butter. Other beverages and their approximate calories are:

Cola: 8 ounces, 105 calories (usual can is 12 ounces)
Diet cola: 6 ounces, 1 calorie

Wine: (dry) 65–95 calories
Wine: (sweet) 120–160 calories

However, tabulation of calories can be very misleading because caloric requirements of individuals vary greatly. The thing to remember is that alcohol contains sugar and carbohydrates. Our bodies need carbohydrates, depending upon the amount of activity. If we don't get enough carbohydrates, then the body burns up protein to get energy. If we get too many, the body stores the surplus as fat.

There was a tendency several years ago to use the cocktail party as a means of allowing everyone to relax. Those days are almost gone. There are ways, however, *not* to give the appearance of being a prohibitionist and yet control consumption.

Controlling Consumption

1. Reduce the length of before-dinner cocktail parties to 30–45 minutes.
2. Serve mineral water or water with a twist of lemon during dinner.
3. If you serve wine with the meal, one to two glasses per person is plenty. (Serving a dry wine will fulfill the obligation and create the image while controlling sugar and calorie intake. And, today, the proper wine for the food being served is not as important as it used to be.)
4. Provide a cash bar in the dining room. (Remember from Appendix E, "Cocktail Party Basics," that consumption decreases at a cash bar.)
5. Eliminate cocktails before luncheons if you have a working session following.
6. With a meal, in place of alcoholic beverages, try serving a cold fruit soup (how about iced sour-cherry soup?), a fruit frappé, or a nonalcoholic punch using a natural fruit juice that contains only fructose (the form of sugar that doesn't give a sudden "charge" to the brain.)
7. Make certain that at every beverage function you provide a variety of alternatives to alcoholic beverages.
8. Schedule some "light exercise functions" following a food function where alcoholic beverages are served. [These can be short (30-minute) affairs, maybe with some competition, that lead into a working session. Attendees will burn off the carbohydrates and calories.]

Many times you will be required by the organization to hold some type of function that includes serving alcohol. This is acceptable, but you can still work in controls; over a period of time, the productivity of your approach, in terms of meeting objectives, will probably influence the organization decision makers.

Summary

This chapter has covered *guidelines* for food and beverage functions in the future—the 1990s and the 21st century. The guideline approach was used because many of the specifics of what is healthy are changing rapidly in the light of new research. Where specifics were given, they were given in terms of accepted research findings. Food guidelines, stressing a healthy approach, started the discussion. Emphasis was placed on planning in terms of your meeting objectives, your meeting agenda, and a basic knowledge of foods and nutrition. A discussion of beverages began with definitions of alcoholic beverages that briefly explained the processes of distilling and fermenting (with an indication of when sugar was added in the process). Caloric content was considered, but a calorie-only approach to planning either food or beverages is not wise, since caloric requirements vary so much from person to person. Again, guidelines for planning the use of beverages were presented. Both the use and nonuse of alcoholic beverages were covered, and guidelines supplied for both approaches. From this chapter, plus additional reading from the bibliography, you should have a strong foundation on which to build your planning of food and beverage functions.

WHAT YOU SHOULD HAVE LEARNED FROM THIS CHAPTER

1. The role of more health-conscious attendees in terms of food and beverage factors.
2. Consideration of protein and carbohydrate consumption to secure maximum mental and energy levels during sessions.
3. The need to serve protein foods and beverages before carbohydrates.
4. How to plan food and beverage functions in relation to meeting objectives and the agenda of a meeting.
5. The importance of holding sugary foods to a minimum during working sessions.
6. How to provide adequate food without producing a "stuffed" condition for attendees.
7. The importance of carbohydrates in evening meals to assist the attendees in unwinding from the day's activities.
8. The importance of providing an assortment of beverages, alcoholic and nonalcoholic, at hospitality functions.
9. The alternatives that permit planner control of the consumption of alcoholic beverages for serious working groups.
10. The importance of avoiding sweet rolls and Danish during nutrition breaks because they "calm" attendees and can produce sluggishness.

REVIEW QUESTIONS

1. Do foods and beverages influence the brain or the body?
2. Should you serve both decaffeinated and regular beverages during a break?
3. How can short breaks be used to benefit the attendees? How long should they be?
4. How can a synergistic approach be used in planning food and beverage functions?
5. What is meant by mind-enhancing and energy-enhancing nutrition breaks?

6. What kinds of foods produce a calming effect that can lead to sluggishness?
7. If you decide to control food and beverage for health and energy reasons, how can you get your attendees to accept the approach?
8. If you have a partying group, what would you do to counteract the effects of partying?
9. What kind of a balance, in terms of protein and carbohydrate, would you seek in planning a meal?
10. How would you use calorie, protein, and carbohydrate limits and targets in planning your food and beverage functions?

APPLICATION EXERCISE

Plan food and beverage functions for Corporate Meeting 3 using both the material given in Appendix D and the guidelines given in this chapter.

Chapter 10

Developing and Organizing the Meeting Plan

Chapter 10 is a much shorter chapter than the other chapters in this book. Yet, the meeting plan itself may be two or three times the length of this entire text. The answer to this seeming contradiction is that most of the work for the meeting plan has already been done in the previous chapters, so Chapter 10 needs simply to focus and organize the material into an operational document. Thus, many of the pages in this chapter are forms that you may use in developing your own plans.

The recommended format for the meeting plan follows this pattern:

1. A list of arrivals and departures, including meeting staff, VIPs, and attendees.
2. Registration procedures, personnel, and equipment and supplies needed.
3. Sleeping room assignments if needed.
4. VIP list with names and titles.
5. Meeting staff list with names and titles.
6. Accounting and billing procedures, including names of those who may charge to the master account.
7. A daily schedule sheet (including consecutive event numbers).
8. Function sheets for the daily schedule sheet.
9. List of food and beverage functions with menus, room setups and any special details such as decorations, provision for a head table, number of people at the head table, number of covers per waiter, time of guarantee, and procedure and amount of gratuity.
10. List of special events such as recreation or dances, including location, contact persons, phone numbers, and costs.
11. List of audiovisual equipment, when and where needed, and costs.

12. List of other equipment, including number of chairs, podiums, tables, and risers for each event (even though much of this will be on the function sheet).
13. List of local suppliers and servicepeople with addresses and telephone numbers. Include bus companies, destination-management company, car-rental agency, decorators, florists, talent agents or brokers, drayage company, travel agents, the local offices of the major airlines you will be using, and so on. If your meeting is offshore, include the addresses and phone numbers of the U.S. Embassy and currency exchange offices, simultaneous translators, and interpreters.
14. List of key hotel personnel, particularly the convention service manager discussed in Chapter 11. Include location and phone numbers. Include with this list convention bureau personnel you might need to contact, including the director of the bureau's convention services.
15. An addendum of miscellaneous information you think you might need.
16. Copies of all contracts and correspondence (for in-house distribution and use only).

Following is a form for a daily events schedule. The heading contains the name of your organization, the name of the meeting, the name of the meeting manager in charge, the dates of the meeting, and the date and day of the event.

The events listing has columns for time (you may use the 24-hour clock if it is better for you or the property), the number of the event (in consecutive order), the name of the function, the location of the function, the number of people you anticipate will attend, and the page number of the function sheet applicable to the event. The list of events and the numbers of the events should come from the meeting pattern you developed in Chapter 7.

Function Sheets. An example function sheet follows the daily events listing example. Notice that we again have a detailed heading that indicates name of event, number of event, person in charge, location, date, times, number of people, and a word description of the setup. The space for special instruction could include the audiovisual equipment required, any nutrition to be in the room, decorations, risers, podiums, disconnected telephones, and so on.

If there is to be a head table, indicate this with the number of people to be seated. If there is no head table, simply state "none."

Essential on the function sheet is the room diagram. Sometimes, particularly in offshore meetings, you will find setup crews who do not read English. Even if the setup crew reads English, by giving them a visual you are reinforcing communication. On the right of the setup diagram is a list of equipment with the symbols you might use in drawing the setup and space for indicating the numbers of each item of equipment.

DAILY SCHEDULE SHEET EXAMPLE

Organization Name						
Dates of Organization Meeting				Meeting Day and Date		
Time		Function	Number	Location	No. of people	Page
A.M.	7:					
	8:					
	9:					
	10:					
	11:					
	12:					
P.M.	1:					
	2:					
	3:					
	4:					
	5:					
	6:					
	7:					
	8:					
	9:					
	10:					

The two forms, daily events schedules and function sheets, are the most critical for your meeting. Undoubtedly the hotel will include some function sheets with their version of your contract. However, for your meeting plan and the official function sheet, *do your own.*

There are other forms you may want to develop for yourself to include in your meeting plan. The following pages include some possibilities. Feel free to create your own adapted to your organization and your particular meeting needs.

When you have all the forms and lists completed, it is time to assemble the completed plan. Index tabs on the copies for you and your staff and for the main hotel contact people (such as the Convention Services Manager) are helpful. Set a target date for getting the copies of the meeting plan to the hotel of one month before the meeting. This gives the hotel an opportunity to ask questions.

Also, depending on the size of the meeting, arrive at the hotel two days (for a large convention, several weeks) before the start of the meeting. Go over every detail of the meeting plan with the hotel(s) staff who will be involved in the meeting—this includes the head housekeeper, who needs to be briefed on gratuity policy and details of how the sleeping rooms are to be made up. There is no way to overcommunicate and the more detail on which you can secure

Sample Function Sheet

Organization: ______________ Name of Meeting: ______________

Name of Person in Charge: ______________ Headquarters Room: ______________

Post Function Name as: ______________ From: ________ To: ________

Room No. or Name: ______________ No. of People: ________ Set up by: ______________

Special Instruction: pads ________ pencils ________ ash trays ________ telephone(s) ________

Head Table: ______________ No. of People: ______________ Risers: ______________

Room Set-up Diagram

Equipment Needed

Equipment	Symbol	
Easel	(/\ )	______
Easel and flipchart	( )	______
Chalkboard	(CB)	______
Table mike	(●)	______
Floor mike	(⦿)	______
Chairs	(∩ ∩)	______
Podium	(P)	______
Lectern	(L)	______
Gavel	( )	______
35mm projector	(35)	______
8mm projector	(8)	______
16 mm projector	(16)	______
Opaque projector	(OP)	______
Overhead	( )	______
3-inch by 4-inch projector	( )	______
Tape recorder	( )	______
Cassette recorder	(●●)	______
Pointer electric	( )	______
Telephone	( )	______
Iced water	( )	______

mutual understanding, the better opportunity you will have for a smooth meeting. Without the detailed meeting plan in hand, there is no sure way to secure mutual understanding.

Sample Registration Form

Organization person in charge ______________________________

Hotel person in charge ______________________________

Date of function __________ Function number __________ Time __________

1. Location __________

2. Number of tables __________ Rounds? __________ Banquet __________

3. Signs (list) __________

4. Number of chairs ______ 5. Boxes for envelopes (number and type) ______ __________ 6. Typewriter __________ 7. Computer __________

8. Telephone(s) ______ 9. Chalkboard(s) ______ 10. Tackboard(s) ______

11. Bulletin boards __________ 12. Special lighting __________ ______________________ 13. Local literature __________

14. Promotional literature __________ 15. Attendee packets __________

16. Additional requirements ______________________________

Sample Reception Form

Organization official in charge __________

Hotel official in charge __________

Date of function __________ Time __________ Location __________

Alternate location __________ No. of people __________

Number of hors d'oeuvre tables __________

Number and type of hors d'oeuvre __________

Number of bars __________

Types of drinks at bars ______________________________

Size of bar drinks __________ Number of bartenders __________

Brands of liquor ______________________________

Costs: Drinks __________ Hors d'oeuvre __________

Types of hors d'oeuvre ______________________________

Costs of drinks per person ______ Costs of hors d'oeuvre per person ______

Decorations __________

Flowers __________

Music __________

Cost of music __________ Additional requirements __________

Sample Meal-control Form

Organization official in charge ________________
Hotel official in charge ________________
Date of function ________ Time ________ Time of final guarantee ________
Type of meal: Breakfast ________ Lunch ________ Dinner ________
Cost per person ________
Location ________ Event no. ________ No. of people ________
Type of seating ________ Menu ________
Gratuity ________ Head table ________ No. of people at head table ________
Head table on riser ________ Decorations ________
Number of tables ________ Number of servers ________ Music ________
Cost of music ________ Lectern ________ No. and type of mikes ________
Photographer ________ Cost of photographer ________ Dance floor ________
Size of dance floor ________ Lighting ________
Centerpieces ________
Air-conditioning ________ Light and temperature control and location ________
Proximity and no. of restrooms ________
Additional requirements ________________

Room layout ________________

Sample Speaker Checklist

Name ________ Address for correspondence ________
Phone number(s)( ) ( )
Title of presentation ________
Event no. ________ Location ________
Name of organization person in charge ________
Room setup ________________

Equipment needed ________________
Flashlight pointer ________ Lectern light ________ Floor mike ________
Roving mike ___ Extension pointer ___ Easel ___ Flipchart and stand ___
Chalkboard and stand ________ Bulletin board ________
35mm slide projector ________
Film-strip projector ________ 16mm projector ________
VCR monitor(s) ________
Overhead projector ________ Opaque projector ________
3 × 4 slide equip. ________
Lectern ________ Podium ________
Biographical sketch received ________ Handout material submitted ________
Photographs for promotion ________

WHAT YOU SHOULD HAVE LEARNED FROM THIS CHAPTER

1. That the meeting plan brings together all the plans and research you have conducted.
2. How to organize the meeting plan in an operational form that permits efficient use both before the meeting and during the meeting.
3. That the most important content of the meeting plan is the daily events schedules and the function sheets.
4. That the daily events schedule comes from the meeting pattern developed before the meeting manager ever contacts the hotel.
5. That other lists and forms need to be developed that fit the organization and the particular meeting.
6. That the meeting plan serves as a vital communication link between the hotel and the meeting manager and the manager's staff.
7. That there is no way to overcommunicate the details of the meeting, both internally and with hotels and other suppliers.

REVIEW QUESTIONS

1. Where would you get details of room setups to include on your function sheet?
2. Where would you get details of food and beverage functions to include on your function sheet?
3. What additional forms would you develop to include in your meeting plan?
4. Why is the meeting plan such an important document for a meeting manager?
5. To whom would you distribute copies of your meeting plan? Include both internal and external people.
6. Is there any way you can think of to predict how many copies of your meeting plan you should have printed? What influences your decision on the number of copies?
7. It is important that decision-making officials of your organization read and understand your meeting plan. How would you ensure that the plan is both read and understood?

APPLICATION EXERCISES

Develop an outline of the content you would include in a meeting plan for Corporate Meeting 1.

Develop an outline of the content you would include in a meeting plan for Corporate Meeting 2.

Develop an outline for the content you would include in a meeting plan for Corporate Meeting 3.

Discuss specific differences that exist among the three plans and why the plans are different.

Chapter 11

Working with Destination and Site Services

When the meeting plan has been collected and organized in loose-leaf binders, we must direct our attention to the people at the destination and the site we have selected, since they will play an important role in the success of our meeting.

These services have been divided into categories for easier consideration:

1. Transportation services
2. Destination coordination services
3. Destination supplier services
4. Site services

Transportation Services

The first of the transportation services is the airline and other transportation involved in providing access to the destination. Airlines are more frequently used than train or bus companies, so we discuss airlines as a pattern that may be used even if other forms of transportation may be involved. In recent years, airlines have made major efforts to serve and market their services to the meeting industry because meetings represent a significant market for them.

As with any destination or site service, discover a *key person* with the organization. You will find airlines have group travel sections geared to assisting the meeting manager. Early in your planning, establish the account executive with whom you will work.

Airlines normally like to have a minimum lead time of six months for bookings. The airline account executive will work with you to ensure you have considered all aspects of travel. For instance, when you are first projecting your budget, the airline will frequently suggest you examine whether your meeting will fall during "peak" or "off" seasons. Peak seasons will result in significantly higher airfares, which may indicate you should change either your meeting dates or destination. Not all destinations have a peak season except during vacation times. For instance, peak seasons for ski destinations are not the same as for historic destinations such as Washington, D.C. Also, if you meet during peak seasons and have a large group, the airline may need to place additional aircraft into service to handle the projected volume your meeting would produce.

Cost Analysis. Remember, when we first projected our budget, we used the *Official Airline Guide* to give us estimates of costs. When the research phase of your budget begins, the airlines can provide you with a cost analysis for transportation given the number and points of origin of the attendees. They can even pinpoint times of the year when discount fares might be available.

Computer Service. Airlines, particularly for association meetings, will set up a toll-free number that the attendee may call for everything ranging from reservations and seat assignments to rental cars and requests for dietary meals. You will need to be prepared when talking with the airlines about this service. For instance, you will need to know your destination if selected, what help you think you need, whether you are the decision maker, projected attendance and whether companions will be attending, hotel(s) and convention centers you plan to use, start and finish dates of the meeting, past attendance, any pre- or postmeeting tours or events, and whether you are using a travel agent. Of course, if you have already contacted an account executive with the airline, the account executive will assist you.

Promotional Assistance. Most airlines will have direct mail support available to you. This will include full-color shells that promote the destination plus posters and other literature. The airline will tailor this information to your meeting and mail it to prospective attendees to assist you in creating enthusiasm. If you have a relatively large group (500 or more), airlines will consider providing free courtesy items.

Pre- and Postmeeting Tours or Trips. Frequently your attendees will wish to take an extended vacation before or after your meeting or make your meeting a stop on a series of planned individual business meetings. Most airlines are geared to assist your attendees if you have prepared the airline for this type of request.

Hospitality Rooms at Airports. These hospitality rooms can serve as assembly areas for groups of attendees who live or work around a given point of origin. Also, they can serve as a special amenity lounge area, which makes your attendees happy.

Reservation and Reconfirmation Desks. These desks may be located at your meeting hotel or at the convention or conference center you will be using.

Special Baggage Handling. If you have a group traveling together, you might want to keep them together by providing last on–first off baggage handling. The airline can arrange this service to expedite traffic flow for your group. For example, at ski-destination meetings, groups of people can be collected at an airport near the destination. It is a nice amenity to have the hospitality room as a gathering point and last on–first off baggage handling to collect skis and other baggage for the group before they are transported to the ski area. Lost skis make attendees very unhappy and can spoil the meeting for them.

Custom Check-In Counters. If you have a large group, custom signs, a special check-in counter, and an airline official to greet and expedite movement of arriving and departing passengers are available to the meeting planner.

Destination Site-Inspection Visits. Destination site-inspection visits were mentioned in Chapter 8 and are one more service of the airlines. You will discover other services as you work with the airline contact you have established.

Communication is very important. *You* must take it upon yourself to contact the airline(s) and make these arrangements with a key person (decision maker) of the airline(s). When your meeting plan is complete, it is a good idea to take a copy to each airline's key person and go over all transportation arrangements with that person. This gives you a double-check on the arrangements and gives the airline contact person a perspective on your entire meeting. (The airline likes to have copies of these meeting plans to extract key data on your group to store in their computer for use in future meetings.)

Travel Agent Cooperation. Nothing that has been said in any way precludes your use of a travel agent. Frequently, the travel agent can provide services not provided by the airlines. Also, the airline likes to work with travel agents on support details of the meeting, and you get the benefit of a transportation team that can even help you in coordinating local tours and other ground transportation needs. As with the airlines, give a copy of your meeting plan to the travel agent and go over every detail of the plan with the agent.

Destination Coordination Services

Chief among the destination coordination services is the convention and visitors bureau at your selected destination. The convention bureau has information about most support services you will need. For instance, they can provide insight about various drayage companies, local talent agents and brokers, decorating companies, audiovisual suppliers, destination management companies, college, university, and high-school sources for part-time help and school art departments, computer hardware suppliers for your computer network, electricians, union rules and requirements, employment agencies for part-time help, caterers, and so on.

Again, as with all agencies with which you work, find a key person. (In convention bureaus, you will find convention services directors.) Communicate frequently with this key person from the time of your original selection of the destination and throughout the actual meeting. Also, be certain the key person at the convention bureau receives a copy of the meeting plan and that you go over every detail—including changes made in the plan before and during the meeting.

One last word of advice about convention bureaus. (Some are located in or *are* the local Chamber of Commerce.) No meeting is too large or too small for the convention bureau to be involved, *but don't expect the bureau to recommend a single supplier.* The bureau will recommend several, if available, and you will have to make the selection. (Bureaus are usually supported by a membership fee and the recommending of a single supplier represents unethical treatment of the other member suppliers.)

You will find other destination coordination services as you deal with the convention bureau. Their type and number will vary with the destination. Contact the convention bureau and take it from there. No matter how small the involvement, get a copy of your meeting plan to the key person with the supplier and go over it in detail.

Destination Supplier Services

There are hundreds of supplier services you may need. Probably the most frequently used are destination management companies, decorating firms, unions, and local ground operators. Only these four are discussed, but the principles apply to dealing with all suppliers.

There are four principles to follow in working with suppliers. These are: *contact, negotiate, contract,* and *communicate.* These principles can be used with all suppliers discussed here as well as with the others you may need.

Destination Management Companies. Destination management companies are a relatively new phenomenon in the meeting industry. Their purpose is to make available to the meeting manager the destination management requirements the meeting manager may have, without the necessity of the meeting manager having to make frequent trips to the destination. Of course, this service will cost money and be allocated to the administration budget category. However, you may save money in the long run because of the reduced expense in frequent trips to the destination.

Do thorough research before selecting a destination management company because many are inexperienced. The founders and owners of these companies may have been hotel sales or convention services people or have worked for organizations as meeting planners before forming their own companies. The local convention bureau can give you general information, you can check with other planners who may have used such a service, and hotels can also be good sources of information.

Unless you know the people and the company, write to them, give a general sketch of what services you are seeking, and ask for a proposal, in writing. The proposal must include their experience and references. Then contact their references in writing and ask for a written response concerning the quality of work done. (Remember, they will list only those references they believe will be favorable). These written references should be balanced against information you have secured from other sources.

Finally, spell out the actual service you want and submit a contract to the destination management company. Once the contract is signed, the destination management company becomes privy to *most,* not all, of the information about the meeting. (For instance, they don't need to know your entire budget—just that with which they will be involved.) Always include in your contract the right of final decision so that you retain control.

The destination management company, once contracted, must be included in your communication network. It gets a copy of your meeting plan, which you go over in detail to ensure the company completely understands its role in relation to the total meeting.

Decorating Firms. Decorating firms are used primarily when you have exhibits. There are several national decorating firms, such as Freeman and Greyhound, whose experience and performance are relatively easy to check. Sometimes, however, if the national firm does not have a warehouse at the destination, it is a good idea to explore using a local company, since the local company will have a warehouse and the equipment readily available and, if a quality company, can provide service at lower cost.

Decorating firms can set up booths, carpet, and drapes; supply signs for the exhibits and meeting; store vender material shipped in advance; supply tables and chairs (usually for less than you could rent them if the tables and chairs are part of the total exhibit package); make necessary arrangements with applicable unions; arrange drayage; and create some very innovative designs for the exhibit hall and/or meeting.

Again, communicate the meeting plan to these firms and go over the details to secure mutual understanding.

Unions. A meeting manager who goes to a destination without a thorough investigation of the unions and union requirements is naive. In some cities you can have this scenario.

> A union picks up your shipped material. Another union loads it on a truck. Another union drives the truck to the site. Another union unloads the truck on the dock and another union moves the equipment to its general location at the site. Equipment must then be unpacked and set up. You must deal with the electrical union for setup of electrical equipment, the plumbers' union, the gas workers' union, and, of course, the unions of the personnel and workers at the meeting site.

This may seem to be a horrendous challenge. It is, but the benefits of previous agreement give you an insurance of a smooth operation. When a problem arises, contacting the on-site union steward gets instant action to remedy or accomplish a task.

It may take several days at the destination to meet with each union and discuss your general requirements. Once you have a knowledge of the extent and depth of the union's capability and can reach an agreement, the vital next step is a contract spelling out all details. With contract in hand, you should have little trouble in a union city or property. In fact, some meeting managers prefer to go to a union city or property because they have a basic assurance of job accomplishment. Your success or failure in dealing with unions will depend upon you as an individual.

Site Services

The first person you will encounter at a hotel or meeting site is a salesperson. Usually, this person knows what facilities and services are available to you. Once you have negotiated a contract with this person and have it signed by the hotel, your meeting will usually be turned over to a convention services executive, manager, or director. Since you are now knowledgeable about communication, you should have identified a potential communication barrier. You spoke with one person and negotiated a written contract that both you and the salesperson understand. However, words are mere symbols and thus subject to interpretation. To find out if the convention services person has the same interpretation, meet face-to-face with that person and discuss your contract.

When your meeting plan is complete, the convention services person gets a copy, and you go over it in detail to ensure maximum understanding. *Here is where you may actually make some changes in your meeting plan based on input from convention services.* You may find that the convention services person knows more about the property and its capabilities than the salesperson with whom you originally dealt.

At the time of this meeting with convention services, determine what other department heads will be involved in your meeting (catering, food and beverage, housekeeping, engineering, reservations and front desk, accounting, operations, and so on). You should have carried a supply of meeting plan copies with you; now you can distribute them personally to the involved department heads. Always indicate to the department head that you will want to meet with all heads prior to the meeting to go over the plan and any changes that may have been made.

The meetings with department heads provide an opportunity to get to know each one on a more personal level; frequently, the heads will take the time to look at your plan as it affects them. When they do, they may have more valuable suggestions. Listen. You can learn something new every time you talk with a department head because each hotel has a slightly different management approach coming from the general manager. The interpretation and implementation of this management approach is up to the department heads, and so we have different approaches not only for *general* operations but also for *department* operations.

If a sales or convention services person leaves the convention bureau or the property, there is no assurance the details and understandings of your meeting will be communicated. Therefore, extremely important in using destination and site services is the idea of constant and continuing communication, even if your meeting is several years away. This communication can be as simple as holiday greeting cards or a postcard from another meeting destination saying you are thinking of them and your meeting with them because something or other at your current meeting reminded you of them. If these cards are returned because the addressee is unknown, you have an indication of personnel change. Another way of keeping track is a phone call every six months as a friendly gesture rather than checking up—even though it does check up.

What will you do if your destination management company files bankruptcy and you are not notified? Again we have the need for constant and continuing communication.

An additional method of keeping in touch is to schedule your flights to other meeting destinations through the destination for that meeting and arranging for a half-day layover as a flight interruption. Drop in on the property or the convention bureau.

Summary

This chapter has covered four areas; transportation services, destination coordination services, destination supplier services, and site services. In each case, four principles have been stressed: contact, negotiate, contract, and communicate. Although the services may be different or may be influenced by union agreements and requirements, these principles remain constant. There is a saying in the meeting industry, "Get it in writing." This is very true, but whatever is in writing must be mutually understood, and there is no substitute for following up written communication with face-to-face communication.

WHAT YOU SHOULD HAVE LEARNED FROM THIS CHAPTER

1. The four principles to follow in using services: contact, negotiate, contract, and communicate.
2. The four categories of services: transportation, destination coordination, destination supplier, and site services.
3. The role of the meeting plan in the communication and use of destination and site services.
4. The importance of continuing follow-up through face-to-face and written communication, even though original contracts are in writing.
5. The possibility of changes in site and destination personnel, resulting in potential communication barriers and/or problems during the meeting.
6. The importance of selecting key personnel with each service, so you have one decision-making person as a communication link.

REVIEW QUESTIONS

1. What are ten important services an airline may provide a meeting manager?
2. How would you involve both airline(s) and travel agents in providing transportation needs for your meeting?
3. What function(s) does an airport hospitality room serve?
4. What specific airport hospitality service would you have the destination convention bureau and/or the airlines provide?
5. What do you believe would be the most important consideration(s) for a meeting manager in dealing with destination unions?
6. Why is the selection of key personnel with a destination service considered crucial?
7. What is wrong with the following statement? "Once you have worked with three different hotels, future properties will all be the same."
8. What six possible tasks or jobs would you assign to a destination management company?
9. What procedure would you use in selecting a destination management company and why?
10. Would you use a convention bureau or a destination management company to make arrangements with a union, or would you do it yourself? Why?

APPLICATION EXERCISE

Turn to Appendix C. Decide which of the three corporate meetings would most require the services of a destination management company (DMC). Then, decide what you would have the DMC do for that meeting. Finally, establish a procedure for selecting and contracting with a DMC at that destination.

Chapter 12

Planning Publicity, Promotion, and Public Relations for a Meeting

There is an adage in the meeting profession that *all meetings, no matter how small require promotion.* Chapter 12 directs your attention to the multiple considerations that must be evaluated as you approach promoting a meeting.

The first consideration is whether to restrict yourself to publicity, which is simply collecting and transmitting the *facts* about what is going to happen to the attendees. This may be sufficient if your meeting is a corporate meeting where attendance is required. Even though attendance is required, promotion that emphasizes getting *potential* attendees to attend is valuable. And public relations, increasing the *image* of the program and organization for the public, should be an essential part of any business. Public relations is particularly important for meeting managers, since we are striving to enhance both our own image and that of the profession with organization executives and the general public. Our meetings are a medium for this enhancement.

Publicity

Fundamental to our process is publicity. We must collect and organize the *facts* about our meeting and the organization. But what kind of facts do we need? Consider the following list as a guide to securing the facts and to the kind of material that you will need for promotion and for public relations:

1. Site and destination facilities and attractions.
2. Site and destination special events.
3. Meeting special events: banquets, entertainment, tours, recreation, featured speakers, entertainment groups, sports figures, competitions, etc. (These should come from your meeting pattern or your meeting plan.)

4. Special agenda or content features (new and different information, problems to be solved, special teleconference persons, etc.).
5. Speaker and/or artist biographies and pictures.
6. The meeting theme.
7. Companion activities, sessions, or events.
8. Weather information for the destination.
9. Clothing recommendations.
10. Terminal-to-site transportation information.
11. Air or ground transportation information (if not controlled and handled by meeting management) and recommended procedures.
12. Meeting schedule (from meeting pattern or meeting plan).

This 12-item list is a starting point. You will discover that you will add to or delete from the list for each meeting you do.

Promotion

Once you have collected the facts, it is time to plan your promotional strategy. An effective marketing program is based on *two* vital considerations: (1) a thorough market study and (2) a marketing plan. We conducted our marketing study, without labeling it as such, in Chapters 3 and 4. We should now know our group characteristics and the needs of the group, since we had to know needs to write our objectives. The marketing plan is our promotional and public relations plan. The plan should address the *what* and the *when*. The *how* comes later.

The 12-point checklist should give an idea of substance. It does not give an indication of the *medium* to be used. The medium may be either *direct mail* or *media*. Each has its own specifics.

Direct Mail. Direct mail may include:

1. Meeting "alert" cards.
2. Response cards.
3. Brochures.
   (a) Early brochures with general details.
   (b) Brochures with agenda and registration data.
   (c) Promotional brochures just prior to the meeting to secure attendance from the "procrastinators" and the "undecideds."
   (d) Brochures for the media.
4. Destination, site, and transportation literature.

Each of the direct-mail possibilities should be carefully evaluated in terms of cost and effectiveness. Cost will involve both the printing and the postage. If printing and mailing can be done in-house, then it may become an indirect cost, where you don't list it as a line item in the budget but account for it in the income and expense statement and the meeting balance sheet. Whether done in-house or out-of-house, it is a cost factor that must be considered.

Effectiveness is considered in terms of the potential attendees, their characteristics, and their needs. Media brochures are evaluated in terms of the media to be used and the audience reached by the media.

Alert and response cards may not be needed, although they can be of value in creating early interest and permitting potential attendees to plan their budgets for attendance.

Destination and site and transportation literature and promotional materials should not represent a major cost factor, since the destination and site and transportation companies should handle the printing (usually the mailing) and your cost is in producing mailing lists.

Brochures require careful planning. The following are two guidelines for developing brochures:

1. Make the cover interesting to the reader so it isn't immediately placed in the trash. There is nothing worse than sending a brochure that is so bland it is totally ignored. The cover should contain an interesting and provocative title that captures interest *and* attention. The cover should also contain something about the attendee for whom the meeting is designed, the name of the organization or group sponsoring the meeting, a short summary (one or two sentences) of the program and concise information on date(s) and location.

2. The inside of the brochure must provide complete information. Repeat from the cover the title, sponsoring groups, dates, time (completeness and detail depends on whether it is the initial brochure or a later mailing), location (destination and site), meeting schedule, featured speakers (names, titles of their presentations, affiliations, and positions), fees and what is included with the fee, the reduced fee for early registration if applicable, companion activities (if any), child-care information, provisions for handicapped, special events, lodging information (including cost), why people should attend, and a registration form to be returned.

This information is a minimum. Such items as clothing, suggestions, weather contingency plan for outdoor events, and (if it is a professional conference) suggestions for premeeting reading can be included. The design and layout of the brochure is an art in itself and it is recommended you read some of the material in the bibliography before starting or use a graphic artist once you have your information assembled. Sometimes the design and layout can be handled by your in-house facility.

Evaluation of the cost and effectiveness of direct mail must also include *printing*. A meeting manager needs to have a rudimentary knowledge of printing in order to deal with printers. The following information will serve as a basis for further reading in the bibliography of this book and for discussions with printers.

Before we can discuss relationships with printers, we need to mention the importance of *scheduling* promotion. It is generally accepted that the first mailing should occur about one year before the meeting and is normally a meeting alert card or announcement. After this, the schedule should look like this:

Six to nine months before the meeting: Send the first press release to related organizations.

Five to seven months before the meeting: Advertisements should be placed in meeting-related publications.

Four to six months before the meeting: Mail the first brochure to potential attendees.

Three to four months before the meeting: Send a follow-up brochure or reminder.

Two to three months before the meeting: Send a final brochure or reminder.

Two to six weeks before the meeting: Send tickets to social events and final program. Include a short promotional item on one or more of the meeting events.

With our promotional schedule in place, we can begin to deal with the printers. The first area with which we must be familiar is typesetting.

There are three general approaches to typesetting. The first is what is called *hot type,* which is used for large headings and posters. This may be done by hand but it is normally done by machine. The second is usually done by typewriter and is called *cold type.* The third and most commonly used is photographic. Advances in typesetting have been so rapid that additional approaches appear almost yearly. The latest is the use of a computer. Copy is put on a computer using a floppy disk; with the development of the 3.5-inch diskette, more copy can be placed on one disk than with the old 5.4-inch diskette. Desktop publishing software makes editing and production of copy for printing much more inexpensive than older methods because much of the work can be done in-house by you or a competent secretary.

Of the three methods of printing (letterpress, gravure, and offset) the offset method is the most commonly used for brochures. Paper can be run through the presses several times for the application of additional colors. However, the more colors used, the greater the cost. Well-designed two-color brochures can be just as attractive as multicolor productions. (This depends on the original layout and graphics.) If you are faced with hundreds or thousands of copies, you should probably look for a printer with a web press. These presses can print up to 30,000 copies per hour and do as many as 200,000 copies of multiple pages—such as 16, 24, and 32 sections—at one time. Web presses combine folding and cutting, so production time is greatly reduced.

When you deal with printers, there are also guidelines.

1. Get a minimum of three bids.
2. Set deadlines for the printer two or three weeks prior to when you need the finished material.
3. Avoid cutting paper stock. Cutting costs money, so try to fit your printed material on standard stock sizes. By careful layout, this can be done and will save on waste as well as cutting costs.
4. Make certain the printer has enough stock for your job and ask the printer to reserve additional stock from the same batch for any additional needs you may have. Paper color and consistency will vary slightly from batch to batch.
5. Make certain the size of your finished direct mail piece will fit a standard envelope, or make the direct mail piece a self-mailer. (Self-mailers are more easily discarded without reading than the same material enclosed in an envelope—but they save money.)

6. When requesting bids:
   a. Supply complete information on your requirements (volume, paper stock, type faces, page size, type of binding, when you will submit copy, when you want the finished copy, etc.).
   b. Request that the printer's proposal to you includes a detailed list showing prices for elements of production (paper, composition, etc.), major contract terms outlined, including penalties for printing errors, and a production schedule.
   c. Check out the printer for the quality of work and performance background, financial stability, management and labor quality, and stability.

Media. Media may include press releases to both the print and electronic media where the organization is headquartered, the destination for the meeting, and hometown newspapers of the attendees.

1. Press releases should be typed and double-spaced on white paper (preferably on a single page).
2. Place the words *For Immediate Release* at the top of the page unless you want to set up a schedule of releases or want a release held until a certain date. (Remember, when you ask the media to hold copy, it may be forgotten.)
3. Make your release interesting to the editor who receives it. (Competition for space or time is tremendous, and you need to catch the editor's eye and make it easy for him or her to use your release.)
4. Always use the *inverted pyramid* style of writing. By this I mean include who, what, when, where, and why in the first two or three lines of the release. Then, elaborate by giving the most significant or attention-getting ideas first, moving to less and less important details as the release progresses.
5. Place the number 30 at the end of the release.
6. Add, after the 30, *For more information, contact:* and the name of the contact person.
7. If you wish to submit pictures:
   a. Use 5-inch by 7-inch photos.
   b. Find out if glossy or matte finish is preferred.
   c. Put on your release *W/PIX*.
   d. Write what is called a *cutline* identifying what the picture is about and who the people are from left to right. (Put their names, addresses, and phone numbers at the top of the cutline page.)
   e. Use a soft lead pencil or grease pencil to write the same information on the back of the photo.
   f. Put an abbreviation on the photo to identify it with the cutline.
   g. Put the abbreviation *W/PIX* at the top of the page where the photo is to be used.
   h. Make certain all the people in the picture have signed a form permitting use of the picture.
8. Schedule your releases in such a way that they add interesting details, which tend to build interest and importance. Build to a crescendo at the meeting time.

9. Prepare a pressroom for the use of the media personnel. Include the following:
   a. Desks, worktables, and chairs.
   b. Typewriter, extra ribbons, correction tape *and* fluid, white paper, scratch pads (usually legal size), pencils, legal and 9-inch by 12-inch envelopes, paper clips, and staplers.
   c. A complete set of meeting handout materials, including registration materials, for each reporter.
   d. A banner with your organization logo and meeting theme on the wall.
   e. Coffee and juice, a wall clock, bulletin board, and coatrack.
   f. Electrical outlets for typewriters and computers.
   g. Wastebaskets, ashtrays, and matches.
10. If the room is to be used for a press conference or if you schedule a separate room for press conferences, include the following:
    a. Logo and meeting theme on a large, tasteful sign.
    b. Comfortable chairs for both interviewers and interviewees.
    c. A tasteful and dignified backdrop for photographers and television.
    d. Interview tables (either set up in advance or provided as needed).
    e. Adequate electrical outlets, current, and jack adapters for television.

Public Relations

Although most of the elements of promotion can also be used for publicity, there are additional factors to consider. Of course, the press releases and pressrooms are important, but even more important is the care and feeding of destination VIPs and members of the press corps. Assign a knowledgeable and personable member of your staff to "VIP relations."

There are certain bits of information that need to be relayed to the VIPs, such as how many dollars the attendees will be spending at the destination, human-interest stories about a few of the attendees or organization executives, unusual events of the meeting (particularly those using local sites or events), or some prominent speakers who might be available for interview.

Start building interest in the meeting two or three weeks in advance. Let the media know you are coming with special events, human interest, and features for their use. Let them know there will be a pressroom for their use.

Your VIP relations person must make a point of meeting each important person (including media), try to find out something about each to serve as a basis of communication, and make absolutely certain these people don't get lost trying to find their way around the meeting and the property.

If you should have a nationally or internationally famous person who has special security, your problems are magnified. You need to make every effort to facilitate their work. Learn as much as you can about security requirements and procedures. You'll discover procedures and requirements vary from person to person, so you can't rely upon previous experience. You will be amazed at how thoughtful handling of security people produces spin-off effects that are excellent publicity.

Sometimes you will encounter a new reporter. Make every effort to help these individuals feel welcome, to supply information and ideas, and to make certain that their job is made easier. (Think back to the strain you were under doing your first meeting.)

Obviously, what has been discussed under the heading of publicity is really a matter of good human relations. Anyone can be taught human relations, but some people have a personality that makes human relations easier. This is the kind of person to seek out to handle VIP relations. *A word of caution:* Some people who appear natural for human relations are not discreet. Any organization has certain information that should not be shared—particularly with visiting dignitaries who are not members of the organization or the press. Thus, judgment on your part and on the part of your VIP relations person is extremely important.

There is much more material that could be covered under this chapter. However, it is recommended you pursue those publications cited in the bibliography so you may secure more in-depth coverage of each of the areas.

Summary

Publicity, promotion, and public relations each have distinct roles in ensuring a successful meeting. Publicity secures and releases data, promotion focuses on attendance, and public relations centers on organization and meeting *image* enhancement. We covered general guidelines for each, giving specifics about designing brochures and using direct mail. The planning of a promotional schedule is essential before you begin working with printers so that you have some idea of printing deadlines you must establish. Areas of concern in dealing with printers are typesetting, the type of press to be used for your material, and requirements for receiving proposal bids and evaluation of those bids.

Public relations focused on media relations, both print and electronic. Press releases must be carefully structured to gain attention and be easy for the editor to use. Submission of photos has certain guidelines, with the most important (for protection of the meeting manager) being securing of releases to print the photos.

Media relations at the time of the meeting are extremely important. Materials must be prepared for each media representative and a pressroom set up that contains equipment possibly needed by reporters. If necessary, a separate interview room with provision for both still photography and television should be arranged.

The chapter concluded by directing your attention to *human* relations as the key underlying factor in both promotion and publicity.

WHAT YOU SHOULD HAVE LEARNED FROM THIS CHAPTER

1. The three general considerations for letting people know about a meeting: publicity, promotion, and public relations.
2. Guidelines for developing an effective brochure.
3. An approach to scheduling promotion and public relations.
4. The three kinds of typesetting.
5. The three kinds of printing.
6. The importance of the type of printing press to be used for each type of printing need you have.

7. Criteria for bid proposals from printers.
8. How to evaluate proposal bids.
9. Guidelines for the writing of press releases.
10. Guidelines for submitting photos with press releases.
11. How to set up and equip press and interview rooms.
12. The role of human relations in relating to VIPs and members of the press.

REVIEW QUESTIONS

1. What are the differences among publicity, promotion, and public relations? What do they have in common?
2. What do you believe is the most important element of a brochure for a meeting?
3. What would you include in a first mailing to potential attendees?
4. How are *marketing* and *promotion* similar?
5. What kind of typesetting is becoming most frequently used?
6. What are key cost factors to consider with promotional materials?
7. What is meant by the *inverted pyramid* approach in writing press releases?
8. You have a photo of the organization president and a television drama star. Describe what you would do when including the photo in a press release.
9. You are managing an 800-attendee meeting. To whom would you send your press releases?
10. You are holding a meeting in a hotel where the vice president of the United States will be speaking. How would you go about working with the vice president's security people?
11. The Canadian ambassador is to speak at your meeting. Describe procedures you would take to set up a press conference for him or her.

APPLICATION EXERCISE

The chapter described publicity, promotion, and public relations considerations. Most of these would be more applicable to an association meeting. However, a corporate meeting must also include some of, if not all, the considerations. Set up a publicity, promotional, and public relations *plan* for a corporate meeting. (You may use one of the corporate meeting descriptions from Appendix C or create your own meeting.)

Chapter 13

The Law and the Meeting Professional

When you read this chapter and discover the many aspects of law for which you must be accountable, you will probably agree with Michel de Montaigne, the sixteenth-century French philosopher, when he said:

> I am further of the opinion that it would be better for us to have (no laws) at all than to have them in so prodigious numbers as we have them.

What is covered in this chapter must not be regarded as a substitute for legal opinion. Therefore, it is recommended that you seek out a reputable attorney for interpretation of specific legal situations and conditions. The guidelines in this chapter cover, in a general manner, the legal concepts with which you should be familiar: liability (tort) law, contract law, and insurance to protect you and your organization.

Liability Law

You as the meeting manager may be held responsible to some degree for the behavior of your group, for damages caused by you or the attendees, for violation of laws such as liquor laws, and for cancellation of a meeting that causes damage to the host property.

Liability is based upon negligence, the degree of negligence, or what is called "comparative" negligence. In non-English-speaking countries the legal code is based on civil law, which is different than the common law of English-speaking countries. For instance, under civil law, you are guilty until proven innocent. (This is why Americans have been jailed for possession of drugs and remain jailed for a period of time before a trial is held and they can attempt to prove their innocence.)

The following chart places the elements of tort law in a layperson's perspective.

Types of Torts	Duty Required?	Breach	Proximate Cause	Damage
Intentional	Yes	Intentional act, e.g., striking or libeling another	Necessary	Necessary with a few exceptions
Unintentional	Yes	Negligent act: person has not conformed to "reasonable person" standard	Necessary	Necessary
Strict Liability	Yes	Don't have to *prove* negligence or intent	Necessary	Necessary

Duty. A law *imposes* some kind of duty, which then becomes *obligatory conduct.* We have a tort when someone fails, or *breaches,* that obligatory conduct. Supposing one of your attendees is the victim of an accident that you did not cause. Even though you are an eyewitness, you have no legal obligation to assist that person because a *moral* obligation is not recognized by the courts in a situation like this. The same is true of a medical doctor at the scene of an accident. (In fact, in our litigious society, the doctor could be sued for malpractice if a victim dies because of his humanitarian act.) Duty is an extremely flexible concept that changes with social conditions.

Breach of Duty. If it is established that a duty exists, a violation of that duty must exist if there is to be a *breach.* This violation of that duty may be by negligence or intention.

Proximate Cause. Proximate cause simply means that negligence, to be a *cause,* must be the *next* or nearest cause of any resulting injury or damage. For example, a meeting attendee at a food function has food spilled on his clothing by a waiter. The attendee sends the suit to a dry cleaner outside the hotel. If the suit is ruined by the dry cleaner, the attendee cannot expect compensation from the waiter, the hotel, or the meeting planner because the negligence of the dry cleaner intervened to break the chain of causation, and the dry cleaner becomes the *proximate cause.*

Damage. Without damage, injury, or loss, there can be no recovery. For instance, if you drive through a stop sign, there are no other vehicles or people in the intersection, and there is no damage or injury, you are guilty *only* of running a stop sign. If, on the other hand, there is an accident and damage or injury, then you have committed a tort and are what the law calls a *tort-feaser.*

The meeting manager can easily become guilty of a tort against personal rights. There are several possibilities:

1. Assault and battery. *Assault* is a threat to inflict bodily harm or injury. There must be a real or apparent ability to inflict the harm, and the person threatened must have a reasonable fear of physical harm.

Battery is intentionally or wrongfully touching another person without the person's consent. Battery must include a threat, or assault.

2. *False Imprisonment.* If one person confines another without the second person's consent *and* there is no means of safe escape, false imprisonment results. Be careful. A police officer may make an arrest with a *warrant;* if the person is later found innocent, no action can be taken against the police officer.

3. *Defamation.* This is the injuring of another person's good reputation without good reason. There are two types of defamation; here is where the meeting manager must be careful. *Slander* is defamation by *words* or *gesture.*

Libel is defamation by use of information in printing or pictures. However, the statement or material must be communicated in such a way as to be heard or read by a third person. For example, a meeting manager tells a hotel accountant that the accountant "cheated" on the master account by charging tax on gratuity. If the words are spoken in the privacy of the accountant's office and no one hears, there is no libel. If, on the other hand, the remark is made at the front desk within hearing of others and the tax on gratuity was not illegal, we have libel and defamation of character.

If our meeting manager tells other meeting managers that the hotel is dishonest in accounting and the statement results in a decline of business for the hotel, malicious intent occurs, and the manager is guilty of slander.

To make it more complicated, there are occasions where damage to reputation does not have to be proved. For example, where there is damage to a person in his or her profession, or where false charges of an individual having a disease or committing a crime are involved, there is no need for proof. *If a statement can be proven true, it cannot be considered either slanderous or libelous.*

4. *Malicious prosecution.* This is an intentional tort when a person brings criminal action against another with no valid reason and with the intent to cause damage or injury. The charged person must be proven not guilty and prove that damages resulted before filing for recovery.

5. *Right of privacy.* This is the last of the intentional torts against personal rights. Courts generally consider violations to cause mental anguish.

Of particular interest to the meeting manager is that any pictures, names, or statements made by an individual cannot be used in advertising or promoting a meeting without that individual's permission. This permission should be in writing. (Remember, in Chapter 7 we told you to have written permission to use pictures in advertising.)

One business tort that is important is *copyright.* A copyright gives an exclusive right to the copyright holder to reproduce that material. A copyright is valid for the life of the holder plus an additional 50 years.

Therefore, if a speaker at a meeting reproduces copyrighted material without written permission, whether it is distributed or just used in quotation form, he or she is liable if damages can be proved.

Next we will briefly discuss three aspects of *unintentional torts,* which may be the most important area of tort law for the meeting manager:

Negligence. This was referred to earlier. It frequently involves breach of duty. As long as a person takes every reasonable precaution, he or she will probably avoid negligence. Of course, "reasonable" is subject to legal interpretation by the courts for each individual case. Ignorance, honest mistakes, and physical disabilities *are not* legal excuses for negligent behavior. *Be very careful.* If in doubt, consult an attorney. It is better to spend some money on an attorney before the fact than *much more money* if you make a mistake.

Contributory negligence. Sometimes a victim of a negligent act is found to have *contributed* to the injury or damage resulting from the negligence of another person. In this case, many states do not permit the victim to recover damages.

Comparative negligence. Contributory negligence is more strict than comparative negligence. Some states have adopted a standard that the jury determines *just how negligent* the plaintiff was and the verdict is reduced by the amount of negligence. [Usually *percentages* of negligence (10, 20, 30, and so on) are used.]

It is hoped that you will now be careful and use the reasonable person standard when dealing with hotels, other suppliers, and your attendees. One way of protecting yourself beyond the reasonable standard is through a rudimentary knowledge of *contract law.*

Contract Law

The contracts we, as meeting managers, encounter are covered by the Uniform Commercial Code (Article 2: Sales) in all states except Louisiana, which has not adopted the code. There are five *forms* of contracts, which you should read for yourself and/or learn via a course in business law. Therefore, here we will do no more than list them and then go to the contents of the contracts with which we deal. The five categories of contracts are these:

1. Formal and simple contracts
2. Unilateral and bilateral contracts
3. Express and implied contracts
4. Valid, void, voidable, and unenforceable contracts
5. Executed and executory contracts

Terminology and Legal Requirements of Contracts

The six legal requirements of contracts are offer, acceptance, mutual assent, consideration, competent parties, and a legal purpose.

Offer. An offer is a promise by one party to perform an act upon acceptance by another party. If you, as a meeting manager, make an offer to a hotel, you are the *offerer.* The hotel becomes the *offeree.*

To determine whether an offer has been made, the courts use three criteria: intent, certainty of terms, and communication.

Intent. An offer must be made in good faith and the parties must indicate real intent that their promises can be enforced. (If I say, "For a nickel, I'd sell this watch," and you say, "I'll take it," there is no obvious intent on my part to sell the watch for that price. Therefore, there is no offer or contract basis.)

Certainty of Terms. Terms must be clearly and completely stated. There must be no chance of misunderstanding. Therefore, if a hotel offers you a contract, make *absolutely* certain that every term is clear and understandable to you. If not, ask the hotel to clarify and/or modify the unclear parts. (For instance, careful analysis of many hotel contracts will show they are designed to protect the hotel but not the meeting organization or the manager. Ask for reciprocity, such as a penalty for noncompliance.) Also remember there are conditions such as: If overbooked, the hotel will secure equal accommodations for your attendees. The term *equal* is ambiguous and should indicate the meeting manager will be involved in the determination of the meaning of equal. If you submit your own contract, make certain the terms are mutually understood by both you and the hotel.

Communication. This is the requirement that an offer, to be valid, must be made known to the offeree. For example, if an offer is extended by letter, the letter *must be received* by the offeree. If the offer is lost in the mails, no offer exists. (This is the reason for using "return receipt requested" service when making an offer.) Note also that *only* the offeree may accept the offer. That is, a hotel sends a contract to you for your organization. In the contract the organization is the offeree. Can you, as the meeting manager, accept the offer? Who can sign for the hotel?

Termination. When an offer has been properly extended, it can be terminated (ended) in one of several ways. In contracting with any supplier, make certain one or more provisions for termination are included.

Revocation. Usually an offer can be *revoked* at any time before it is accepted if proper notice is given to and received by the offeree. However, if the offerer promises to keep the offer open, it must be kept open.

Occasionally an offerer and offeree agree to hold the offer open over a given period of time. This is known as an *option* and usually involves a *binder,* such as payment of money. Many hotels are now requiring a binder. The amount may be negotiated. Also, an offer is *under seal* until a stated period of time elapses.

Lapse of Time. Lapse of time is the second way an offer may be terminated. If an offer is extended with a specified time limit for acceptance and the time limit expires, the offer is said to *lapse* and cannot be accepted by the offeree. When no time limit is specified, the offer expires after a "reasonable" amount of time, as determined by the courts.

Death or Insanity. When either the offeror or offeree dies or is declared mentally incapacitated, the offer is terminated because, when both parties agree and accept terms, there is a *meeting of minds,* which is impossible upon death or with insanity. (Fortunately, we do not encounter this problem very often in the meeting professions.)

Destruction of Subject Matter. If, for instance, there is an offer from a hotel to make its facilities available for a meeting and the hotel is destroyed by fire, explosion, or other disaster before the offer is accepted, the offer is terminated. If the calamity happens after the offer is accepted, any binder must be returned and the meeting manager has to find an alternate property.

Intervening Illegality. If an offer is made and the subject matter of the offer becomes illegal before acceptance, the law declaring the subject matter illegal is said to *come between* (intervene) between offer and acceptance. This terminates the offer. Normally we don't encounter this with hotels, but we do with transportation rules and regulations that affect the airlines or other modes of transportation.

Rejection by the Offeree. When an offeree refuses to accept (rejects) the offer, the offer is terminated. *Note that the offeree cannot accept that same offer at a later date.*

Counteroffers. When an offeree submits changes to the original offer he or she is said to make a *counteroffer.* When the "counter" is submitted, the original offer is terminated. Keep this in mind because sometimes a hotel or a meeting manager desires to make changes in an original contract. When these contract changes are submitted, the original contract is terminated, and a new meeting of the minds must occur.

Acceptance of an Offer

When you agree to the terms of the offer and agree to be bound by the terms, you are said to *accept* the offer. An acceptance, as with the offer, is bound by certain requirements. These are silence and words or actions, performance, and correspondence.

Silence and Words or Actions. Generally, silence does not indicate acceptance. Acceptance should be communicated to the offerer by words or actions according to the terms of the contract.

Performance. Performance, such as an offer of a reward usually appears with unilateral contracts.

Correspondence. If acceptance requires a return promise, that promise must be done through correspondence. A contract like this becomes effective when the acceptance becomes effective. Note that the Uniform Commercial Code permits acceptance in any reasonable manner by any reasonable method when the contract involves *sale of goods,* but the code does not apply to all other contracts.

We have now discussed contracts in a general manner. There are other details of course, but you have enough basis here to be able initially to pursue your career in the meeting profession. Again, it is strongly recommended you read a good business law book, take a course in business law, or consult with an attorney when you have doubt.

Insurance Coverage

No matter how careful we are, problems can arise. For this reason, the meeting manager needs an understanding of insurance that is available for protection.

Most properties and convention centers now require that an organization have insurance up to a specified dollar amount. Further, you will find that hotels and convention centers include a *hold-harmless* clause that releases the property from responsibility for any damages to or destruction of the organization's materials and equipment, whether owned or rented. You, as meeting manager, should require that all your major suppliers and contractors indemnify (hold harmless) the organization in a manner similar to that of the hotels and convention centers. Spend some time with an attorney to assist in drawing up indemnity language to include with all contracts signed. Having accomplished the hold-harmless clause in all contracts, we can look at specific insurance policies.

There are professional liability policies for the planner. These policies protect you from damages that may result "by reason of any wrongful act" by you or your staff. (One should not have any knowledge of this wrongful act before the policy goes into effect.) Coverage includes attorney's fees incurred as a result of a suit, bonds, investigation expenses, adjustments, appeals by another insurance company, and most other reasonable fees. It is strongly recommended that you secure a professional liability policy for yourself, and if you work for an organization, determine what coverage you have under the organization's policy. (No organization should hold a meeting without at least $1 million in insurance coverage.)

You should also explore securing meeting-cancellation insurance. These policies will cover such things as cancellation, curtailment, postponement or abandonment of conventions, exhibitions, meetings, and conferences. You can also get coverage for the nonappearance of entertainers and speakers. Remember that entertainers cannot be the main reason for holding the meeting.

Since you have your own regular insurance policies, you are aware of the *exclusions* that appear. The same happens with meeting-cancellation policies. They usually exclude financial insolvency or bankruptcy of an organization or an individual, variations in exchange rates for off-shore meetings, not enough sales or attendance, and lack of exhibitors or sponsors. Coverage of physical loss while shipping and moving to the destination and site is available. There will also be exclusions on property loss, so go over every detail with your agent.

There is one other area of both law and insurance of which you should be aware, which is *liquor liability.* Most cities and states now have their own liquor laws, which are called *dram shop laws.* If you plan to host functions where liquor is consumed, you *must* check out the local dram shop laws. When we deal with hotels, we quickly discover there is a difference between a guest and an invitee. People who are registered guests of the hotel are guests. A local person attending your meeting but not registered in the hotel falls in the category of invitee. The responsibility and liability of the hotel is usually different for an invitee than for a guest. If an invitee is injured in an accident on the way home after an alcohol function at your meeting, you usually discover that you and your organization are liable rather than the hotel. Also, if a guest is injured as a result of your negligence, the idea of comparative negligence will probably apply.

Therefore, talk to your insurance agent to discover if your professional liability policy or the meeting-cancellation policy can be extended (at an additional premium amount) to cover liquor liability. (Of course, you should find out if the property or the caterer carry what is called *host liquor legal liability.* If the property or caterer is not covered, you should make every effort to be covered under your own policy.

As long as you are talking with your agent, find out if you can get additional coverage for fire, burglary, robbery, accidental death or dismemberment, and even malpractice. You may end up "insurance poor," but that is superior to the kinds of financial loss you could suffer if you are not covered.

Summary

This chapter has given you a very basic orientation concerning the legal aspects of meeting management, including liability law, contract law, and insurance coverage. It was stressed throughout the chapter that the meeting professional should augment the material in this chapter by reading books on business law, taking a course in business law, or *consulting with an attorney when in doubt.* Contract law is the area in which meeting managers are most frequently involved because, as an adage in meeting management says, "get it in writing." The quality and completeness of that writing depends on the contracts you sign and the complete mutual understanding of the terminology used.

Insurance coverage was stressed because no matter how careful we may be, accidents happen; insurance coverage helps in these eventualities.

WHAT YOU SHOULD HAVE LEARNED FROM THIS CHAPTER

1. The differences among intentional, unintentional, and strict liability torts.
2. What duty, breach of duty, proximate cause, and damage are.
3. How duty, breach of duty, proximate cause, and damage impact liability law.
4. What the torts against personal rights are and how they apply for the meeting manager.
5. How copyright law affects the meeting professional.
6. The differences among negligence, contributory negligence, and comparative negligence.
7. The five categories of contracts.
8. The six legal requirements of a contract.
9. Definitions of offer, intent, certainty of terms, communication, and termination.
10. The three ways in which a contract can be accepted.
11. Two major types of meeting insurance.
12. The importance of knowing dram shop laws where you hold your meeting.

REVIEW QUESTIONS

1. What is a tort?
2. Define negligence, comparative negligence, and contributory negligence. How might each relate to the meeting profession and the meeting manager?
3. Give a narrative example of a meeting contract that meets the six requirements of a contract. (You do not need to write a contract; just indicate how each should be met in a meeting contract.)
4. What is a dram shop law? Do your city and state have dram shop laws, and, if so, where can a copy be secured for careful reading?

5. What should be covered in a professional meeting liability policy?
6. What should be covered in meeting-cancellation insurance? What additional coverages should be explored with an insurance agent?
7. What is the difference between a guest and an invitee at a meeting? How can this difference affect a meeting manager?
8. If a contract offer is received through the mail, how should it be accepted?

APPLICATION EXERCISE

Call three or four agents representing insurance companies and find out if their company provides any of the types of meeting insurance you might need and the cost of $1 million coverage. Find out what the exclusions of their policy(s) are. Also, find out if the policies cover international meetings. Do they cover you in transit to the meeting? Do they cover you for a meeting in Hawaii or Alaska?

Chapter 14

Meeting Evaluation

Evaluation is an essential—but frequently overlooked—task of the meeting professional. Betty Richardson, *Meeting Manager,* June 1985, cited findings of her research on use of evaluation. Many meeting managers use evaluation, although a much smaller percentage utilize their findings for future meetings. She also found that female managers tend to use evaluation in planning of future meeting less often than do male planners.[1]

Evaluation will provide three essential pieces of information: (1) how your meeting compared to previous meetings, (2) what your attendees thought of the sessions, presenters, and the total meeting, and (3) how well your meeting accomplished the meeting objectives.

Chapter 14 considers four areas basic to evaluation: (1) what to evaluate, (2) when to evaluate, (3) how to evaluate, and (4) how to analyze, interpret, and use evaluation findings.

What to Evaluate

There are two *general* areas that should be evaluated. These are the site (property) where you hold your meeting and the program of the meeting. Findings in each area should be compared with findings of the two previous years if you have the data from the earlier meetings.

Site (Property) Evaluation

Sites are usually very interested in receiving evaluations from both you and your attendees. Many actually use evaluation results to improve or change their services and facilities. You should include ratings of sleeping rooms, food, facilities for movement (such as stairs, escalators, and elevators), check-in and checkout procedure, personnel, in-house shops, meeting rooms, access to the hotel and parking, the destination city or area, recreation facilities, entertainment, and weather conditions. A possible evaluation form follows this discussion, but you should create your own for your particular meeting and your organization.

Sleeping rooms should be rated on such considerations as attractiveness, cleanliness, comfort, equipment, and service. Food ratings should probably include tastiness, whether it was served efficiently, promptly, and correctly, whether the number of people at the table was conducive to comfort and effective service, if the menus provided variety and food to attendees' liking, and whether the items on the menus were conducive to good health. House food and beverage facilities should be evaluated (restaurants, lounges, and so on) on cleanliness, product quality, and service quality.

Internal facilities may be evaluated on ease of movement from one area to another and whether equipment was adequate. (For instance, is there seating in the lobby where attendees could wait to meet friends from outside the meeting?) Of course, the adequacy and availability of restrooms should be considered under facilities. Don't forget to include signs indicating where meeting rooms are and how helpful the hotel signs are in finding the meeting rooms.

Check-in and checkout procedures are important to the attendee and should be carefully rated. Consider efficiency of procedure and personnel, courtesy of personnel, and clearness of registration and checkout instructions.

Service personnel can make or break a property and should be rated as precisely as possible. Include door and bellpeople, room clerks, room service, housekeeping service, and concierge service, if available.

In-house shops (gift shops, drug stores, and so on) are important to attendees. Ask them to rate whether in-house shops were adequate in number and kind and the service. (To rate prices is a waste of time. Attendees always rate in-house shops as too expensive.)

Include on your ratings evaluations of meeting-service personnel such as setup crews, convention services, and food-service personnel, from food and beverage managers to food serves and the chef. (You, as the meeting manager, and your staff will probably be the only ones to rate these people because attendees are not usually familiar with meeting-service people.)

Ask your attendees if meeting rooms were easy to find, well equipped, comfortable, appropriate for the type of presentation, and well lighted and if they had adequate acoustics. Were the chairs comfortable? Were there distractions such as noise, heat, glare from windows, mirrors, pictures, or overcrowding?

Did they find the property easy to reach by automobile or from the airport, train, or bus terminal? Was parking adequate? What about the neighborhood in which the facility was located? Did attendees feel secure and comfortable when they went off the property?

Were recreation and entertainment facilities adequate, clean, accessible, and run by efficient, courteous personnel?

How friendly were the people in the destination city? Did the "natives" (taxi drivers, retail clerks, police, and so on) make the attendees feel welcome? What about recreation, entertainment, and cultural activities and facilities? Include the weather.

Following is an example property evaluation form.

Sample Site/Destination Evaluation Form

Heading: (include name of property/destination, name of organization, date(s) of meeting)

Sleeping rooms. (For the items indicated below, please rate their quality and importance to you by checking the appropriate blank.)

ITEM	QUALITY: VERY GOOD	QUALITY: ADEQUATE	QUALITY: POOR	IMPORTANCE: VERY IMPORTANT	IMPORTANCE: SOMEWHAT IMPORTANT	IMPORTANCE: NOT IMPORTANT
Comfort						
Attractiveness						
Cleanliness						
Equipment						
Housekeeping						
Room Service						

Meeting food and beverages. (For the items indicated below, please rate their quality and importance on a scale from 1 (very poor) to 5 (very good.)

ITEM	QUALITY	IMPORTANCE
Breakfasts		
Menu(s)	______	______
Service	______	______
Healthiness	______	______
Tastiness	______	______
Please list any special likes or dislikes. ______		
Lunches		
Menu(s)	______	______
Service	______	______
Healthiness	______	______
Tastiness	______	______
Please list any special likes or dislikes. ______		
Dinners		
Menu(s)	______	______
Service	______	______
Healthiness	______	______
Tastiness	______	______
Please list any special likes or dislikes. ______		
Nutrition Breaks		
Menu(s)	______	______
Service	______	______
Healthiness	______	______
Tastiness	______	______
Please list any special likes or dislikes. ______		
Hospitality/Cocktail Functions		
Beverages served		
Alcoholic	______	______
Nonalcoholic	______	______

Food served		
Hot foods	_______	_______
Cold foods	_______	_______
Munchies	_______	_______
Service		
Bar	_______	_______
Food	_______	_______
Please list any special likes or dislikes.		
Internal Facilities/Equipment		
Stairs, escalators, elevators	_______	_______
Restrooms	_______	_______
Direction signs	_______	_______
Relaxation areas (lobbies, etc.)	_______	_______
Lighting	_______	_______
Decor	_______	_______
Please list any special likes or dislikes.		
Check-In/Checkout		
Front desk		
Procedure	_______	_______
Service	_______	_______
Door people/Bellpeople		
Efficiency	_______	_______
Courtesy	_______	_______
Knowledge of property	_______	_______
Cashiers		
Procedure	_______	_______
Service	_______	_______
Please list any special likes or dislikes.		
Meeting-Room Evaluation		
Room setup for program		
Session 1	_______	_______
Session 2	_______	_______
Easy to find	_______	_______
Comfortable		
Seating	_______	_______
Temperature	_______	_______
Lighting	_______	_______
Sound	_______	_______
Please list any special likes or dislikes.		
On-Premise Shops for Your Special Needs		
Adequate number	_______	_______
Adequate type	_______	_______
Accessibility	_______	_______
Service and courtesy	_______	_______
Please list any special likes or dislikes.		
On-Premise Restaurants and Lounges		
Adequate number	_______	_______
Food	_______	_______

Beverages	_______	_______
Service	_______	_______
Please list any special likes or dislikes. ____________________		
Property Accessibility/Parking		
From terminal where you arrived	_______	_______
Service available	_______	_______
Accessibility if you drove	_______	_______
Parking	_______	_______
Self-parking	_______	_______
Valet parking	_______	_______
Please list any special likes or dislikes. ____________________		
Recreation/Entertainment at the Property		
(List types available)		
Adequacy	_______	_______
Equipment	_______	_______
Service	_______	_______
Accessibility	_______	_______
Please list any special likes or dislikes. ____________________		
City (Area) Where Meeting Was Held		
Friendliness of people	_______	_______
Cleanliness	_______	_______
Entertainment available	_______	_______
Cultural activities	_______	_______
Safety	_______	_______

Obviously this property destination evaluation form could be expanded or reduced. Also, the approach might be changed, as will be discussed under *how* to evaluate. You should note the form includes *three* evaluation approaches, the check mark, the five-point rating scale, and the open-ended question, where additional remarks may be made.

Program Evaluation

Program evaluation is probably *more* important to the meeting manager than site/destination evaluation, although the site/destination evaluation will give you very important data on your group, as discussed in Chapter 3 in the section on data collection.

There are many aspects of a program that may be evaluated. These aspects may be used to determine the format of your evaluation approach. For instance, do you wish to direct your evaluation in such a way as to discover your success or failure in accomplishing *meeting objectives?* Do you wish to evaluate *individual presentations* (speakers)? Do you wish to determine if your meeting met *attendee needs?* Do you wish to rate your *agenda* or your overall *meeting pattern?* Or do you wish to have a *comparison of these four elements,* or would a *comparison of this year's meeting with the previous year(s)* be of more value?

Thus, the first step in program evaluation must be a decision on your part about *what you want to find out.*

The second step consists of preliminary planning of the design of a questionnaire to determine accurately the information you have decided you need. Here are some questions for you to answer as you begin to plan the design of your questionnaire:

1. Will I want to use a computer to store and analyze the data?
2. Will I want to evaluate *each* session, each speaker, each presentational method?
3. Will I want an overall evaluation of the total meeting?
4. How much *time* do I want my attendees to spend on evaluation?
5. How knowledgeable and/or skillful will my attendees be in the use of questionnaires?
6. Can I motivate my attendees to complete the questionnaire?
7. How objective or subjective do I want the collected data to be?
8. How much analysis and interpretation of the data do I intend to do?
9. How will I use the data I collect?
10. Who else will see my collected data?

An example of how to approach the evaluation of each session is as follows:

1. Break down the agenda into each agenda item and have it rated.
2. Break down the agenda into individual presenters and have each rated.
3. Break down the agenda into presentational methods, such as speaker, symposium, round table, audiovisual, problem solving, and hands on. Then have each method rated individually or in comparison to each other.
4. Decide on the method(s) of analysis or interpretation to be used.
5. Decide on whether you want to evaluate each session, speaker, or presentational method or evaluate by purpose (enlightenment, belief, motivation, etc.).
6. Decide if you want to ask a simple question as to whether the attendee would attend a similar session or presentational method or hear a similar speaker in the future.

When to Evaluate

There is a great difference of opinion as to the best time(s) to evaluate:

a. At the end of each session?
b. At the end of the meeting?
c. By mail-out evaluation form designed to arrive at the attendee's office or home shortly after the attendee's return?
d. A composite of two or more of these alternatives?

There are pros and cons in each case, so a manager must make the decision in terms of the individual meeting and the manager's personal preference.

At the End of the Session

The advantage is that the content, presentation, and method are fresh in the mind of the attendee.

The disadvantages are these: (1) If emotions are aroused in the session, the attendee may respond emotionally rather than objectively, (2) additional time for evaluation has to be provided for each session, thus skewing the agenda unless this has been built into the original meeting pattern, and (3) attendees may be in a rush to leave and get to the next session, so they don't give needed time to the evaluation.

At the End of the Meeting

The advantage is that attendees are able to view each session and event in terms of the overall picture. They can see how one session is related to another and get a fairer perspective.

The disadvantages are similar to those of evaluating at the end of a session: (1) Attendees are in a hurry to leave and may ignore part or parts of the questionnaire, (2) if the final session is highly motivational, emotions may prevail that distort the objectivity of the response, and (3) time for the evaluation must be provided (in a large block, since the whole meeting will be covered).

A Mail-Out to the Attendees's Office or Home

The great advantage here is that the attendee has had time to think back on the entire meeting during the trip home. Further, the attendee may complete the evaluation form in a more leisurely manner, giving greater thought to each item.

The greatest disadvantage is that when an attendee returns to work, the paperwork has piled up during the attendee's absence and the evaluation is placed at the bottom of the stack until it is too late to return it. Also, with a large convention, your mailing costs can be very great.

You might wonder, why not give the evaluation form to the attendee at the time of departure and have it returned. Attendees collect a great deal of material during a meeting. When they return home, they place it in a "to-do" stack, and then much of it is discarded. The evaluation form may not go into the wastebasket immediately, but its *importance* is lost.

You might use a combination of techniques. You could evaluate at the end of each session but use a monitor from your staff who has been trained in how to motivate questionnaire completion; that person can hand out, motivate, and collect the evaluations. On the last day, a similar approach can be used for the entire meeting (a *much* shorter questionnaire) and for the site/destination evaluation. The cashier might even collect the forms as attendees check out (of course, people have to be told they need to produce the completed form at checkout).

If exhibits are used, interviewers from a local college can be recruited and trained for random evaluation of both the entire exhibition and to select those most striking exhibits. This is combined with an evaluation from each exhibitor, who evaluates the management and the value of exhibiting. Attractive, well-dressed young people are very effective in getting results if forewarned not to be too aggressive in achieving the quota of interviews or evaluations assigned.

How to Evaluate

Naturally, any evaluation uses words, and words are simply symbols, in communication theory, to which people assign meaning based on their backgrounds. Therefore, the most difficult task in preparing any questionnaire is the wording to be used. We have all taken tests where we complain that the instructor's question was not clear and we didn't know what he or she wanted. If we are not using *objective* questions and permit the attendee to write out a response, the development of questions is much easier, since answers can be qualified. Notice that the questions at the end of each chapter in this book are a combination of those that ask for a specific answer from the chapter and general questions, which usually begin with "What do you believe?" These *text questions* illustrate what is meant.

Now, refer back to the sample property evaluation form. Attendees are asked to rate items on a three-point or five-point scale (objective). At the end of each block of questions, there appears this statement: List any specific likes or dislikes. This statement permits subjective responses, which qualify the objective answers. The objective question ratings may be used for statistical analysis, whereas the subjective comments may be stored in the computer and used for *clarification* of the objective ratings.

The layout of the questionnaire is important. We need to provide respondents with a feeling of accomplishment. This is done by the use of white space—space not covered by questions. Many questions can be used if they are spaced or laid out in such a way that the respondent feels he or she is moving through the questionnaire and getting to the end. A questionnaire with *ten* pages containing *six* questions is more conducive to completing the questionnaire than one of *six* pages with *ten* questions because there will be more white space. Also, the use of check marks encourages more responses than having to rate an item by writing numbers.

The use of *words* only in evaluation will create problems. For instance, what *precisely* is meant by such words as "poor," "good," and "excellent"? Very few people will have the same interpretation. Therefore, when you compile your responses, you will be unable to determine exactly what these words do mean. This can be illustrated by asking what is really meant by "good food."

Similar problems can occur with numbers, but giving a wide-enough range gives an opportunity to be more precise. But observe what happens with these different point scales. The direction is: Rate breakfast the first morning on the following scale, with 1 being extremely poor and n being extremely superior. Place a check (√) on the blank under the number that is *your* rating.

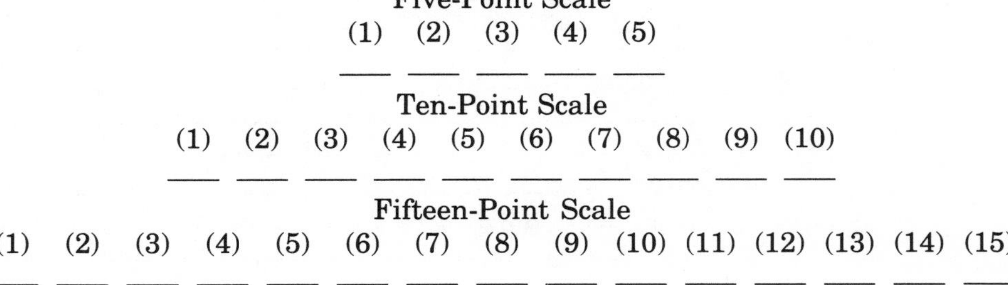

The wider the range of the scale with this layout, the less white space there is. If you wish to use a 15-point scale, it can certainly be done, but you will have to be creative in your layout. You might place the items to be rated across the top and the numbers down the side:

		Item														
		1	2	3	4	5	6	7	8	9	10	11	12	13	14	15
	1															
	2															
R	3															
	4															
A	5															
	6															
T	7															
	8															
I	9															
	10															
N	11															
	12															
G	13															
	14															
	15															
	Total															

This type of matrix makes it very easy for you to make a quick analysis. However, you should probably eliminate the total at the bottom and type item names vertically at the top to eliminate confusion for the respondent and keep the total on a separate form for your use.

The preceding examples should give you an idea of what creativity in layout can enable you to do. There are, of course, many more ways that you will think of as you encounter the requirement of your individual meeting.

Before we leave the subject of how to construct your evaluation form, there are two additional suggestions: (1) You may want to determine the usefulness of the material presented at the conference and/or how the attendee will *use* the material, and (2) you will want to consider what kind of form your interviewers use.

A very simple (open-ended) set of questions permitting subjective feedback on use of material is recommended. An example follows:

How will you use the material from the conference?

Problem solving at work? ______________________________

____

____

Feasibility studies and marketing? ______________________________

____

____

In hobby or part-time job? ______________________________

____

____

Informally? ______________________________

____

____

Other? ____
____
____

While you may get simple yes or no answers, the use of the lines *encourages* more explicit responses.

Now you need to determine the kind of form to be used by the interviewer. You may use a form identical to the one you would create for a distributed questionnaire, or you may create a more condensed form that anticipates respondent questions so your interviewer has material and knowledge to respond to any interviewee questions.

How to evaluate is much easier if you have gone through the process of determining what to evaluate and when to evaluate. The suggestions given in both sections give you a head start. Make the what and the when an *automatic* part of your evaluation planning.

How to Analyze and Interpret the Evaluation Results (Data)

Analysis and interpretation of data cause more consternation among meeting managers than any other aspect of meeting evaluation. They panic over such words as statistics, standard deviation, and analysis of variance. Many meeting managers feel uncomfortable with mathematics. Such reactions need not serve as a deterrent to evaluation analysis and interpretation because of computers, which are discussed in depth in Chapter 15.

Statistical packages can do all the work and mathematical calculations in a few seconds. Statistical software is available for all computers, from personal computers to mainframes. The use of the software is covered in the documentation that accompanies it.

Most statistical procedures start with determining an average, or *mean*. Sometimes it is necessary to discover the mode, which is the score, or rating, that occurs most frequently. (If there are 40 ratings of 3 and no other rating occurs more than 40 times, then 3 is the mode.) Meeting managers very seldom use the *median,* which is the middle point of the collected data. If you use a 5-point scale you can safely assume the median will be a 3. The *standard deviation* is the average amount by which ratings deviate from the mean. The *analysis of variance* is a procedure to determine how much individual ratings vary from each other.

When you get the results from the computer, you need to interpret them. Ask someone to help if you can't figure it out from the documentation. Or, if you cannot find someone to help, here is another approach that is not as sophisticated but will still give you an interpretation.

Let us say we receive 100 responses (N) and there are 5 questions. We can determine the average rating. Then we can find out what *percentage* of people rated the question 2, 3, 4, and so on. Place these percentages in a table and you will have a good idea of what each percentage means in terms of the total. Following is one question with percentages to give you the idea. Let's say you wanted to find out how much people learned from a session. If you used a 5-point scale and assigned *words* to each rating, you would have a table that looks like this:

Mean	Question	Very Much (5)	Quite a Bit (4)	Some (3)	Not Much (2)	None (1)
3.65	Feasibility studies	23%	39%	29%	6%	3%

Looking at these results, we see that only 9% received little or nothing from the session, whereas 62% received more than the average of 3.65. This would indicate the session was above average in producing attendee learning. A procedure like this is very helpful. However, you must realize it is not as exact as if we knew how the ratings were distributed around the average, what the *probability* of the scores occurring again would be, and so on. Your approach can be determined somewhat by the amount of sophistication and accuracy your organization demands and how you intend to use the results in planning your next meeting.

When you are making your decision on the type of analysis and interpretation you will do, remember your organization. Suppose you went into your supervisor and said the meeting was a success. What if he or she happened to be a marketing person with a statistical background and asked for proof? Can you give the kind of answer demanded? This is the reason you need to do careful and thorough evaluation of your meeting.

Summary

Chapter 14 covered four factors of evaluation: what, when, how to evaluate, and how to interpret the results of evaluation. There are two categories to be evaluated: the destination/site and the program. An example evaluation form was given for destination/site evaluation that illustrated three different approaches to evaluation, the check mark, the rating scale, and the open-ended question.

Program evaluation uses the three approaches but first requires careful planning to determine just what should be evaluated for a particular meeting. This planning provides a basis for the next steps, which are the when to evaluate (during, after, or a combination), and how to evaluate. Rating scales were discussed, with consideration given to the degree of accuracy of response desired such as 5-, 10-, and 15-point rating scales. Formats, rather than specific examples, were presented along with the cautions one must use in developing the finished instrument.

The final area of discussion was devoted to analysis and interpretation of the data (results) received from the evaluation. Statistics and the use of a computer for collection and interpretation were covered, with the emphasis being on the *ease* with which data can be interpreted if the meeting manager lets the computer do the work. The use of percentages of response was illustrated for the benefit of those without a computer or who did not need the degree of sophistication that statistical analysis and computer interpretation can provide. The last word of caution emphasized the need to determine what your organization wants and needs. This last caution really determines the thoroughness of the evaluation process to be used to determine if the meeting met its purposes and objectives and the needs of the attendees.

WHAT YOU SHOULD HAVE LEARNED FROM THIS CHAPTER

1. Why there must be evaluation of meetings.
2. What should be evaluated.
3. When evaluation should take place.
4. How the evaluation instrument can be developed.
5. How the collected results (data) from evaluation can be analyzed and interpreted.
6. Formats and procedures that may be used in constructing the evaluation instrument.
7. The planning questions to be answered *before* constructing the questionnaire or other instrument to be used.
8. The use of monitors in conducting evaluation.
9. The advantages and disadvantages of conducting evaluations at different times during the meeting and after the meeting.
10. Basic statistical terms used in analysis and interpretation.

REVIEW QUESTIONS

1. What are the two categories of a meeting that should be evaluated?
2. Why should you conduct site/destination evaluation, and to whom should you submit copies of the evaluation?
3. What areas of the meeting program may be evaluated other than the sessions?
4. Areas of destination evaluation were discussed. What *additional* areas do you believe should be covered?
5. What is an open-ended question, and how would you use such questions in your evaluation instrument?
6. When might you use a "monitor" in the evaluation process, and where would you look for monitors you think would be qualified?
7. What would you plan to evaluate if you had exhibits? What kind of evaluation approach would you use?
8. Where would you look for interviewers to conduct evaluations?
9. What characteristics and qualities would you emphasize in selecting and training interviewers?
10. Assuming you did not want to perform a statistical analysis of your collected information, what would you do?
11. What are the most important governing factors in the evaluation and analysis of a meeting?
12. How would you use the results of this year's evaluation in the planning and management of next year's meeting?

APPLICATION EXERCISE

Develop a site/destination evaluation form for the *destination* you selected for Corporate Meeting 2.

What, when, and how would you develop and administer evaluations of Corporate Meeting 3? Develop a complete *plan* for evaluation of this meeting.

References

1. Betty G. Richardson, "The Meeting Evaluation Process," *Meeting Manager* (June 1986): pp. 31–32.

Chapter 15

Computers and Meeting Management

Meeting managers range from those who have never used computers to those who are sophisticated and experienced computer experts but who could benefit from meetings applications and interfacing/networking ideas. Therefore, this chapter includes information ranging from basic to the advanced in a vocabulary elementary enough for the beginner. No particular products are recommended, or endorsed. If a specific computer or program is mentioned, it is simply to guide your thinking. Also, any recommendations would be quickly outdated with the constant revision, expansion, and updating of material currently on the market.

It is recommended that you not consider any meeting-related software unless you have a computer with a minimum of 256 kilobytes (KB) of memory. Many programs can be used if you have this minimum. In general, the more kilobytes of memory you have, the more comprehensive is the software you may use. Another recommendation is that your computer be IBM compatible because of the nature of materials on the market. If you have a MacIntosh personal computer (PC), you will find some very usable programs, particularly in the realm of design, that may be used with a mouse for freehand drawing. Your best approach, regardless of my comments, is to do a thorough analysis of your needs and then select both hardware and software that meet these needs regardless of the manufacturer.

This chapter is divided into two sections: (1) needs analysis and (2) software shopping. These are the two essential areas for effective computer utilization in meeting management.

Needs Analysis

Meeting managers, like managers in other areas of business, face the problems of identifying *what* they want to do with their computers. As a result, they frequently don't know where to start and have difficulty communicating with programmers, systems analysts, and software salespeople. If you are not careful, it is possible to spend several thousand dollars on useless programs that do not meet specific needs.

This section presents the most common meeting management uses of computers under the general categories of planning, registration, financial and accounting, printing, menu planning, administrative, and customizing. You will discover there is an overlapping of needs from category to category. This overlapping organization is done intentionally to assist you in perceiving where a software program may have more than one utilization in meeting your needs.

Planning

Planning is a general-use area that encompasses development of schedules such as PERT and Gantt discussed earlier. Planning schedules can be developed for your agendas, meeting patterns, printing, promotion, and personnel. The value of planning software is the flexibility it gives you in quick management monitoring and revision of sublevels of meeting development while at the same time maintaining a perspective on the entire plan.

Very few of the existing meeting-focused programs on the market provide more than Gantt or checklist capability. Exceptions would include the new, easy-to-use InstaPlan priced around $300. Specific PERT programs for large computers cost several thousand dollars.

Planning Needs

1. Schedules
2. Agendas
3. Meeting patterns
4. Printing
5. Promotion/advertising
6. Personnel
7. Conflict checking

Please note item 7 in the list. *Make certain that the scheduling software you are contemplating buying permits you to check scheduling conflicts.* You will waste hours in checking potential conflicts unless the software permits you to check on a continuing basis as well as after you finish the schedule.

Registration

Registration is divided into *Pre*registration and On-site registration. These two divisions naturally overlap, but in determining your needs you must consider needs peculiar to each and yet be able to visualize where they overlap when you begin searching for software.

Preregistration Needs

Confirmation letters
Sleeping room assignments
Session assignments
Name badges
Fee receipts
Cancellation acknowledgments
Food function reservations
Recreation reservations
Special event reservations
Registration area design

On-Site Registration Needs

Session assignments and tracking
Name badges
Fee receipts
Food function reservations *and* tracking
Recreation reservations *and* tracking
Special event reservations *and* tracking
Message center control

Look over the lists and note which items appear on both lists. This will mean that you will have to have a computer on-site that uses the same disks and program or that can access your home-based computer through what is called a *modem.* A modem permits you to use a telephone line to connect your computer to another computer some distance away from you. (It is even possible to use a modem to link your on-site computer when you are doing a meeting in Europe with your home-based computer in the United States.)

Accounting and Finance

Finance and accounting seem to create difficulties for many meeting managers, particularly when they need to make software selections. In most cases, the reason seems to be a lack of understanding of basic *bookkeeping* rather than accounting procedures. Terminology appearing in the following lists is not difficult to comprehend. If you have questions, refer back to Chapter 5, where the terms are defined. Accounting and finance needs may be divided into general, or management, needs and bookkeeping/accounting needs. Therefore, the following lists emphasize these areas.*

Financial Management Needs

Meeting budget summaries
Year-end budget summaries
Fee (registration/exhibit) tracking cash flow

*All these categories may be further subdivided: For instance, program costs, operations and overhead, committee(s), speaker honoraria, and the like.

Credit card processing
Check processing
Costs per attendee
Rental (car, audiovisual, etc.) tracking
Billing tracking
Indirect- and direct-cost tracking

Bookkeeping/Accounting Needs

Income
Registration fees received
Exhibits fees received
Food function payments received
Recreation payments received
Entertainment payments received
Payments due to you (outstanding accounts)
Interest payments due to you
Debits
Salaries/wages
Payments to be made
Supplies
Rental costs
Interest payments due
Equipment purchases
Advertising costs
Travel costs
Space costs

You have noticed the use of the word *tracking*. Tracking means the constant monitoring on a day-by-day or week-by-week basis in order to provide the most current information or status of the budget.

A word of caution: Because computers can make so much data available, you may have a tendency to collect useless data. One hotel food and beverage manager received an 800-page computer report each week; by the time he read it, there was no time left to do his regular job. It was found the report detailed how many spoonsful of sugar were used in each day's pastries. As you gain experience, you discover just what the most useful data is. However, when you begin, you should err on the side of too much rather than not enough data.

Printing

Printing is a category of needs that may or may not include many items. For instance, if you are working for a corporation and have in-house printing capabilities, much of the detail work is handled by others, and your needs will be focused on scheduling material and possibly designing material for each meeting. If you must go out-of-house, lead time and detail increases, as do your computer needs. For instance, in the following list, you find desktop publishing, which is rapidly emerging as a time-saving and frequently cost-saving computer capability. Desktop publishing permits you to design, lay out, and print much of the material normally sent to a printer. However, weigh any differences in appearance between what a desktop publishing program can produce and what a professional printer can produce. You may be assured that you get what you pay for in software, and professional printing costs might be a wise investment.

Printing Needs

Handouts for speakers and program
Signs
Name badges
Brochures
Folders
Advertising/Promotion
Desktop publishing
Questionnaires
Certificates

Menu Planning

Many meeting managers do not utilize this category. With our modern diet-conscious society, failure to do careful menu planning can produce many attendee complaints that must be taken seriously. Elements of nutrition such as calories and cholesterol are serious matters to health-conscious attendees. Therefore, the accumulation of a databank on foods seems practical with a computer because of computer capability to sort and select information you need almost instantaneously. When a databank on nutrition is merged with data on menus from previous meetings, you are in a position to provide enough variety so that attendees look forward to gastronomic experiences at your meetings.

Before listing menu planning needs, we refer to Chapter 3. You undoubtedly remember the numerous forms concerning personal data and preferences that included likes and dislikes of foods. If these data are compiled and stored as part of your menu-planning needs, you have a basis for designing menus that are not only nutritious, but also well liked by your attendees.

Menu-Planning Needs

Menu tracking (history of meals)
Nutrition break tracking (history of nutrition break foods)
Hospitality function tracking (liquor and food used)
Menu storage
Nutrition (calories, cholesterol, etc.)
Attendees' preference data

Administrative

This area of computer needs may seem to be a catchall. The previous areas of needs all relate to management and could easily be classed in this category. However, the needs that follow can be considered primarily administrative, or management, needs.

Administrative needs are divided into categories such as design, document, roster, and scheduling so that we may view them separately from the needs areas previously listed. However, please recognize when you start purchasing software to fulfill your particular needs that there may be overlap.

Administrative Needs

1. Design needs
   Meeting-room specifications
   Meeting-room setups
   Exhibit-area layouts
   Exhibit design
   Brochure and logo design
2. Document needs
   Contracts
   Correspondence
   Proposals
   Destination data
   Property data
   Member records
   Reports
   Survey results
   Storage of evaluation results
   Statistical analysis packages and results
   Attendee data and preferences
   History of previous meetings
3. Roster needs
   Attendees lists
   Session lists
   Mailing labels
   Vendor lists
   Speaker and speaker bureau lists
   Cancellation lists
   Continuing education unit (CEU) lists
   Room occupancy lists
   Arrival/departure lists
   Equipment lists
   Recreation event lists
   Entertainment lists
   Talent lists
4. Scheduling
   Event and session tracking
   Meeting-room scheduling
   Conflict checking
   Personnel scheduling

The preceding lists are by no means complete. However, they should serve as a basis for your own thinking and analysis. They do provide you with the basis for a shopping list when you begin to examine software. The following section of this chapter is designed to guide you as you begin shopping for computer software.

Shopping for Computer Software

Throughout this chapter you have noticed many references to software but few to hardware. The reason for this is that, unless your organization has already purchased a computer (hardware), you are well advised to determine your needs first and then select your software. Once you have the software, you can look for hardware that will handle your selected software in the most economical way. There is no need to purchase a computer that is too large or too small, since in either case you would be wasting your money.

Prioritize Your Needs

As a starting point it is recommended that you prioritize your needs. This will permit you to operate most effectively within budgetary limitations by purchasing the most essential software first and then adding to it as your budget permits. Also, your total needs list will serve as an indicator of the capacity you need if you have to purchase a computer or will help you limit your list to the capacity of the computer you may already have.

Determine How Many Terminals (People) You Want to Be Able to Use the Software at One Time

Some of the existing programs are single-user only, which means they can be used by only one single person or terminal at a time. Earlier the text referred to having an on-site terminal for your meeting that could be used to contact your home computer via a modem. If someone else is using your home computer, you will not be able to use your on-site computer if you have a single-user package.

At the end of this chapter is a list of companies who are presently marketing meeting-package software. Their packages have different capabilities, but it would be useless to indicate what their packages can do because companies are constantly changing and modifying what they have to offer. Therefore, contact the companies directly for their latest listings.

If none of the meeting-package companies can meet your needs list, examine discrete software programs. Discrete programs are those that address particular areas such as word processing, graphics, or accounting. Let us examine some of these areas.

Spreadsheets. Spreadsheet packages are probably used for financial analysis more than any other program. The value of a spreadsheet is that it can permit you to say, "What if I were to change my cost allocation for recreation and allocate a part of the cost to food and beverage?" The computer, with the use of a spreadsheet program, will recalculate the entire spreadsheet and show you what the impact would be on your other *line items,* or individual cost areas.

Lotus 1-2-3 has been the best-selling spreadsheet for several years, and there are many additions currently available that expand the 1-2-3 capabilities. However, other software, such as VP-Planner Plus, Quattro, Microsoft Excel, and Surpass, is available. Each competes by either offering enhancements or by being faster than 1-2-3. As mentioned earlier, the JOE Spreadsheet is less expensive, although it will not perform all the functions included in the programs mentioned earlier.

Data Base Management. Data base management is very popular among computer users and meeting managers. Its popularity is exceeded only by word processing and spreadsheets. Meeting managers tend to use what is called the *flat-file,* which stores all your data in one file. However, there are restrictions with the use of only one file, since meeting managers are called upon to store many data that may require more than one file, and the flat-file does not permit comparison of one file with another. There are two other forms of data base management, relational data base and free-form data base.

Relational data base permits you to compare one file with another as long as the files have something in common, such as a city or a number. Free-form data base permits you to search multiple files without any restriction. Both relational and free-form data bases are more complex and are not as user-friendly.

Accounting/Finance Software

If your needs analysis indicates you could use general ledger, accounts payable, accounts receivable, inventory, purchase orders, billing, payroll forecasting, and job costing, there are several well-established, multifeatured programs available. These include Peachtree Complete Accounting and Dac-Easy. If, on the other hand, you need only single-entry accounting with something similar to an electronic checkbook, then Quicken could be your answer.

Graphics Programs. Graphics programs seem to be becoming more important all the time. Several meeting managers are using computer-aided design (CAD) to lay out meeting rooms and exhibit and registraiton areas to scale. There is presently an effort being made by some companies to add a data base to CAD so that you can also handle registration lists, session assignment lists, and so on.

In addition to desktop publishing, you may want to secure a graphics package that will produce name badges and meeting signs or even permit you to do freehand drawing with the use of a mouse. A mouse is a small hand-controlled device that sits on a desktop, is connected to your computer, and as you move the mouse, lines are drawn on your monitor. In short, you become an artist on a computer and, if you have a printer that prints in color, you can produce some artistic masterpieces for logos or just to liven up the registration area of your meeting.

Still another aspect of graphics programs is called *presentational graphics*. These are programs that permit you to create transparencies and other material for the presenters at your meetings. Some of the graphics programs on the market are MacDraw, Aldus Freehand, Harvard Graphics, Freelance Plus, and Windows Draw.

Communications Programs. Communications programs allow a personal computer to exchange files with other personal computers, send and receive electronic mail, and retrieve data from data bases. Crosstalk Mk.IV and Smartcom III are two of the most popular communication programs on the market. However, MicroPhone II, ProComm, and PC-Talk4 are very effective. ProComm and PC-Talk4 are less expensive than Crosstalk Mk.IV and Smartcom III.

Integrated Programs. Integrated software offers two or more applications in one program. Many of the meeting-specific programs fall in this category. The integrated programs generally include word processing, spreadsheet, data base management, and communications. An advantage is that the various modules can be loaded into your computer at the same time so you can switch from one to the other without complications of changing drives or booting (loading) each module when you wish to use it. An example of one of the more effective integrated programs is Open Access II, which, in addition to word processing, has versatile relational data base management and telecommunication aspects. Enable 2.0, Microsoft Works, and PFS:First Choice are also effective lower-cost programs.

Multitasking Programs. Multitasking programs are the latest entries in the software sweepstakes. They are still developing, although several are on the market and appear to be effective. Multitasking programs do such things as allow you to run word-processing, spreadsheet, and communication programs at the same time.

Word-Processing Programs. *Whatever your identified computer needs,* you should begin with a good word-processing package. Whether the word-processing package is a separate program such as WordPerfect or WordStar or integrated into other packages, *make certain you have word processing.* This text does not offer a complete list of programs because there are so many.

Contact Users

Once you have identified possible programs, contact people who have used the program. The company trying to sell you the software will identify several previous purchasers (not just one) whom you may contact, Further, contact the Meetings Industry Microcomputer Users Group (MIMUG), who will be most happy to share pros and cons of their member experiences with different programs.

Check After-Sales Support

If you adopt the philosophy that nothing is perfect, you will have taken a major step toward becoming a computer veteran. Thus, before you purchase any program, make certain the manufacturer has a strong after-sales support program. If you are a beginner, the psychological assistance gained from calling a toll-free number and discussing the problems you have will really help you overcome the frustration you are certain to have as you begin to use your equipment. If you are an experienced user, you already know the advantage of after-sales support. However, a word of advice to both the beginner and experienced person: When you call for sales support be able to give step-by-step or key-by-key descriptions of what occurs just before and/or during you problem. Also, try to place your phone next to the computer so that you can actually implement what you are being told.

Sources of Meeting-Specific Software

Advanced Solutions, Inc.
1332 Walnut Street
Philadelphia, PA 19107
(215)985-0285

Association Management Software
2801 Far Hills, #309
Dayton, OH 45419
(513)298-9752

Aztech Corp.
1621 Connecticut Ave. N.W.
Washington, DC 20009
(202)232-5500

Computerized Reservations Systems
634 30th Street
San Francisco, CA 94131
(415)648-1107

Conference West
383 E. 1800
South Orem, UT 84058
(801)378-4787

Congrex USA
c/o DLB Associates, Inc.
P.O. Box 19172
Washington, DC 20036
(301)588-3231

Delta Software Systems
28 East Rahn Road, Suite 114
Dayton, OH 45429
(513)435-2644

InstaPlan Corporation
655 Redwood Highway
Suite 311 R
Mill Valley, CA 94941
(800)852-7526

Information Breakthroughs
445 W. Main Street
Wyckoff, NJ 07481
(201)891-8405

K/M Data Systems, Inc.
P.O. Box 10844
Greensboro, NC 27404
(919)370-2130

MAST Software Systems
2363 E. Stadium Blvd.
Ann Arbor, MI 48104
(313)662-8422

Meeting Systems, Inc.
777 Canterbury Road
Westlake, OH 44145
(216)892-8928

Peopleware
1715 114th Ave. S.E. Suite 212
Bellevue, WA 98004
(206)454-6444

Phoenix Solutions
Attn.: Corporate Products Division
480 Second Street
San Francisco, CA 94107
(415)495-7440

System Dynamics
P.O. Box 4031
Santa Barbara, CA 93140
(805)963-9626

The Association Store
P.O. Box 8420
Silver Springs, MD 20907
(301)588-3345

Topitzes & Associates
6401 Odana Road
Madison, WI 53719
(608)273-4300

Summary

Chapter 15 has given you an overview of computers and their applications in the meeting profession.

Preliminary to the selection of software or hardware was a system of needs analysis for meeting management. As a minimum, the analysis should cover planning, registration, accounting/finance, printing, menu planning, and administrative needs.

Once your needs have been determined, they should be prioritized and then a determination should be made of the number of terminals needed.

When this groundwork has been completed, the software which contains packages permitting multiple uses related to meeting should be your first consideration. If these multiple program packages do not meet your needs, it was recommended that you examine specific programs such as spreadsheets, data base management, accounting/finance, graphics, communication, integrated and multitasking programs, and word processing.

It was then recommended that you should contact users and carefully examine after-sales support before making a final decision on the software to be purchased. The software selected will help determine your selection of computer hardware.

WHAT YOU SHOULD HAVE LEARNED FROM THIS CHAPTER

1. Six categories for analysis of computer needs.
2. The importance of including provision for checking scheduling conflicts in the software for planning.
3. Five guidelines to use in shopping for computer software.
4. Eight general categories of computer software.
5. Sources of meeting-specific software.

REVIEW QUESTIONS

1. What is the minimum computer memory capacity needed to run software programs for meetings? Why?
2. What are the most common uses of computers in meeting management? Can you think of any uses not covered by the text?
3. What are the seven planning needs? Which one do you believe is most important and why?
4. Why would a meeting manager consider purchasing one or more modems?
5. Do you believe meeting managers should consider financial management needs or bookkeeping/accounting needs more important? Why?
6. What would you use as a guide in deciding whether to produce work through desktop publishing software or sending the work to a printer?
7. What kind of information should be stored in a computer to use in menu planning?
8. Would a computer graphics program be more valuable as a meeting planning tool or an administrative tool? Why?
9. Why do you believe a meeting manager would want an on-site terminal capable of accessing the home-base computer?
10. Do you believe a communication software program could aid a meeting manager using an on-site terminal? If so, how?

APPLICATION EXERCISE

Go back through the application exercises you developed for Chapters 3 through 15 and determine your computer needs if you were to use the programs you developed. Place the needs in the six categories of computer needs. Then, discover which of the eight general categories of computer software you would need to examine in order to meet your identified needs.

Appendix A

Meeting and Related Industry Organizations

American Hotel & Motel Association
888 Seventh Street
New York, NY 10106
(212)265-4506

American Society for Training & Development
1630 Duke St., P.O. Box 1443
Alexandria, VA 22313
(703)683-8100

Convention Liaison Council
1575 I St. N.W., Ste. 1200
Washington, DC 20005
(202)626-2764

Foundation for International Meetings
1726 M St. N.W., Ste. 1002
Washington, DC 20005
(202)457-0909

International Fed. of Women's Travel Organizations
4545 N. 36th St., Ste. 126
Phoenix, AZ 85018
(602)956-7175

American Society of Association Executives
1575 I St., N.W.
Washington, DC 20005
(202)626-ASAE

Assn. of Independent Meeting Planners
1012 Atlantic Ave.
Atlantic City, NJ 08401
(609)347-8683

Exposition Service Contractors Association
1516 So. Pontius Ave.
Los Angeles, CA 90025
(213)478-0215

Hotel Sales and Marketing Association
1300 L St. N.W., Ste. 800
Washington, DC 20005
(202)789-0089

Insurance Conference Planners
18 Chestnut Street
Worcester, MA 01680
(617)793-5828

International Assoc. of
Auditorium Managers
500 N. Michigan Ave., Ste. 1400
Chicago, IL 60611
(312)661-1700

International Assoc. of
Convention & Visitor Bureaus
1809 Woodfield Dr.
Savoy, IL 61874
(217)359-8881

Meeting Planners International
1950 Stemmons Freeway
Dallas, TX 75207
(214)746-5222

Professional Convention
Management Association
100 Vestavia Office Park,
Ste. 220
Birmingham, AL 35216
(205)823-7262

Society of Company Meeting
Planners
2600 Garden Rd., Ste. 208
Monterey, CA 93940
(408)649-6544

Trade Show Bureau
8 Beach Rd.
East Orleans, MA 02643
(617)240-0177

International Assoc. of
Conference Centers
45 Progress Parkway
Maraly Heights, MO 13604
(314)469-9093

International Assoc. of Fairs &
Expositions
P.O. Box 985
Springfield, MO 65801
(417)862-5771

National Assoc. of Exposition
Managers
334 E. Garfield Rd.
P.O. Box 377
Aurora, OH 44202-0377
(216)562-8255

Religious Conference
Management Association
One Hoosier Dome, Ste. 120
Indianapolis, IN 46225
(317)632-1888

Society of Government Meeting
Planners
1133 15th St. N.W., Ste. 620
Washington, DC 20005
(202)232-6883

Western Fairs Association
1329 Howe Ave., Ste. 202
Sacramento, CA 95825
(916)927-3100

Appendix B

Group and Organization Analysis Form

I. Personal Attendee Data

Category	No. of Males	No. of Females	Total Number
A. Age			
1. Under 18	______	______	______
2. 19–25	______	______	______
3. 26–45	______	______	______
4. 46–65	______	______	______
5. Over 65	______	______	______
B. Food preferences			
1. Breakfasts			
Continental			
Dietetic	______	______	______
Eggs and meat	______	______	______
Hotcakes/waffles	______	______	______
Gourmet (croissants, pastries, etc.)	______	______	______
Vegetarian	______	______	______
Kosher	______	______	______
Dislikes			
______________________	______	______	______
______________________	______	______	______
______________________	______	______	______
2. Lunches			
Salads	______	______	______
Sandwiches	______	______	______
Fruit	______	______	______
Substantial (meat, potatoes, etc.)	______	______	______
Dietetic	______	______	______

Category	No. of Males	No. of Females	Total Number
Vegetarian	______	______	______
Kosher	______	______	______
Dislikes			
____________________	______	______	______
____________________	______	______	______
____________________	______	______	______
3. Dinners			
Fish	______	______	______
Ham	______	______	______
Beef	______	______	______
Lamb	______	______	______
Poultry	______	______	______
Shellfish	______	______	______
Vegetables			
Corn	______	______	______
Peas	______	______	______
Beans	______	______	______
Carrots	______	______	______
Beets	______	______	______
Cauliflower	______	______	______
Broccoli	______	______	______
Desserts			
Ice Cream	______	______	______
Fruit pies	______	______	______
Cream pies	______	______	______
Cakes	______	______	______
Mousse	______	______	______
Custards	______	______	______
Fresh fruit	______	______	______
Cheeses	______	______	______
Dietetic			
Vegetarian	______	______	______
Kosher	______	______	______
Dislikes			
____________________	______	______	______
____________________	______	______	______
____________________	______	______	______
C. General preferences			
1. Music			
Classical	______	______	______
Semiclassical	______	______	______
Pop	______	______	______
Rock	______	______	______
Hard rock	______	______	______
Disco	______	______	______
Country and western	______	______	______
Ballroom	______	______	______
Dislikes			
____________________	______	______	______
____________________	______	______	______
____________________	______	______	______

(continued)

Category	No. of Males	No. of Females	Total Number
2. Recreation			
Team sports			
____________	____	____	____
____________	____	____	____
____________	____	____	____
Individual sports			
Golf	____	____	____
Tennis	____	____	____
Swimming	____	____	____
Racquetball	____	____	____
Handball	____	____	____
Shuffleboard	____	____	____
Skiing	____	____	____
Fishing	____	____	____
Sailing	____	____	____
Waterskiing	____	____	____
Other			
____________	____	____	____
____________	____	____	____
____________	____	____	____
3. Political			
Democrat	____	____	____
Independent	____	____	____
Libertarian	____	____	____
Republican	____	____	____
Other			
____________	____	____	____
____________	____	____	____
____________	____	____	____
4. Speakers			
Humorous	____	____	____
Motivational	____	____	____
Subject content	____	____	____
Other			
____________	____	____	____
____________	____	____	____
____________	____	____	____
5. Religious			
Agnostic	____	____	____
Atheist	____	____	____
Catholic	____	____	____
Fundamentalist	____	____	____
Jewish	____	____	____
Protestant	____	____	____
Other			
____________	____	____	____
____________	____	____	____
____________	____	____	____
6. Tours			
Historical	____	____	____
Landscape	____	____	____

Category	No. of Males	No. of Females	Total Number
Museum	_____	_____	_____
Hiking	_____	_____	_____
Jeep	_____	_____	_____
Shopping	_____	_____	_____
River rafting	_____	_____	_____
Other			
____________________	_____	_____	_____
____________________	_____	_____	_____
____________________	_____	_____	_____
7. Cultural			
Musical concerts	_____	_____	_____
Painting	_____	_____	_____
Sculpture	_____	_____	_____
Theatre	_____	_____	_____
Other			
____________________	_____	_____	_____
D. General Geographical			
1. Home residence			
Urban	_____	_____	_____
Small city (under 50,000)	_____	_____	_____
Rural	_____	_____	_____
Suburban	_____	_____	_____
2. Home point of origin			
United States			
East Coast			
Northeast	_____	_____	_____
Southeast	_____	_____	_____
Midwest	_____	_____	_____
Rocky Mountain	_____	_____	_____
Southwest	_____	_____	_____
West Coast	_____	_____	_____
Alaska	_____	_____	_____
Hawaii	_____	_____	_____
Puerto Rico	_____	_____	_____
European country			
____________________	_____	_____	_____
____________________	_____	_____	_____
____________________	_____	_____	_____
Middle Eastern country			
____________________	_____	_____	_____
____________________	_____	_____	_____
____________________	_____	_____	_____
African country			
____________________	_____	_____	_____
____________________	_____	_____	_____
____________________	_____	_____	_____
Central/Latin American/Caribbean country			
____________________	_____	_____	_____
____________________	_____	_____	_____
____________________	_____	_____	_____
Mexico	_____	_____	_____

(continued)

Category	No. of Males	No. of Females	Total Number
Asian country			
Japan	______	______	______
China	______	______	______
Taiwan	______	______	______
Australia	______	______	______
New Zealand	______	______	______

II. Organization Data; Previous Meetings.

Organization name ______________ Address ______________

______________________________ Phone __________

A. General data

1. Location and sites of previous two meetings: (include evaluative notes)
2. Length of previous two meetings (days/nights)
3. Decision maker (give name, title, phone number)
4. Committees: __________ used __________ not used
   (give committee members' names and chair with name of committee)
5. Methods of evaluation used
6. Transportation to site (Who paid costs—organization, individual, or combinations? Were group rates used? What percent of meeting budget was used for transportation of attendees, meeting staff, executives, shipping, freight?)
7. How far in advance
   Were meetings scheduled __________
   Were meetings planned __________
   Was the site selected __________

B. Objectives of the meeting (list for each meeting)

C. Attendance at previous meetings

1. Preregistered
   a. General sessions ______
   b. Break-out sessions ______
   c. Companions ______
   d. Entertainment ______
   e. Food functions ______
      (i) Breakfasts ______
      (ii) Lunches ______
      (iii) Dinners ______
      (iv) Banquets ______
   f. Hospitality functions ______
   g. Recreation ______
   h. Tours ______
   i. Premeeting events ______
   j. Postmeeting events ______
2. Walk-in (on-site) registration
   a. General sessions ______

Category	No. of Males	No. of Females	Total Number
b. Break-out sessions	______		
c. Companions	______		
d. Entertainment	______		
e. Food functions	______		
(i) Breakfasts	______		
(ii) Lunches	______		
(iii) Dinners	______		
(iv) Banquets	______		
f. Hospitality functions	______		
g. Recreation	______		
h. Tours	______		
i. Premeeting events	______		
j. Postmeeting events	______		

3. Average age of attendees at each meeting

4. Sex: Male ______ Female ______

D. Equipment used

1. Audiovisual

Types	Number
______	______
______	______

2. Office equipment

Typewriters	______	Telephones	______
Reproduction	______	Beepers	______
Paper (reams)	______	Walkie-talkie	______
Carbon	______	Recorders	______
Pens	______	Computers	______
Pencils	______	Name badges	______
______________	______	______________	______

E. Facilities used

Sleeping rooms		Costs
Singles	______	______
Doubles	______	______
Queen suites	______	______
King suites	______	______
Parlors	______	______

Meeting Rooms		Costs
Break-outs	______	______
General session	______	______
Food functions	______	______
Exhibits	______	______

F. Organization

Special likes

Special dislike

Special characteristics

G. Attach policy data

Appendix C

Corporate Meetings

Corporate Meeting 1
Publishing Firm

Attendance: 64 sales personnel whose points of origin are from Chicago and St. Louis on the east to Salt Lake City and Phoenix on the west and from Fargo, North Dakota, on the north to San Antonio, Texas, on the South.

30 women, 34 men

Purpose: Enlightenment and motivation about six new books just published by the firm.

Goal: To produce $1 million gross sales of the new books in one year.

Dates and place of meeting: February 13–15, 19— in Denver, Colorado.

Food and beverage: Breakfast and lunch daily. Awards dinner February 14, cocktail party each evening. Nutrition breaks.

VIPs: president, chairman of the board, and national sales manager (single occupancy).

Sales personnel: Double occupancy

Transportation, lodging, food, and beverage paid by corporation and placed on master account.

You have freedom to add to these basic facts except for attendance. *You may not eliminate any of the basics.*

Corporate Meeting 2
GREATEST CORPORATION
Headquarters: Chicago, Illinois, USA
Information for Corporate Sales Meeting

Purposes:

To inform sales people of new electronic products
To motivate sales people to increase gross sales 6% in one year after conclusion of meeting.

Length of meeting: Six days, five nights, plus travel time.

Number of sales people: 100, average age is 37 years.

38 females
62 males

Corporate executives:
Chairman of the board: male, age 57 years
Corporation president: female, age 48 years
Vice presidents: 3 females, 2 males
Electrical engineers: 1 male and 1 female
Executive secretary: 1 female

Attendee points of origin. No Companions Permitted:

Chicago, Illinois	10	(all corporate executives)
Boston, Massachusetts	9	
New York City, New York	11	
Washington, D.C.	9	
Miami, Florida	5	
Atlanta, Georgia	3	
St. Louis, Missouri	5	
Chicago, Illinois	11	(salespeople)
Dallas, Texas	7	
Denver, Colorado	5	
Phoenix, Arizona	5	
Los Angeles, California	14	
San Francisco, California	10	
Seattle, Washington	6	
Total	110	

Room arrangements:
Double occupancy for all salespeople
Single occupancy for corporate executives except chairman and president
One-bedroom suites for chairman and president

Food functions:
All meals paid by corporation
Breakfasts: 6
Lunches: 6
Dinners: 4 plus final night banquet with entertainment and dancing. (*Note:* At each dinner and at the banquet, there will be wine on the table or served. People get choice of red or white. No rosé wine will be served.)

Meetings:

One general session each day
Six break-out meetings on four days.
One exhibit area (very high security required. Exhibit area will be open and used two hours per day for four days. Exhibits will be electronic equipment).

Entertainment:

One all-day tour
One half-day golf tournament (low score wins)
Hosted cocktails before each dinner and the banquet
Entertainment show and dancing; Entertainment (orchestra) during banquet and then entertainment and dancing after banquet

Nutrition breaks:

One nutrition break each morning and one nutrition break each afternoon on each meeting day. *Note:* Each break is to have a variety, with no two breaks having the same food except for beverages. For instance: fresh fruit one time, pastries another, and so on. Keep nutrition in mind.

Audio-visual requirements:

Overhead projector and screen in each break-out room
Slide projector and screen for each general session
16-mm projector and screen for each general session
VCR and monitor in each break-out room each day
Flip chart and easel in each break-out room

Other requirements:

1. Awards
   a. Eight awards for recognition of previous year's sales.
   b. Three trophies (first, second, and third) for golf tournament.
2. Headquarters room with:
   a. Two electric typewriters
   b. Two desks
   c. Two tables (6-foot or equivalent)
   d. Two telephones (long-distance)
   e. One telex
   f. One high-speed photocopier with a backup available
   g. One accurate local typist. Speed and excellent English required
   h. Four "beeper" walkie-talkie radios
3. Billing and accounting
   a. Corporation will pay all meeting-related expenses.
   b. Chairman of the board and meeting manager are only people authorized to sign for expenses to the master account.
   c. Hotel will bill corporate headquarters directly within 10 working days after completion of the meeting. Corporation will pay within 30 days after receipt of the bill.
   d. Master account portfolio will be audited by the meeting manager each morning.
   e. All personal expenses of attendees are to be paid by the attendees at time of checkout.

Services needed:

1. A DMC to:
   a. Meet attendees at airport and assist attendees through customs.

b. Provide round-trip transportation from the airport to the hotel.
c. Provide corporation headquarters with information on airport departure taxes and assist attendees through departure customs.
d. Arrange and conduct tour and arrange golf tournament.
e. Secure entertainment, including band, and decorations for banquet.
f. Secure security as follows:
   (i) Bonded, bilingual, and armed 24-hour security guard for exhibit room
   (ii) Electronic "debugging" of exhibit and general session rooms each morning
g. Provide written estimate of cost of all services no later than six weeks before meeting date.
h. Bill corporate headquarters directly within 10 working days after meeting departure.

2. Prekeying and registration by the hotel.
3. One limousine with driver for use by chairman of the board and corporate president. Fluent bilingual driver required.
4. One automobile with driver for use by meeting manager. Bilingual driver required.

Computation of Meeting Budget for Mazatlan, Mexico

Step 1: Compute airfares for most-distant cities:

City	Airfare	Number of People	Total Cost
Boston	$ 1350	______	$______
New York	$ 1250	______	$______
Washington, D.C.	$ 1050	______	$______

Step 2: Compute airfares for nearest cities:

City	Airfare	Number of People	Total Cost
Phoenix	$ 400	______	$______
Los Angeles	$ 250	______	$______
San Francisco	$ 325	______	$______

Step 3: Step 1 plus Step 2 totals ______ ______

Step 4: Divide total cost by number of people from above:

$$\frac{\text{Total cost}}{\text{Number of people}} = \textit{average} \text{ transportation cost}$$

Step 5: Multiply total number of attendees (110) by Average transportation cost:

$$\text{Total transportation cost} = \text{Total attendees} \times \text{average transportation cost}$$

Step 6: Assume transportation equals 50 percent of total budget for meeting.

$$\text{Total transportation cost} \times 2 = \text{total meeting budget}$$

Computation of Meeting Budget for Nassau, The Bahamas

Step 1: Most-distant cities:

City	Airfare	Number of People	Total Cost
Seattle	$ 1600	____	$____
San Francisco	$ 1450	____	$____
Los Angeles	$ 1250	____	$____

Step 2: Nearest cities:

City	Airfare	Number of People	Total Cost
Miami	$ 150	____	$____
Atlanta	$ 195	____	$____
Washington, D.C.	$ 155	____	$____

Step 3: Step 1 plus Step 2 totals ____ ____

Step 4: Average transportation cost $____ (total number of people attending: 110)

Step 5: Total transportation cost $____

Step 6: Total meeting budget $____

Computation of Meeting Budget for San Jose, Costa Rica

Step 1: Most-distant cities:

City	Airfare	Number of People	Total Cost
Seattle	$ 1450	____	$____
Chicago	$ 1200	____	$____
Boston	$ 900	____	$____

Step 2: Nearest cities:

City	Airfare	Number of People	Total Cost
Miami	$ 400	____	$____
Atlanta	$ 480	____	$____
Dallas	$ 530	____	$____

Step 3: Step 1 plus Step 2 totals ____ ____

Step 4: Average transportation cost $____ (total number of people attending: 110)

Step 5: Total transportation cost $____

Step 6: Total meeting budget $____

Corporate Meeting 3

Attendees:	20 males and 15 females plus one male and one female meeting-management personnel. VIPs: Chair of the board (female), president (male), two vice presidents (male), one guest trainer (male). Double occupancy where possible except for corporate executives and the two meeting-management personnel.
Age:	36 years *average*. Executives as follows: Chairman: 59 President: 47 Vice president 1 51 Vice president 2 45 Guest trainer 63
Occupations:	Corporate marketing
Hobbies:	Golf, tennis, handball, racquetball, fishing, sailing, skiing, partying, dancing, gliding, and ultralight piloting.
Arrival:	First day by 5:00 P.M.
Departure:	1:00 P.M. last day
Duration:	Five days, four nights
Time of year:	Spring
Goal:	Corporation has shown a decline in gross sales and profits of 18% in the last fiscal year. Thus, the goal is to increase gross sales enough to show a profit and find out why sales have declined.
Purpose:	To address sales problems and motivate the 35 regional marketing executives to increase sales to the point needed.
Food functions:	Full American plan paid by corporation
Hospitality functions:	Host bars before dinner
Recreation:	One afternoon and evening. Afternoon to involve strenuous exercise and evening to be extremely social and addressed to the meeting theme.
Exhibits and security:	None needed.
Expenses:	Corporation pays all *meeting* expenses including transportation. (All personal expenses must be charged to individuals.)
Accounting:	Master account folio, charges to master account subject to approval of meeting administrator (not meeting manager) and corporate president only. Provide for daily audit of master account.
Awards:	Each attendee except meeting staff and executives are to receive a *quality* recognition memento of the meeting.

Airfares for meeting 3

Points of Origin	Number of Attendees	Possible Destinations		
		Atlanta	Dallas	Denver
Boston, MA	2	$460	$725	$650
New York, NY	1	420	675	525
Philadelphia, PA	3	325	405	595
Tampa, FL	2	100	315	540
Birmingham, AL	2	75	310	495
Louisville, KY	2	125	340	520
Springfield, IL	3	201	360	199
San Antonio, TX	3	325	100	199
Rapid City, SD	2	514	345	165
Billings, MT	1	535	340	211
Tucson, AZ	5	721	340	211
Salt Lake City, UT	4	611	560	120
Boise, ID	2	634	572	165
Casper, WY	2	625	322	125
St. Louis, MO	(execs. 1st class)	220	186	216
Denver, CO	(meeting managers)	298	166	0

Hotel selection possibilities

Atlanta

Group rates	Hotel A EP	Hotel A MAP	Hotel A FAP	Hotel B EP	Hotel B MAP	Hotel B FAP
Sleeping rooms						
Single	$ 80	$ 97	$126	$ 85	$ 96	$109
Double	90	107	136	95	105	119
Suites						
1 bedroom	125	142	171	130	141	154
2 bedroom	150	167	196	140	150	164
Parlor	90	117	146	NONE		
Complimentary rate:	1 per 40 rooms			1 per 35 rooms		
Meeting space:						
Break-out rooms	2 @ 325 ft² $80 per day 2 @ 425 ft² $90 per day 4 @ 650 ft² $125 per day			4 @ 400 ft² $100 per day None 2 @ 600 ft² $125 per day		
Dividable room	1 @ 900 ft² $150 per day			None		
Ballrooms	1 @ 14,000 ft² $2000 per day			1 @ 12,000 ft² $2500 per day		
(No meeting-space charges when a food function is held in the meeting room—both properties)						
Recreation:	Indoor pool, athletic club 1 block away, $15 per person per day			Complete athletic club with pool. Hotel guests free		
Menus:						
Breakfast	$4.00++* continental to $8.95++ for steak			$3.60++ continental to $11.25++ steak		
Lunch	$6.50++ salad to $14.50++ steak and lobster			$5.00++ salad to $14.25++ steak		
Dinners	$12.50++ chicken to $45.00++ chateaubriand			$11.95++ ham to $42.50++ steak and lobster		
Wine	Extra @ $12 per bottle for house wine			Extra @ $6.50 per bottle for house wine		
Ground transportation:						
Limo	$25 one way			Complimentary (hotel)		
Taxi	$30 one way			$30 one way		
Helicopter	$50 one way			None		
Bus	$15 one way			$15 one way		
Location:	Hotel A Downtown			Hotel B Downtown		

*++ means plus tax and gratuity, which would change a budget.

EP = European plan
MAP = Modified American plan (two meals)
FAP = full American plan (three meals)

Dallas

Group rates	Hotel A EP	Hotel A MAP	Hotel A FAP	Hotel B EP	Hotel B MAP	Hotel B FAP
Sleeping rooms						
Single	$ 80	$180	$155	$ 85	$ 96	$110
Double	90	110	165	100	111	125
Suites						
1 bedroom	110	130	181	120	128	145
2 bedroom	135	154	195	140	155	180
Parlor		NONE		105	115	130
Complimentary rate:	1 per 35 rooms occupied			1 per 40 rooms occupied		
Meeting space:						
Break-out rooms	3 @ 250 ft² $80 per day; 2 @ 350 ft² $95 per day; 3 @ 500 ft² $105 per day			4 @ 300 ft² (board rooms) $85 per day; 2 @ 400 ft² (board rooms) $95 per day; 1 @ 600 ft² (board room) $100 per day		
Dividable rooms	1 @ 1200 ft² divides into 3 $160 per day total for 3			4 @ 1000 ft² divide into 4 each of 250 sq. ft. $150 total for 4		
Ballrooms	None			1 @ 8000 ft² $775 per day		
(No meeting-space charge when a food function is held in the room—both properties)						
Recreation:	Outdoor pool. Golf 15 minutes away. $5 per person green fee			Indoor and outdoor pools. Will assist coordinating recreation at no charge.		
Menus:						
Breakfast	$4.05++ continental to $9.95++ steak			$3.75++ continental to $8.45++ steak		
Lunch	$4.95++ salad to $14.50++ steak			$4.25++ salad to $11.95++ steak		
Dinners	$12.50++ chicken to $24.95++ steak and crab			$12.50++ chicken to $41.25++ steak and lobster		
Wine	Extra @ $10 per bottle house wine			Extra @ $7.50 per bottle house wine		
Ground transportation:						
Limo	$8 one way			$20 one way		
Taxi	10 one way			30 one way		
Helicopter	NONE			40 one way		
Bus	Complimentary shuttle (14-passenger)			Complimentary shuttle (14-passenger)		
Location:	5 minutes from Dallas–Fort Worth airport			Near downtown Dallas and freeway		

Denver

Group rates	Hotel A EP	Hotel A MAP	Hotel A FAP	Hotel B EP	Hotel B MAP	Hotel B FAP
Sleeping rooms						
Single	$ 70	$ 90	$115	$ 85	$110	$115
Double	85	105	130	90	115	139
Suites						
1 bedroom	95	$115	$140	$100	$125	$150
2 bedroom	125	145	165	125	150	175
Parlor	85	145	165	90	115	139
Complimentary rate:	1 per 40 rooms occupied			Sliding scale and rates commissionable		
Meeting space:						
Break-out rooms	3 @ 375 ft² 1 raised theater front and rear projection. Seats 225. $300 per day			5 @ 480 ft² $180 per day 3 @ 600 ft² $200 per day		
Dividable rooms	2 @ 1000 ft² 500 ft² each after division $450 per day for 1000 ft²			4 @ 900 ft² divide into 3 $90 per day each after division		
Ballrooms	None. Tennis court 12,000 ft² $450 per day			1 @ 2000 ft² $3000 per day		
(No meeting space charges when a food function is held in the room—both properties)						
Recreation:	Indoor pool, athletic club indoors. Use fee: $1.00 per day registered hotel guests.			No recreational facilities. Have access to nearby athletic club (six blocks away)		
Menus:						
Breakfast	$4.25++ continental to $8.85++ steak			$4.25++ continental to $10.50++ steak		
Lunch	$5.50++ salad to $9.85++ vol-au-vent			$4.65++ salad to $11.45++ creamed lobster		
Dinners	$11.75++ chicken to $26.50++ steak and lobster			$11.50++ ham to $35.50++ steak and lobster		
Wine	Extra. @ $6 per bottle house wine			Extra. @ $7.50 per bottle house wine		
Ground transportation:						
Limo	None			$12 one way		
Taxi	$12 one way			10 one way		
Helicopter	None			None		
Bus	$12.50 one-way shuttle			City bus $3 one way		
Location:	Southeast near freeway			Downtown		

Notice: All rates and food charges have been negotiated.

Appendix D

Meeting Checklists

Planning Checklist

I. Preliminary Questions

A. Objectives:

1. What is the audience composition?
2. After the meeting, what do we want the audience to do?
3. What do we have to provide to enable them to do it? (Information, training, motivation, change in job concept, technical information, etc.)
4. What can the audience gain—what is in it for them?
5. Specific objectives for the meeting or event(s).

   a. ______________________________
   ____

   b. ______________________________
   ____

   c. ______________________________
   ____

   d. ______________________________
   ____

   e. ______________________________
   ____

6. The group facts:

   a. What are the categories of job or professional responsibilities? (Salespeople, managers, executives, professional people—doctors, teachers, lawyers)

   b. How familiar with the subject(s) are the members of the group?

c. Are there any expected negative attitudes? (If so, why?)
d. Is it a homogenous group?
e. How sophisticated are they about communication techniques?
f. What specific possibilities are there to promote their interest before the meeting?
g. What are organization policies concerning the meeting? (Location, time of year, dress, executive presence and speeches, etc.)

II. Meeting Planning

A. Administration

- ______ 1. Objectives decided
- ______ 2. Objectives written
- ______ 3. Budget developed
  - ______ a. Preliminary budget
  - ______ b. Budget researched
  - ______ c. Final budget developed
  - ______ d. Final budget approved
  - ______ e. Accounting/control system developed
- ______ 4. Personnel needs decided
  - ______ a. Planning personnel
  - ______ b. On-site personnel
  - ______ c. Postmeeting personnel
  - ______ d. Secretarial
- ______ 5. Contracted services decided
  - ______ a. Audiovisual
  - ______ b. Exhibits
  - ______ c. Decorating firm
  - ______ d. Travel
    - ______ (i) Destination travel
    - ______ (ii) Ground operators
  - ______ e. Destination management firm
  - ______ f. Shipping
  - ______ g. Insurance
  - ______ h. Catering
  - ______ i. Printing
  - ______ j. Promotion/marketing
  - ______ k. Signage
  - ______ l. Equipment rental
  - ______ m. Attorney
  - ______ n. Passport/visa
  - ______ o. Currency exchange
  - ______ p. Simultaneous translation
  - ______ q. Interpreters
    - ______ (i) Sign language
    - ______ (ii) Foreign language
- ______ 6. Negotiations
- ______ 7. Contracts
- ______ 8. Exhibits
- ______ 9. Floor plans
- ______ 10. Emergency procedures

_____ 11. Medical provision
_____ 12. Provision for handicapped

B. Food and beverage
- _____ 1. Food
  - _____ a. Nutrition breaks
  - _____ b. Breakfasts
  - _____ c. Lunches
  - _____ d. Dinners
  - _____ e. Banquets
  - _____ f. Box lunches for tours
  - _____ g. Space requirements
- _____ 2. Beverage
  - _____ a. Nutrition breaks
  - _____ b. Receptions
    - _____ (i) Beverages
    - _____ (ii) Hors d'oeuvre
  - _____ c. Hospitality functions
    - _____ (i) Beverages
    - _____ (ii) Hors d'oeuvre
- _____ 3. Special events
  - _____ a. Tours
  - _____ b. Companion functions
  - _____ c. Exercise events
  - _____ d. Tournaments
  - _____ e. Dances, etc.

C. Space requirements
- _____ 1. Sleeping
  - _____ a. Single occupancy
  - _____ b. Double occupancy
  - _____ c. Suites
    - _____ (i) 1 bedroom
    - _____ (ii) 2 bedroom
    - _____ (iii) Parlor
  - _____ d. VIP accommodations
- _____ 2. Program
  - _____ a. Rooms
  - _____ b. Setups
  - _____ c. Size
  - _____ d. Location
  - _____ e. Traffic flow
  - _____ f. Recreation
  - _____ g. Entertainment
- _____ 3. Registration
- _____ 4. Meeting headquarters
- _____ 5. Food functions
  - _____ a. Hospitality
  - _____ b. Nutrition breaks
  - _____ c. Breakfasts
  - _____ d. Lunches
  - _____ e. Dinners
  - _____ f. Banquets

- ______ g. Receptions
- ______ h. Dances
- ______ i. Entertainment

______ 6. Press room

- ______ a. Size
- ______ b. Setup
- ______ c. Telephones
- ______ d. Electrical (typewriters, computers)

D. Program

______ 1. Objectives

- ______ a. Objectives planned each session
- ______ b. Objectives written

______ 2. Agenda schedule

______ 3. Speakers

- ______ a. Number
- ______ b. Auditioned
- ______ c. Briefing/training
- ______ d. Hosting/procedure
- ______ e. Contact/contract
  - ______ (i) Initial contact
  - ______ (ii) Contracted
  - ______ (iii) Follow-up communication procedure established
- ______ f. Support requirements
  - ______ (i) Audiovisual
  - ______ (ii) Special room setups
  - ______ (iii) Handicapped communications
  - ______ (iv) Simultaneous translation
  - ______ (v) Printing/reproduction

______ 4. On-site management

- ______ a. Agenda control procedures
- ______ b. Session traffic control procedure
- ______ c. Signage
- ______ d. Session chairmen
- ______ e. Communication procedures
  - ______ (i) During sessions
  - ______ (ii) Between sessions
  - ______ (iii) Emergency messages

______ 5. Emergency alternatives for program

______ 6. Space requirements

E. Transportation

______ 1. Air travel

- ______ a. Round trip
- ______ b. Organization paid
- ______ c. Attendee paid
- ______ d. Costs
- ______ e. Ticketing
  - ______ (i) Itinerary change provision
  - ______ (ii) Refunds
  - ______ (iii) Cancellation
- ______ f. Special for VIPs

_____ 2. Bus/train/steamship
- _____ a. Round trip or ???
- _____ b. Organization paid
- _____ c. Attendee paid
- _____ d. Costs
- _____ e. Ticketing
  - _____ (i) Itinerary change provision
  - _____ (ii) Refunds
  - _____ (iii) Cancellation
- _____ f. Special for VIPs

_____ 3. Ground operations
- _____ a. Tours
  - _____ (i) Costs
  - _____ (ii) Guides
  - _____ (iii) Food/beverage provision
  - _____ (iv) Restrooms
  - _____ (v) Insurance
- _____ b. Hospitality transportation
  - _____ (i) Air/ground terminal to meeting facility and return
  - _____ (ii) Rental cars
  - _____ (iii) Drayage
  - _____ (iv) Special event transportation
    - _____ (a) Fishing
    - _____ (b) Golf
    - _____ (c) Exercise facility
    - _____ (d) Off-property dinners, etc.

_____ 4. Contract with travel agency

_____ 5. Transportation done in-house

III. Program Planning

A. Content material to be covered

_____ 1. New products
_____ 2. Old-product information
_____ 3. New concepts
_____ 4. New problems to be solved
_____ 5. Old problems to be solved
_____ 6. Advertising programs
_____ 7. Marketing objectives
_____ 8. New policies
_____ 9. Old policies
_____ 10. Orientation
_____ 11. Training program
_____ 12. Scholarly material
_____ 13. Professional material
_____ 14. Other subjects

B. Types of presentations to be used

_____ 1. General session (single large group)
_____ 2. Panels
_____ 3. Symposiums
_____ 4. Debates

_____ 5. Seminar sessions
_____ 6. Question and answer sessions
_____ 7. Large group discussions
_____ 8. Small group discussions
_____ 9. Workshops
_____ 10. Executive sessions
_____ 11. Teleconferencing
_____ 12. Multilocation
    _____ a. Computer
    _____ b. Closed-circuit TV

C. Methods of presentation
_____ 1. Speeches
_____ 2. Visual-supported (aided) speeches
_____ 3. Slides with professional video or sound recording
_____ 4. Live skits
_____ 5. Demonstrations
_____ 6. Role playing
_____ 7. Musical presentation or show
_____ 8. Dramatic presentation or show
_____ 9. Motion pictures
_____ 10. Panel presentation
_____ 11. Other
    _____
    _____

D. Program facilities required
_____ 1. General sessions with sound system
_____ 2. General sessions without sound system
_____ 3. Small group with audiovisual support
_____ 4. Small group without audiovisual support
_____ 5. Number of people in
    _____a. General sessions
    _____b. Small group sessions
_____ 6. Seating arrangements for general sessions
_____ 7. Seating arrangements for small group sessions
    __________ __________
    __________ __________
    __________ __________
    __________ __________

_____ 8. Number/size of rooms required—general sessions.
    _____ number
    _____, _____, _____, _____,
    _____, _____, _____ sizes
_____ 9. Number/size of rooms required—small group sessions
    _____ number
    _____, _____, _____, _____,
    _____, _____, _____ sizes
_____ 10. Length of general sessions (times in minutes)
    _____, _____, _____, _____
_____ 11. Length of small group session (times in minutes for each)
    _____, _____, _____, _____,
    _____, _____, _____, _____

_____ 12. Subgroup summary

Event Number	Number People	Time	Setup
_____	_____	_____	_____
_____	_____	_____	_____
_____	_____	_____	_____
_____	_____	_____	_____
_____	_____	_____	_____
_____	_____	_____	_____

E. Equipment to be used

_____ 1. Motion picture projectors _____ Number
_____ 2. Slide projectors _____ Number
_____ 3. Computer synchronizers _____ Number
_____ 4. Screens _____ sizes _____ Number
_____ 5. Special lighting
types _____, _____, _____, _____,
number _____, _____, _____, _____
_____ 6. Sound equipment
types _____ , _____ , _____ , _____ ,
number _____ , _____ , _____ , _____ ,
_____ 7. Closed-circuit television
_____ monitors _____ cameras _____ tape equipment
_____ 8. Staging for live events
_____ 9. Podiums
_____ 10. Microphones (number)

F. Program supplementary events

_____ 1. Field trips (list) _____________________
____
____
_____ 2. Companion programs (list) _____________________
____
____
_____ 3. Entertainment (list) _____________________
____
____
_____ 4. Sports activities (list) _____________________
____
____
_____ 5. Other related events (list) _____________________
____
____

IV. Reference Notes

All-Purpose Checklist*

There are so many different kinds of off-premises meetings and each is so distinctive, that for one master checklist to cover all contingencies in every type of meeting would be impossible. *Meetings & Conventions* feels, however, that this "All-Purpose Checklist" (the successor to our highly successful "Checklist to End Checklists") comes extremely close. It moves from such minuscule items as paper clips and erasers to booking aircraft and hotels, and covers virtually everything in between. Altogether, 24 separate areas are broken down into their constituent parts so that the planner can move logically from item to item, making sure that his meeting planning covers all the essentials.

Though the All-Purpose Checklist has been designed to be used for the more frequently held types of meetings, we have developed and included several separate checklists to cover some of the more unusual kinds of meetings that have become increasingly popular. Thus we have separate additional checklists for Incentive Travel meetings, Weekend meetings and Value Season meetings.

Use the checklist as a continual reminder and check off items as work is completed on them. If several people with differing responsibilities are involved, make copies of the checklist for them so they can check off the items for which they are responsible.

To further enhance the use of this All-Purpose Checklist, we have left two empty spaces at the end of each section, so that you can include items your meeting may require that would not be true of any other meeting. In other words, you can tailor this checklist to your own meeting activity.

Warning. A checklist is only valuable if you use it. Keep it immediately available. Check it or write on it frequently. Let it accompany you right up to, during and even after a meeting. It can be your best meeting assistant.

1 FUNDAMENTALS

Name of company/association

Address with zip code

Telephone numbers with area code

Full name and title of organizer (yourself)

Name of overall description of event

e.g., Medical Association convention; 20th Anniversary of corporation; National sales meeting; Annual dinner; etc.

Objective

e.g., To raise more funds; to draw attention to some particular industry; to introduce a new product; to increase sales; for fun; education; etc.

NOTE: An educational theme allows attendees to charge the outlay to "expenses" providing a strong additional incentive to attend.

Overall event separated into segments

e.g., 22 workshops; 1 film show; a discussion group; 3 cocktail parties; 1 music recital; etc.

NOTE: Each segment must be completely organized by itself then combined into the overall event—jigsaw fashion.

Meetings & Convention Magazine.

need to check | checked

Coordination and time schedules

NOTE: A realistic time schedule must be developed for behind-the-scenes workers in respect to each individual segment of your overall event, noting assembly; start; finish; etc.

From this, programs can be developed.

Additionally, an overall time schedule for all pre-event activities; in-progress activities; and post-event activities must be developed, allowing for periodic checks on everything taking place everywhere.

As arrangements become firmed-up, notations should also be made giving dates i.e. confirmed; letter-agreement; contract; etc.

2 TIMING

- ☐ ☐ Day(s) with second and third choice on different days of week
- ☐ ☐ Date(s) with second and third choice
- ☐ ☐ Commencement date AM/PM Departure date AM/PM
- ☐ ☐ Timing free of conflict
  e.g., long weekend; religious holiday; important event elsewhere; tax paying time; heavy vacation time; college jamboree in area; singles weekend; etc.
- ☐ ☐ Timing convenient
  e.g., will not cause attendees to hang around unnecessarily; fits well with tranportation schedules; ties in with last connections on public transportation; etc.
- ☐ ☐ Registration cutoff date
- ☐ ☐ *________________________
- ☐ ☐ ________________________

3 SITE REQUIREMENTS

If no specific location has been determined:

- ☐ ☐ Type place required
  e.g., hotel; club; aboard ship; arena; convention hall; etc.
- ☐ ☐ Type of area
  e.g., country; city; resort; airport; abroad
- ☐ ☐ Climate
- ☐ ☐ Price range
  economical; moderate; expensive; super-luxury
- ☐ ☐ Image needed to emphasize theme
  e.g., deluxe; in need of funds; hyper-modern; old world; international; etc.
- ☐ ☐ Place accessible to most attendees in relation to type of transportation they would be using
  e.g., airport nearby; easy access by road
- ☐ ☐ Good transportation services available
  e.g., frequent, express, non-stop flights etc.
- ☐ ☐ Centrally or conveniently located
- ☐ ☐ Adequate public transportation

*These blank spaces allow you to add additional checkpoints that may apply only to your meeting.

need to check	checked	
☐	☐	Taxis readily available
☐	☐	Charter and sightseeing services available
☐	☐	Rental car services nearby
☐	☐	Dining on premises or nearby
☐	☐	Shops on premises or nearby
☐	☐	Entertainment on premises or nearby
☐	☐	Beauty salon on premises or nearby
☐	☐	Outdoors/Indoors/Outdoors with indoors alternate
☐	☐	Attitude of employees
☐	☐	Efficiency of employees
☐	☐	No interior refurbishing under way nearby
☐	☐	No outside construction nearby—making dust and noise

When specific location determined:

need to check	checked	
☐	☐	Exact name of location
☐	☐	Exact address—with zip code; also cross-streets, identifying landmarks if difficult to find; etc.
☐	☐	Telephone number with area code
☐	☐	Individual rates and block rates
☐	☐	Prices within budget
☐	☐	Well located
☐	☐	Clean and attractive
☐	☐	Sufficient meeting rooms
☐	☐	Adequate sleeping rooms
☐	☐	Adequate dining and function space
☐	☐	All rooms air-conditioned
☐	☐	Sufficient exhibit space
☐	☐	Adequate recreational facilities
☐	☐	Sufficient manpower to service meeting
☐	☐	Sufficient audio-visual equipment
☐	☐	*______________
☐	☐	______________

4 MEETING LOCATION CONTACTS

First and last names with correct spelling; title; floor and office number; telephone number with switchboard extension or direct dial telephone number; intercom number; secretary's or assistant's name, if applicable

need to check	checked	
☐	☐	Hotel manager
☐	☐	Convention manager
☐	☐	Convention salesman
☐	☐	Banquet manager
☐	☐	Service manager
☐	☐	Maitre d'hotel
☐	☐	Bell captain
☐	☐	*______________
☐	☐	______________

5 ATTENDANCE AND ADMISSION

need to check	checked	
☐	☐	Total number expected
☐	☐	Composition and number expected in each category e.g., general public; trade only; members; invited guests; honor guests; press; staff; spouses; children; etc.
☐	☐	Tickets
☐	☐	pre-paid; payable at door
☐	☐	numbered

*These blank spaces allow you to add additional checkpoints that may apply only to your meeting.

need to check | checked

☐ ☐ type of ticket
e.g., engraved, color coded; single roll; double roll
☐ ☐ or other identification
e.g., pocket inserts; pin-on badges; adhesive badges; etc.
☐ ☐ Price for each classification
☐ ☐ Tax exemption obtained/taxable
☐ ☐ Where taxable
☐ ☐ Taxes marked on each ticket
☐ ☐ Instructions given to tear tickets in half
☐ ☐ Deposit box for ticket stubs
☐ ☐ Door prize arrangements
☐ ☐ Tally form
☐ ☐ Re-admission procedure
e.g., hand stamp; pass; scanning light; half-ticket; etc.
☐ ☐ Policy on single ticket sales
☐ ☐ Policy on accepting checks
☐ ☐ *______________________________
☐ ☐ ______________________________

6 REGISTRATION

☐ ☐ Description of work place
e.g., in booth; at table; counter; etc.

NOTE: Bottlenecks must be avoided; make sure of plenty of space for ingress and egress of registrants

☐ ☐ Adequate lighting
☐ ☐ Equipment
e.g., number and location of typewriters; accounting machines; teletypes; photo copiers; telephones; intercoms; cash registers; etc.

need to check | checked

☐ ☐ Hand-out materials
e.g., on table; hostesses to hand out; etc.
☐ ☐ Furnishings
e.g., typists' chairs; desks; shelves; etc.
☐ ☐ Signs
e.g., directional; bulletin boards; etc.
☐ ☐ Cash drawers
☐ ☐ number and size
☐ ☐ Actual attendance figures
e.g., daily; cumulative
☐ ☐ Bank to open with
☐ ☐ Periodic automatic supply of small change
☐ ☐ Periodic automatic removal of large bills
☐ ☐ Forms for accounting purposes
☐ ☐ Pre-printed material
e.g., registration forms; fill-in material; literature
☐ ☐ Printing-on-spot material
☐ ☐ Records and controls
e.g., card files; attendee lists; attendee categories with appropriate fees; policy on refunds; etc.

NOTE: Make certain all personnel know where to obtain existing supplies and order additional supplies in case of shortage.

☐ ☐ Person to approve expenses and ordering
☐ ☐ Policy for registration of attendees after desk is closed
☐ ☐ Correct information on badges; fill-in material; etc.
☐ ☐ Working forms

*These blank spaces allow you to add additional checkpoints that may apply only to your meeting.

need to check	checked	
□	□	Arrangements for prompt receipt of mail
□	□	Arrangements for prompt delivery of messages
□	□	Switchboard operators briefed in writing
□	□	*________________________
□	□	________________________

7 STATIONERY AND OTHER ITEMS

need to check	checked	
□	□	Ashtrays
□	□	Wastebaskets
□	□	Paper clips
□	□	Staplers with staples
□	□	Regular adhesive tape
□	□	Heavy duty adhesive tape
□	□	Rubber bands
□	□	Stick pins
□	□	Scissors
□	□	Tape measures
□	□	Rulers
□	□	Tool kits (pliers; hammers; wire; etc.)
□	□	Extra bulbs, etc. for equipment
□	□	Glue
□	□	Sponge for wetting labels and envelopes
□	□	Rubber stamps and stamp pads
□	□	Typewriter ribbons
□	□	Stapler removers
□	□	Storage cartons
□	□	Pins, needles and cotton
□	□	Letter openers
□	□	Typewriter correction paper and liquid
□	□	Indexes
□	□	Pencils
□	□	regular/colored
□	□	Pencil sharpeners
□	□	Ball point pens
□	□	blue-black/colored
□	□	Letterheads and printed envelopes
□	□	Plain bond
□	□	Onion skin
□	□	Carbon sets
□	□	Labels
□	□	Lined pads
□	□	Scratch pads
□	□	Telephone message pads
□	□	Petty cash slips
□	□	Routing slips
□	□	Folders
□	□	Files
□	□	In-Out boxes
□	□	Dictionary
□	□	Matches
□	□	Date stamp
□	□	Numbering machine
□	□	*________________________
□	□	________________________

8 PERSONNEL

need to check	checked	
□	□	Number in each category of personnel who will have specific stations e.g., stenographers; registration clerks; doormen; etc.
□	□	Number in each category of ambulatory personnel e.g., hostesses; ushers; guides; pages; escorts for VIPs; etc.

NOTE: All personnel, but most specifically ambulatory personnel, MUST be specifically assigned to

*These blank spaces allow you to add additional checkpoints that may apply only to your meeting.

need to check	checked	
		specific areas between specific times to insure they will be where you wish them at the right time.
☐	☐	Wages, salary scales and hourly rates
☐	☐	Policy on mixing with guests
☐	☐	Policy on forms of address
☐	☐	Order of hierarchy in regard to executives, managers and supervisory staff
☐	☐	Number of coordinators
☐	☐	Presence to make decisions
☐	☐	Temporary staff
☐	☐	Employment agencies (names, addresses, telephone numbers)
☐	☐	Number of hours in full day and number of days per week
☐	☐	Shift periods; specific coffee break times; etc.
☐	☐	Overtime arrangemens
☐	☐	Staff training
☐	☐	Staff briefing
☐	☐	Timekeeping e.g., time clocks; cards; sign in and out
☐	☐	Hiring dates
☐	☐	through help wanted ads/agency/department of labor/ temporary agency/etc.
☐	☐	Policy on paying agency fees e.g., by organization/by employee
☐	☐	Expense accounts e.g., person entitled to use and allowable expenses
☐	☐	Staff parking facilities
☐	☐	*______________________
☐	☐	______________________

need to check	checked	
9		**COMMITTEES AND VOLUNTEERS**
☐	☐	Coordination with committees and volunteers e.g., executive; entertainment; finance; program; hospitality; ladies'; public relations; development; etc.
☐	☐	Specific committees and what each has undertaken to do
☐	☐	Specific volunteers and spots they have undertaken to fill
☐	☐	Periodic checks to determine progress and continued interest of said committees and volunteers
NOTE:		Committees and volunteers can be extremely valuable. They should not, however, be heavily relied upon unless they have proven themselves already. It is frequently wise to have standby plans to cover activities of both committees and volunteers
☐	☐	*______________________
☐	☐	______________________
10		**SLEEPING ROOMS**
☐	☐	Approximate rooms needed: Sing. __ Doub. __ Suites __
☐	☐	Room Rates
☐	☐	Reservation confirmation
☐	☐	Arrival date of most attendees
☐	☐	Departure date of most attendees
☐	☐	Arrivals earlier
☐	☐	Arrivals later
☐	☐	Departures ealier

*These blank spaces allow you to add additional checkpoints that may apply only to your meeting.

need to check | checked

☐ ☐ Departures later
☐ ☐ Arrangements for "no-shows"
☐ ☐ Package plans
e.g., American—includes three meals; Modified American—includes breakfast and dinner; European—room only
☐ ☐ Extra cot in room
☐ ☐ Reservation forms for attendees
☐ ☐ Reservation confirmation by hotel management
☐ ☐ Cut-off date
☐ ☐ Location and room numbers of rooms assigned
☐ ☐ to be ready by what time on what day
☐ ☐ to be cleared by what time on what day
☐ ☐ Enough staff to distribute luggage promptly
☐ ☐ Special labels to distinguish luggage
☐ ☐ *________________________
☐ ☐ ________________________

11 MEETING ROOMS

☐ ☐ Number of rooms needed
☐ ☐ Intended use for each room

NOTE: The same information must be compiled in respect to each room to be occupied.

☐ ☐ Approximate size necessary (Length, width, height)
☐ ☐ Shape
e.g., square; oblong; L-shaped; with balcony attached; etc.
☐ ☐ Approximate number of persons occupying room

need to check | checked

NOTE: Do not accept a room overly large for your group; it is better to have a room too small than too big but pay attention to capacity notice on wall of each room which is required by law in many states.

☐ ☐ Activity of persons in room
e.g., standing; sitting; dining; dancing; yoga exercises; etc.
☐ ☐ Door preference
e.g., swing; double; able to be closed securely; able to be locked; see through glass; etc.
☐ ☐ General decor
e.g., Old World with chandeliers; mod with psychedelic paintings; oak paneled; etc. (to emphasize theme)
☐ ☐ Floor covering preferred
e.g., carpeting; polished; etc.
☐ ☐ Air conditioning/heating
☐ ☐ individually controlled; centrally controlled; open windows; etc.
☐ ☐ Arrangement
e.g., U-shape; T-shape; E-shape; V-shape; theater; boardroom; horseshoe; schoolroom; occasional groupings; auditorium; etc.
☐ ☐ Space and equipment required for coffee-break service, if so, inside room/outside room
☐ ☐ Space and equipment required for registration, if so, inside room/outside room.

*These blank spaces allow you to add additional checkpoints that may apply only to your meeting.

need to check	checked	
☐	☐	Room separated from adjoining rooms e.g., solid wall, sliding panels, accordion panels. Noise disturbance?
☐	☐	When will room be available? What is the event immediately preceding ours in the room? At what time? Scheduled completion: Can our equipment be set up the night before a morning meeting? Will there be a staff available to help us? Can we set up equipment in the morning for an afternoon start of meeting?
NOTE:		Avoid a tight schedule. If another group has the room from 9:00 am to 12 noon, and you're due to start at 1:00 pm, there is little likelihood the room will be ready for you.
☐	☐	Is one room to serve both for meeting and luncheon or dinner?
NOTE:		If "Yes," avoid it! Particularly if you're expected to recess at a stated time to permit conversion. However, if room is big enough to permit both a meeting and meal set-up, make sure table setting is done in advance of meeting and that there will be no table setting during program.
☐	☐	Has the seating of attendees other than VIPs been planned? Are attendees to be in one location, or mixed in with VIPs? How are we designating seating plan? In the room—At the registration center—In advance notices
☐	☐	Diagram showing how room is to be set up?
☐	☐	*________________________
☐	☐	________________________

Points to Check Just Before Each Meeting

need to check	checked	
☐	☐	Check room operation
☐	☐	Seating plan as specified
☐	☐	Location of additional seats
☐	☐	Room temperature:
NOTE:		Start with room cool—it will warm up according to number of persons occupying it.
☐	☐	Teleprompter
☐	☐	Lectern and light and gavel
☐	☐	Water pitcher and glasses
☐	☐	Table ash trays, stands, matches, pencils, notepads at conferees' table
☐	☐	Decorations e.g., theme and color scheme
NOTE:		Be sure it conforms with fire regulations.
☐	☐	Floral arrangements and plants
☐	☐	Banners; balloons; etc.
☐	☐	Flags e.g., national, foreign; club; etc.
NOTE:		Be sure flags are correctly placed. The national flag should always be on the right; namely, on the right of the audience if in the audience section; on the right of the stage if on the stage; on the right of a speaker. The canton must

*These blank spaces allow you to add additional checkpoints that may apply only to your meeting.

need to check	checked	
		always be uppermost on the same side as the pole.
☐	☐	Directional signs
☐	☐	Verbatim reporter/tape recorder to record notes
☐	☐	Copies of notes to be delivered to specified persons (list) by what time (state)
☐	☐	Garage facilities and prices
☐	☐	Kitchen and freight elevators not near enough to cause too much clatter
☐	☐	Lighting e.g., overhead; obscured; variable beam; spotlights; strobe lights; special effects; lights with dimmer switches; table lamps; candles; etc.
☐	☐	Position of switches
☐	☐	Tape recorder
☐	☐	Closed circuit T.V.
☐	☐	Radio and TV broadcasting; CCTV—live; taped; etc.
☐	☐	Engineering charges for hookup
☐	☐	Wheelchair accommodations on aisle
☐	☐	Hearing aid equipment at specific locations
☐	☐	Extra long cords and plug-ins for portable telephones
☐	☐	Roving photographers with photographs for sale—or for publicity
☐	☐	Roving cigarette girls
☐	☐	Hat check services

Points to Check after Each Meeting

need to check	checked	
☐	☐	Removal of organization property
☐	☐	Check for forgotten property
☐	☐	Take down signs, banners, etc.
☐	☐	Recovery of films, slides, etc.
☐	☐	*______________________
☐	☐	______________________

12 PRE-MEETING AUDIO-VISUAL CHECKS

need to check	checked	
☐	☐	Acoustics: Clap your hands sharply . . . talk loudly . . . listen carefully.
☐	☐	1. No echo or dead spots present?
☐	☐	2. No drapes or acoustic panels needed?
☐	☐	Audio: Plug in everything, then test it.
☐	☐	1. Public address system working?
☐	☐	2. Feedback at working level?
☐	☐	3. Electrical interference or hum?
NOTE:		Hum often caused by two instruments being placed too closely together.
☐	☐	4. Speaker placement OK?
☐	☐	5. Enough PA mikes?
☐	☐	6. Mike cords long enough?
☐	☐	7. Mike stand heights OK?
☐	☐	8. Tape recorder working?
☐	☐	9. Recording mike tested?
☐	☐	Booth or Projection Station—Do you have to erect a stand or move a table? Also:
☐	☐	1. High enough to clear heads and hats?
☐	☐	2. Wide enough for all equipment?
☐	☐	3. Right distance from screen?

*These blank spaces allow you to add additional checkpoints that may apply only to your meeting.

need to check	checked	
☐	☐	4. Rigid and level?
☐	☐	5. Enough AC electrical power?
☐	☐	6. Circuit breakers or fuses located?
☐	☐	7. Spare fuses or standby circuits ready?
☐	☐	8. Enough extension cords or adapters: AC power? Audio? Remote control?
☐	☐	9. Intercom system tested?
☐	☐	10. Signal light or buzzer needed?
☐	☐	11. Emergency work light ready?
☐	☐	Lectern—Put yourself in the place of the dignitaries
☐	☐	1. Height comfortable?
☐	☐	2. Script light tested?
☐	☐	3. Glare eliminated from stage lights or spots?
☐	☐	4. Mike placement OK?
☐	☐	5. Pointer handy?
☐	☐	Room lights—Don't take anything for granted. This is one of the biggest causes of traffic commotion before showings.
☐	☐	1. All light switches located, checked, labelled?
☐	☐	2. Are power outlets hot when lights are out?
☐	☐	3. Is the room dark enough for projection?
☐	☐	Door—Expect people to come and go during the presentation. Is light from doors prevented from hitting screen?
☐	☐	Estimate how many people will be in the room and how long you expect the meeting to last.
☐	☐	1. Will air change sufficiently with doors and windows closed?
☐	☐	2. Will the temperature remain comfortable?
☐	☐	3. All heating, air conditioning and fan controls tested?
☐	☐	Screen—Know exactly what kinds of materials will be projected, then find out whether the existing screen is suitable
☐	☐	1. Large enough?
☐	☐	2. Horizontal or square format?
☐	☐	3. Keystoning eliminated?
☐	☐	4. Surfacing appropriate for viewing conditions?
☐	☐	5. Electrical controls tested?
☐	☐	6. Stage curtain controls tested?
☐	☐	Seating—Put a typical slide on the screen, then go out and sit where the audience will sit.
☐	☐	1. Front row no closer than two screen widths?
☐	☐	2. Last row no further than six screen widths
☐	☐	3. No row of seats wider than its distance from the screen (except "wide screen")
☐	☐	4. Is the picture bright enough for people in the side seats? Is it distorted?
☐	☐	5. Will everyone be able to see when seats are filled?
☐	☐	6. Right lenses to fill the screen?
☐	☐	7. Vital spares on hand: Lamps? Belts? Fuses? Repair kits?
☐	☐	8. Standby equipment ready?

need to check	checked	
☐	☐	Equipment. A breakdown can spoil the show. Be prepared.
☐	☐	1. Movie Projector: a. 16-mm? b. Regular 8mm? c. Super 8mm? d. Tested and working? e. Spare lamps? f. Extension speaker?
☐	☐	2. Slide projector: Remote control? Remote extension? Focus from remote? Tested and working? Spare lamp?
☐	☐	3. Filmstrip projector. Provision for sound? Tested and working? Remote control? Spare lamp?
☐	☐	4. Tape recorder: Tested and working? Built-in speaker? Extension speaker?
☐	☐	5. Easels, blackboards, chalks, erasers, plexiglas boards, colored grease sticks, chemical erasers
☐	☐	6. AC or DC current?
☐	☐	7. Sufficient extension cords of our own to supplement those provided?
☐	☐	A-V Materials—Inspect everything that's to be used—day before, if possible. Right subject and title? Sequence in program checked? Inspected for cleanliness and condition?
☐	☐	1. Films: Heads out, wound properly? No breaks, tears or weak splices? Sound? Optical, magnetic or silent? Run down to titles? Prefocused and framed?
☐	☐	2. Slides: Sound level determined? Mounts compatible and straight? No dirt or fingerprints? Orientation checked (each slide)? Magazines tested for jamming? Prefocused and framed?
☐	☐	3. Tapes: Heads out, wound properly? Speed checked? Tracks compatible? Cued up? Playback level determined?
☐	☐	People—The greatest variable. Brief and check everyone.
☐	☐	1. Schedule checked with program chairman?
☐	☐	2. Cued scripts; audio man?
☐	☐	3. Presenters checked out on mikes, controls, etc.?
☐	☐	4. Everybody posted, checked out and cued: All equipment operators? Light switch operators? Drape and curtain operators? Door guards.
☐	☐	5. Arrangements made for prompt return of all materials and equipment.
☐	☐	*____________________
☐	☐	____________________
13		**FOOD AND BEVERAGE FUNCTIONS**
☐	☐	Type of function e.g., luncheon; dinner; coffee break; brunch; buffet; etc.
☐	☐	Timing e.g., continuous/specific timing during morning; midday period; afternoon; dinner period; evening; night owl period; etc.
☐	☐	Cuisine e.g., French; Italian;

*These blank spaces allow you to add additional checkpoints that may apply only to your meeting.

need to check	checked	
		Armenian; vegetarian; kosher; etc.
☐	☐	Menu selection e.g., chosen in advance; at time of event (only feasible at small events); choice of one main dish; choice of three main dishes; etc.
☐	☐	Specific menu e.g., soup, fish, entree, etc.
NOTE:		Be sure menu and day do not clash with religious observances or other food taboos, for instance venison served at anti-blood sports function; pork at seminar for rabbis; etc.
☐	☐	Number of persons to be served
☐	☐	Check of number served e.g., collection of tickets by waiter; etc.
☐	☐	Guaranteed minimum
☐	☐	Deadline for adding more names or canceling out
☐	☐	Handling of gratuities
☐	☐	Price to organization per plate
☐	☐	Add taxes
		Wine
☐	☐	Type e.g., red; white; both; French; Italian; Spanish; American; specific name and year; etc.
☐	☐	Number of bottles
☐	☐	Menu and program e.g., especially printed/regular, etc.
☐	☐	Kitchen not too far away—so food does not get cold
☐	☐	*______________________
☐	☐	______________________

need to check	checked	
14		**TABLES**
☐	☐	Head Table
☐	☐	Position
☐	☐	Number to be seated
☐	☐	Shape e.g., square; oblong; circular; apex of horseshoe; top of T
☐	☐	Level e.g., floor level; raised one tier; raised multiple tiers
☐	☐	Steps leading up with risers that are not too steep
☐	☐	Floor covering e.g., parquet; carpet
☐	☐	Underneath table obscured
☐	☐	Seating positions e.g., Who sits next to whom; any feuds between people; central positions; male-female distribution
☐	☐	Microphones in position
		Tables generally
☐	☐	Shape e.g., square; oblong; round; etc.
☐	☐	Usage e.g., meal; coffee; card; conversational groupings; etc.
☐	☐	Number of tables
☐	☐	Number to be seated at each table
☐	☐	Number to be seated in toto
☐	☐	Reserved seating/sit anywhere
☐	☐	If reserved alphabetical seating lists and ushers

*These blank spaces allow you to add additional checkpoints that may apply only to your meeting.

need to check	checked	
☐	☐	Chair types
☐	☐	Table cloths e.g., white; stock colored; special colored; etc.
☐	☐	Sufficient space between tables
☐	☐	Sufficient space between chairs at tables
☐	☐	Placecards
☐	☐	Floral arrangements e.g., on head table; at each other table; in vases around room
☐	☐	Special table decorations other than flowers
☐	☐	Table tents with appropriate legend for special tables e.g., Advisory Committee; Press; etc.
☐	☐	Check location of kitchen, entrance and exit doors, obstructions, etc. in relation to head table and other tables
☐	☐	Diagram of exactly how room to be set up
☐	☐	Firm timetable for reception; receiving line; toasts; serving; clearing away; etc.
☐	☐	*________________________
☐	☐	________________________

15 BAR ARRANGEMENTS

need to check	checked	
☐	☐	Location of all bars—organization and public
☐	☐	Bar service e.g., bar with bartenders serving behind it; hatch service; waiter service; cocktail waitress service; etc.
☐	☐	Who pays e.g., attendees purchase own drinks; organization pays for all drinks; organization pays for limited number of drinks; etc.
☐	☐	How paid for e.g., included in ticket; chit system; cash system; etc.
☐	☐	Guaranteed minimum at bar
☐	☐	required/not required
☐	☐	Full bar/limited
☐	☐	Gratuities included in price of drinks/tip as desired
☐	☐	By the bottle arrangements
NOTE:		Usually have to pay for every bottle opened. Therefore opened bottles not emptied should be requested for own use in hospitality suites, etc.
☐	☐	Corkage charges
NOTE:		These charges apply where attendees win bottles of, say, champagne, and want to open and drink them at the event.
☐	☐	Appetizers e.g., elaborate hors d'oeuvre/simple potato chips, peanuts; etc.
☐	☐	Buffet
☐	☐	Hot/cold and hot; etc.
☐	☐	*________________________
☐	☐	________________________

16 CELEBRITIES, GUEST SPEAKERS AND OTHER VIPS

need to check	checked	
☐	☐	Guest list of celebrities, speakers and other VIPs
☐	☐	Invitations
☐	☐	sent; accepted; etc.
☐	☐	Suites provided
☐	☐	Bars, snacks and complimentary buffets

*These blank spaces allow you to add additional checkpoints that may apply only to your meeting.

need to check	checked	
☐	☐	Limousines/helicopters/private planes provided to meet long-distance transportation; etc.
☐	☐	Welcome arrangements
☐	☐	Special hospitality arrangements
☐	☐	Honorarium
☐	☐	required/prepared; etc.
☐	☐	Reference material about organization supplied to speaker for incorporation in his address
☐	☐	Speeches cleared/spontaneous
☐	☐	Biography and photographs
☐	☐	Special theater tickets, opera tickets, etc.
☐	☐	Arrangements for entourage e.g., how many persons; what relationship to VIP; same or different social status; correct sleeping arrangements; etc.
☐	☐	Special personal preferences of VIP e.g., likes to show off; likes to be quiet; etc.
☐	☐	Thank you letters (afterwards)
☐	☐	Receiving line
☐	☐	"Now speaking" sign on door
☐	☐	Where program is to be run over and over again, or repeated elsewhere:
☐	☐	Time indicator
☐	☐	Hand signals
☐	☐	Appraisal chart
☐	☐	Presentations e.g., bouquet of flowers; citations; plaques; etc.

need to check	checked	
☐	☐	Arrangements for "Questions from the floor"
☐	☐	*____________________
☐	☐	____________________

17 ENTERTAINMENT

need to check	checked	
☐	☐	Type of entertainment e.g., speaker; comic; full show; lecture; movies/slides; awarding of prizes; fashion show; entertainer; soloist; band; etc.
☐	☐	Time schedule with approximate on and off for each act
☐	☐	Program for audience
☐	☐	Signal system if someone is needed to keep track for repeat performances
☐	☐	Use of room for rehearsals and time necessary
☐	☐	Dressing rooms
☐	☐	Equipment for dressing rooms such as hangers, mirrors, costume and wigstands, etc.
☐	☐	Music e.g., for listening; dancing; as accompaniment for entertainer; etc.
☐	☐	Rhythm style(s) e.g., conservative; strict tempo; mod with electrical instruments; Latin; etc.
☐	☐	Band/group/roving accordionists or violinists etc.
☐	☐	Continuous dance music = 2 bands
☐	☐	Dance music with intermissions = 1 band

NOTE: Don't waste the time that the

*These blank spaces allow you to add additional checkpoints that may apply only to your meeting.

need to check	checked	
		band would normally be playing by using it to make speeches, presentations, etc. Let these coincide with band intermissions.
☐	☐	Approximate number of pieces (if union is involved, union specifies number of pieces according to size of room)
☐	☐	Union or non-union?
☐	☐	Rates
☐	☐	License to dance required?
☐	☐	Recorded music—License from ASCAP and/or BMI for public performance of same
☐	☐	Own equipment/rent/already installed
☐	☐	MUZAK as background music, if already installed
☐	☐	*Religious, patriotic and other observances*
☐	☐	Number of interruptions, reasons and timing
☐	☐	Be sure they do not clash with anything
☐	☐	National Anthem
☐	☐	With recording or live musicians
☐	☐	Prayer(s)
☐	☐	Religion(s) Catholic; Jewish; Protestant; other
☐	☐	Toasts
☐	☐	How many
☐	☐	Will refilling of glasses be necessary? If so, prearrange handling of same
☐	☐	Stage/platform/ramp
☐	☐	Stage front curtain e.g., can we operate ourselves/must have union stage hands
☐	☐	Stage backdrop (curtain) fully to floor and non-transparent
☐	☐	Wings or back walkway sufficiently large to wait in, pass along; also wide enough for props to be stored
☐	☐	Positioning of props e.g., chalk marks
☐	☐	Placement of props e.g., prior to program; during; interchanges; upon command
☐	☐	Arrangement for storage of props
☐	☐	Permanent dance floor/roll away dance floor
☐	☐	*Public Address System*
☐	☐	Number of microphones needed and positions
☐	☐	Type e.g., built in; hand; yoke; lapel; stand
☐	☐	Cord—long enough; obscured so no one falls over it
☐	☐	Paging system e.g., in all rooms; specified areas; etc.
☐	☐	Drawings for prizes.
☐	☐	*____________________
☐	☐	____________________

18 EXHIBITS AND FREIGHT ARRANGEMENTS

need to check	checked	
☐	☐	Plan of entire area with entrances; obstructions; etc.
☐	☐	Number of exhibits
☐	☐	regular; special; etc.
☐	☐	Plan for each exhibit with dimensions involved (width, length, height) and usage

*These blank spaces allow you to add additional checkpoints that may apply only to your meeting.

need to check	checked	
		e.g., encyclopedia sales; automobile display; lion in cage; etc.
☐	☐	Type of space e.g., floor space; ceiling space from which something suspended; booth; revolving platform; swimming pool; animal cage; fashion ramp; etc.
☐	☐	Floor e.g., absolutely flat, variations in height; on an incline; arcs or curves, etc.
☐	☐	Floor sufficient to withstand weight of each exhibit and of total event
☐	☐	Ceiling e.g., maximum height; variations; on an incline; arcs or curves, etc.
☐	☐	Ceiling sturdy enough to withstand anything suspended from it
☐	☐	Floor to ceiling measurements sufficient to provide for tallest exhibits
☐	☐	Access to exhibits e.g., allow sufficient room for people circulating around each exhibit
☐	☐	Noise considerations e.g., no inappropriate sound overlapping—for instance discotheque music next to booth selling cemetery vaults; etc.
☐	☐	Competitors e.g., policy re same; do not put close together unless desired; etc.
☐	☐	Livestock and plants

need to check	checked	
		e.g., care and watering; attendants; etc.
☐	☐	Labor e.g., all union controlled; non-union helpers allowed; etc.
☐	☐	Utilities e.g., electrical power; steam; gas; water; draininge; compressed air; etc.
☐	☐	Overall decor, color scheme and theme dominating entire event
☐	☐	Decor for each exhibit e.g., standard; special with details such as partitions; backdrops; sidewalls; carpets; etc.
☐	☐	Assigned number and location for each exhibitor e.g., for labeling of booths and exhibits; for directory listings; directional signals; etc.
☐	☐	Set up dates
☐	☐	Open for inspection
☐	☐	Dismantling dates
☐	☐	Name of display company
☐	☐	Rental charges to organization
☐	☐	Rental charges to individual exhibitors
☐	☐	Hours e.g., opening; closing; all out by
☐	☐	Cleanup arrangements
☐	☐	Exhibition hours throughout; overnight
☐	☐	Special handling items e.g., fragile; alive; etc
☐	☐	Distinctive delivery tags and person to whom all freight and props should be addressed.
☐	☐	Times

need to check | checked

☐ ☐ Earliest time can begin to arrive/latest time same must be off premises with full instructions to whom to address
☐ ☐ All rented equipment to be returned promptly
☐ ☐ Check for anything overlooked before departure
☐ ☐ Storage facilities
e.g., for shipments in advance; for extras and spares; etc.
☐ ☐ Elevators and ramps for freight
e.g., number; location; sufficient to withstand weight of exhibits; etc.
☐ ☐ Elevators–escalators–stairs–ramps—for people.
e.g., number; location; sufficient to provide for ingress and egress of expected number of attendees; attendant operated; self-operated; etc.
☐ ☐ Proper packing of material
e.g., in packages; boxes; crates; etc.
☐ ☐ Double wrapping; labeling inside; padding; corners and edges reinforced; etc.
☐ ☐ Methods of transportation of advance shipments
e.g., mail; rail; air; truck; etc.
☐ ☐ Forward equipment record
e.g., contents of each piece, assigned number and particulars of documents relating to it.
☐ ☐ Personal contacts at offices of all handlers

need to check | checked

☐ ☐ Receipts for delivery
☐ ☐ Personnel and time set aside for packing and checking and unpacking and checking.
☐ ☐ Articles accompanying individuals
☐ ☐ All personal envelopes, brief cases etc., labeled
☐ ☐ *____________________
☐ ☐ ____________________

19 FOREIGN MEETINGS

☐ ☐ Tax law effect
☐ ☐ Passport, visa information
☐ ☐ Interpreters
☐ ☐ Mailing regulations and rates—airmail; first class; printed matter; etc.
☐ ☐ Credit with overseas facility
☐ ☐ Overseas special employees
☐ ☐ Miscellaneous special regulations; money; import; quota; communications set up with home office; etc.
☐ ☐ Simultaneous translation equipment
☐ ☐ Location of cable offices
☐ ☐ *____________________
☐ ☐ ____________________

20 LICENSES, RESTRICTIONS AND OTHER NO-NO's

☐ ☐ Check for anything restrictive in relation to what your group wishes to do
☐ ☐ Hotel "house" rules
☐ ☐ Legal requirements
e.g., local, state, federal
☐ ☐ Union regulations
☐ ☐ Community prejudices

*These blank spaces allow you to add additional checkpoints that may apply only to your meeting.

need to check	checked	
		e.g., in respect to activities; in respect to nationalities; etc.
☐	☐	Liquor licensing e.g., restricted/wide open; etc.
☐	☐	Liquor available e.g., all over at all times/restricted hours at certain places; etc.
☐	☐	Ladies' restrictions e.g., not allowed to sit at bar without an escort/not allowed to sit at bar at all; not permitted to attend during all hours or certain hours; areas not recommended to visit at all or during certain hours; etc.
☐	☐	*________________________
☐	☐	________________________

21 SECURITY

need to check	checked	
☐	☐	Any anticipated trouble e.g., protesters; pickets; hecklers
☐	☐	Security aids e.g., house detectives; guards; guard dogs and handlers; etc.
☐	☐	Agreed upon trouble signal
☐	☐	Police alerted
☐	☐	Bodyguards for VIPs
☐	☐	Any type of bullet-proof protection for VIPs
☐	☐	Special obscure exit or entrance for VIPs
☐	☐	Alternate entrances/exits
☐	☐	Location of fire exits and check to see doors or windows to such exits open easily
☐	☐	Extinguisher locations e.g., Fire sprinklers/foam; etc.
☐	☐	Emergency instructions issued in writing to employees
☐	☐	Walkie-talkie communication
☐	☐	Replacement procedures in case of theft or failure to operate
☐	☐	Alternate transportation arrangements (people and freight) in case of strikes; etc.
☐	☐	Back up personnel in case of mass absences
☐	☐	Protest procedure

NOTE: Some organizations have found it judicious to actually provide space for protest groups, which, at least, keeps the protesters in one place.

need to check	checked	
☐	☐	Complaint procedure
☐	☐	Hold-up procedure
☐	☐	pre-briefing of staff on how to behave
☐	☐	Safe deposit vault
☐	☐	Arrangements when moving large sums of money from one place to another to prevent loss or theft
☐	☐	Locked closets
☐	☐	Out of hours admission—definite policy
☐	☐	Taking items out of building—definite policy
☐	☐	Insurance coverage e.g., damage; fire; liability; accident; theft; etc.

NOTE: Make sure insurance company will cover in case of riots, protests, and so on. Frequently there is an

*These blank spaces allow you to add additional checkpoints that may apply only to your meeting.

need to check | checked

exclusion clause in regard to these instances. Also be sure casual help is insured.

- ☐ ☐ Area well lighted and safe at time of ending of event
- ☐ ☐ Lost and found bureau

Emergency telephone numbers and addresses that are necessary:

- ☐ ☐ Police
- ☐ ☐ Fire
- ☐ ☐ First aid available on premises
- ☐ ☐ Doctors
- ☐ ☐ Hospitals
- ☐ ☐ Private ambulance service
- ☐ ☐ Drug store on premises—hours open; all night drug store location; etc.
- ☐ ☐ *________________________
- ☐ ☐ ________________________

22 PUBLICITY, PROMOTION AND ADVERTISING

- ☐ ☐ Mailing list
- ☐ ☐ Mailing out by self/mailing house
- ☐ ☐ Mailing dates set up
- ☐ ☐ First Mailing
- ☐ ☐ Second Mailing
- ☐ ☐ Third mailing
- ☐ ☐ Feed-back and follow-up
- ☐ ☐ Postal permits for bulk mailing
- ☐ ☐ Form 3514 requested
- ☐ ☐ Is advance release on meeting wanted? If so, date to release
- ☐ ☐ Advance copies of speeches or presentations wanted? If so, available?
- ☐ ☐ Advance releases on major speeches wanted? If so, date to release
- ☐ ☐ If advance copies unavailable, on-the-spot release arrangements OK and made for the benefit of press?
- ☐ ☐ Press conference for a major speaker? TV interview? Radio?
- ☐ ☐ Coverage in home-town papers for delegates? Award winners? Coverage for company house organs on award presentations and the winners?
- ☐ ☐ Follow-up release on outcome of meeting or conference?
- ☐ ☐ As much coverage as possible/restrict coverage
- ☐ ☐ Photographs prior to event/during
- ☐ ☐ Pre-printed promotional material
- ☐ ☐ Publicity kits
- ☐ ☐ Posters
- ☐ ☐ Bulletin board notices
- ☐ ☐ Advertising
  e.g., TV; radio; newspapers; magazines; billboards; wire services; etc.
- ☐ ☐ Publicity
  e.g., TV; radio; newspapers; magazines; house organs; bumper stickers; real telegrams; facsimile telegrams; etc.
- ☐ ☐ Appearance dates coordinated
- ☐ ☐ Press room set aside
- ☐ ☐ Stamped-addressed envelopes/cards; etc.

*These blank spaces allow you to add additional checkpoints that may apply only to your meeting.

need to check	checked	
☐	☐	Information material e.g., placed on audience chairs; display table; rack; handed out upon entering or leaving or during; etc.
☐	☐	*________________
☐	☐	________________

23 LOCAL RECREATION

need to check	checked	
☐	☐	Programs for good weather/bad weather
☐	☐	Bus tours e.g., already organized; chartered especially; etc.
☐	☐	Guide e.g., male/female; speaks foreign language; etc.
☐	☐	Participation sports e.g., tennis; golf; swimming; gambling; etc.
☐	☐	Spectator sports e.g., ball games; horse racing; etc.
☐	☐	Amusements e.g., opera; theater; museums; etc.
☐	☐	Religious services e.g., Protestant; Catholic; Jewish; etc.
☐	☐	Already scheduled local events e.g., town parade; fair; etc.
☐	☐	Reciprocal invitations e.g., Elks; Lions; bridge clubs; garden clubs; etc.
☐	☐	Theater ticket agencies
☐	☐	Swimming pools e.g., indoors/outdoors
☐	☐	Location of after-hours nightspots
☐	☐	*________________
☐	☐	________________

24 SPECIAL PROVISION FOR SPOUSES

need to check	checked	
☐	☐	Baby sitting services
☐	☐	Visits to local industries
☐	☐	Shopping expeditions
☐	☐	Demonstrations e.g., cookery; hobbies; cosmetics; etc. (tie-in with local traders arrange for discounts and souvenirs)
☐	☐	Fashion shows; boat trips; calisthenics classes; dance classes; etc.
☐	☐	Timetable e.g., assembly time; departure; arrival at highpoint; leave highpoint; return; etc.

NOTE: Be sure to return participants in plenty of time to dress for evening events

need to check	checked	
☐	☐	*________________
☐	☐	________________

25 ACCOUNTING

need to check	checked	
☐	☐	Accounting on premises/ accounting material sent back to office daily
☐	☐	Budget allowed
☐	☐	Details of individual events should be carefully listed

NOTE: To aid the accounting department, list all quotations, deposits, minimum guarantees, estimated and actual costs and receipts, refunds and commissions under appropriate headings.

*These blank spaces allow you to add additional checkpoints that may apply only to your meeting.

need to check	checked	
☐	☐	Publicity, promotion and advertising
☐	☐	Personnel rates and costs
☐	☐	Sleeping rooms
☐	☐	Meeting rooms
☐	☐	Meals, food
☐	☐	Beverages
☐	☐	Hired equipment
☐	☐	V.I.P. expenditures
☐	☐	Entertainment
☐	☐	Exhibits and freight expenditures
☐	☐	Transportation—people
☐	☐	Transportation—freight
☐	☐	Phone, cables, mailing etc.
☐	☐	Licenses
☐	☐	Security costs
☐	☐	Insurance coverage
☐	☐	Petty cash
☐	☐	Expense accounts
☐	☐	Gratuities
☐	☐	Taxes (i.e., Federal; State, City; etc.)
☐	☐	Leeway (at least 10% of cost)
☐	☐	Estimated overall
☐	☐	Local credit arranged through regular bank channels
☐	☐	Credit arranged with local businessmen
☐	☐	Procedures for paying in and collecting money from bank
☐	☐	Arrangements for deferred payments and deadline dates.
☐	☐	*________________________
☐	☐	________________________

INCENTIVE TRAVEL CHECKLIST

Pre-Program Considerations

need to check	checked	
☐	☐	objective(s)
☐	☐	budget
☐	☐	tax advantages
☐	☐	quotas
☐	☐	participants
☐	☐	contest length
☐	☐	contest dates
☐	☐	motivational house
☐	☐	travel agent

Choosing a Destination

need to check	checked	
☐	☐	amount available per participant
☐	☐	number of participants
☐	☐	sophisticaton of participants
☐	☐	demographics of participants
☐	☐	sports they enjoy
☐	☐	trips of competitors
☐	☐	promotability of destination
☐	☐	airline availability
☐	☐	hotel availability
☐	☐	restaurants
☐	☐	attractions
☐	☐	night entertainment
☐	☐	ground transportation
☐	☐	language
☐	☐	currency
☐	☐	political stability
☐	☐	inspection trip
☐	☐	special rates (air, hotel, other)

Promoting the Program

need to check	checked	
☐	☐	budget
☐	☐	promotional theme
☐	☐	promotional kick-off
☐	☐	promotional materials
☐	☐	timing and frequency

Logistics

need to check	checked	
☐	☐	getting there
☐	☐	transfer to hotel
☐	☐	booking rooms
☐	☐	booking dining

*These blank spaces allow you to add additional checkpoints that may apply only to your meeting.

need to check	checked	
☐	☐	booking attractions
☐	☐	chartering buses
☐	☐	booking theatres, nightclubs, etc.

Program Evaluation

need to check	checked	
☐	☐	objective(s) attained
☐	☐	trip evaluation

VALUE SEASON MEETINGS

need to check	checked	
☐	☐	objectives
☐	☐	possible dates
☐	☐	possible destinations
☐	☐	package deals available
☐	☐	special air fares
☐	☐	price concessions on rooms
☐	☐	price concessions on food & beverage
☐	☐	price concessions on recreational activities
☐	☐	hotel staff support
☐	☐	weather
☐	☐	restaurants open (hours)
☐	☐	attractions open (hours)
☐	☐	recreational activities available

WEEKEND MEETINGS

need to check	checked	
☐	☐	objectives
☐	☐	previous company policy
☐	☐	areas of resistance
☐	☐	areas of enthusiasm
☐	☐	cost comparison with weekday meetings
☐	☐	special packages available
☐	☐	special concessions available
☐	☐	length of meeting
☐	☐	attendance of spouse
☐	☐	advantages over mid-week meetings

Appendix E

Cocktail Party Basics

Amount of Liquor Per Drink

Mixed group:	$1\frac{1}{4}$ oz
Male group:	$1\frac{1}{4}$ oz
Female group:	1 oz

Drinks Per Liter Bottle

$1\frac{1}{4}$-oz drinks:	27+
1-oz drinks:	34

Drinks Per Person Per Hour: (Computed from data on 215 cocktail parties of each type of group during a 10-year period)

First-day party:		
Mixed group	2.48	
Male group	2.55	
Female group	2.10	
After first-day party:		
Mixed group	2.65	(Percent increase: 6.85%)
Male group	2.87	(Percent increase: 12.5%)
Female group	2.40	(Percent increase: 14.3%)

Averages drop almost one drink per hour if a cash bar is used.

General Suggestions

1. Establish the amount per drink with bartender beforehand.
2. Always monitor bartenders.

3. Ensure bartenders use proper size jiggers for amount per drink agreed upon.
4. Make sure no seals on bottles are cracked before the party.
5. Conduct a bar inventory before and after the party and have inventory signed by the bartender.
6. Consolidate liquors 15 minutes before end of party.
7. Allow no empties near the bar or as water bottles.

Appendix F

Master Gantt Chart*

*From Lois B. Hart and Gordon Schleicher's book, *A Conference and Workshop Planner's Manual*, originally published by AMACOM in 1979 and now available exclusively from Leadership Dynamics, 875 Poplar Ave., Boulder, CO. 80302.

Date of Event

Conference or Workshop Coordinator

What	Who	When
Review Chapter 2	C	10
Review schedules and all materials	C	10
Select committee chairs	C	10
Arrange first meeting	C	10
Hold first planning meeting	C	10
Select committee members	All	10
Decide on exhibits	X	10
Review with program chair	PR	10
Hold first committee meeting	A	10
	E	10
	P	9
	R	9
	PR	9
	X	9
	F	9
Contact convention bureau	A	9
Review information on sites	A	9
Visit sites	A	9

What	Who	When
Review options for promotion	PR	9
Submit key questions and procedures to planning committee	F	9
Establish an account	F	9
Develop first draft of program design	E	9
	P	8
Review draft of design	P	8
Select facility	A	8
Negotiate details	A	8
Confirm arrangements in writing	A	8
Outline promotional plan	PR	8
Review plan with program chair	PR	8
Review plan with fiscal chair	PR	8
Determine preregistration information	R	8
Decide on locations for exhibits	A X	8
Make floor plan	X	8
Develop exhibit rules and contract	X	8
Committees submit budgets to fiscal committee	All	8

What	Who	When
Compile committee budgets	F	8
Critique evaluation instrument	E	8
Develop evaluation instrument in final form	E	7
Revise first draft of program design	P	7
Select resource people	P	7
Prepare room-needs request form	A	7
Finalize promotional plan	PR	7
Identify monetary registration procedures	R F	7
Prepare sample registration form	R	7
Give registration form to promotion chair	R	7
Decide who should exhibit	X	7
Contact exhibit sources (first letter)	X	7
Present budget to planning committee	F	7
Present budget to planning committee	F	7
Contact suggested resource people	P	6
Send confirmation letter to resource people selected (first letter)	P	6
Include room-needs checklist in program committee's letter	A	6

What	Who	When
Process preregistration applications	R	6
Send confirmation letter to preregistered participants	R	6
Send second letter to exhibitors	X	6
Accept and confirm exhibitors	X	6
Assign space	X	6
Order supplies and equipment	A	6
Send contracts to confirmed exhibitors	X	6
Decide on exhibit hours	X	6
Review program plans with fiscal chair	P	5
Check feedback from resource people	P	5
Follow up where needed	P AR	5
Send second letter to all resource people	P	5
Coordinate with promotion committee	P	5
Prepare program book	PR P	5
Serve as liaison to printer for other committees	PR	5
Identify on-site registration needs	R	5
Decide on "traffic builders"	X	5
Coordinate efforts with promotion chair	X	5

What	Who	When
Give evaluation form to promotion chair for printing	E	5
Decide on distribution procedures	E	5
Coordinate with arrangements committee	P	4
Select facilitators	P	4
Reserve use of AV equipment	A	4
Coordinate with promotion committee	A	4
Confirm site arrangements with facility in writing	A	4
Confirm lodging for resource people	A	4
Arrange special transportation	A	4
Determine site food and beverage needs—confirm arrangements	A	4
Coordinate registration setup with arrangements committee	R	4
Determine exhibitors' needs and assign tasks	X	4
Coordinate printing of final program with promotion committee	P	3
Obtain list of restaurants	A	3
Arrange for preparation of necessary signs	A	3
Arrange for registration personnel and equipment	R	3
Coordinate exhibitors' needs with arrangements committee	X	3

What	Who	When
Prepare letter of welcome for resource people	P	2
Arrange transportation for resource people	A	2
Obtain list of participants from registration committee	X	2
Monitor arrival of exhibits	X	2
Arrange for receipt of monies at site	F	2
Check on supplies	A	1
Confirm final site arrangements	A	1
Final meeting between committee members and site staff	A	1
Supervise delivery of equipment, supplies, program books	A PR	1
Prepare registration lists	R	1
Prepare instructions for registration staff	R	1
Check last-minute registration needs	R	1
Supervise exhibit setup	X	1
Check with committees about bills	F	1
Day of Event		
Inspect session rooms	P A	0

What	Who	When
Monitor transportation arrangements	A	0
Distribute and collect evaluations	E	0
Following Event		
Review evaluation results	E	+1
Send letters to resource persons	P	+1
Send thank-you letters to resource persons, facilitators, members of planning committee	P	+1
	A	+1
	PR	+1
	R	+1
	X	+1
Review bills	F	+1
Return supplies and equipment	A	+1
Letter to committee members	A	+1
Ensure return of equipment	X	+1
Send follow-up evaluations	E	+1
Tabulate evaluation results	E	+2
Arrange for closing account	F	+2
Prepare final reports	A	+2
	P	+2
	PR	+2
	R	+2
	X	+2
	F	+3

Appendix G

Site Inspection Checklists

This checklist is designed for a comparison of three properties at the selected destination. It is recommended that each item on the list receive a rating on a ten-point scale, where 1 represents *extremely poor* and 10 represents *extremely superior*. When the inspection is completed, the ratings are added together and an average rating for each property is secured. The average ratings are used for a comparison guide to assist in final selection.

Name of property 1 ____________ Contact person ____________
Name of property 2 ____________ Contact person ____________
Name of property 3 ____________ Contact person ____________

Property 1	Property 2	Property 3
Sleeping Rooms:	Sleeping Rooms:	Sleeping Rooms:
Singles # ______	Singles # ______	Singles # ______
Doubles # ______	Doubles # ______	Doubles # ______
Suites	Suites	Suites
1 bedroom # ______	1 bedroom # ______	1 bedroom # ______
2 bedroom # ______	2 bedroom # ______	2 bedroom # ______
Parlors # ______	Parlors # ______	Parlors # ______
	Handicapped Accessibility	
______	______	______
Comments ____________	____________	____________
____________	____________	____________
____________	____________	____________
____________	____________	____________

(continued)

Property 1	Property 2	Property 3
	Bathrooms	
Clean? ______	Clean? ______	Clean? ______
Amenities? ______	Amenities? ______	Amenities? ______
Lighting? ______	Lighting? ______	Lighting? ______
Handicapped accessibility? ______	Handicapped accessibility? ______	Handicapped accessibility? ______
Tub/shower	Tub/shower	Tub/shower
Caulking ______	Caulking ______	Caulking ______
Shower head ______	Shower head ______	Shower head ______
Grab bar ______	Grab bar ______	Grab bar ______
Traction in tub ______	Traction in tub ______	Traction in tub ______
Shower mat ______	Shower mat ______	Shower mat ______
	Sleeping Rooms	
Clean? ______	Clean? ______	Clean? ______
Size? ______	Size? ______	Size? ______
Decor ______	Decor ______	Decor ______
Television	Television	Television
Color? ______	Color? ______	Color? ______
Movies? ______	Movies? ______	Movies? ______
Cable? ______	Cable? ______	Cable? ______
Closet space? ______	Closet space? ______	Closet space? ______
Worktable/desk? ______	Worktable/desk? ______	Worktable/desk? ______
Fire detector? ______	Fire detector? ______	Fire detector? ______
Sprinkler system? ______	Sprinkler system? ______	Sprinkler system? ______
Heat/cooling? ______	Heat/cooling? ______	Heat/cooling? ______
Hotel directory? ______	Hotel directory? ______	Hotel directory? ______
Bed comfort? ______	Bed comfort? ______	Bed comfort? ______
Telephone? ______	Telephone? ______	Telephone? ______
Charges?	Charges?	Charges?
Local? ______	Local?______	Local?______
Long-distance? ______	Long-distance? ______	Long-distance? ______
Message light? ______	Message light? ______	Message light? ______
Chairs? ______	Chairs? ______	Chairs? ______
Luggage rack? ______	Luggage rack? ______	Luggage rack? ______
Writing paper, etc. ______	Writing paper, etc. ______	Writing paper, etc. ______
Coat hangers? ______	Coat hangers? ______	Coat hangers? ______
Sound	Sound	Sound
Outside noise ______	Outside noise ______	Outside noise ______
Through walls ______	Through walls ______	Through walls ______
Carpet wear ______	Carpet wear ______	Carpet wear ______
Drapery condition ______	Drapery condition ______	Drapery condition ______
Windows clean ______	Windows clean ______	Windows clean ______
Local literature ______	Local literature ______	Local literature ______
Lighting ______	Lighting ______	Lighting ______
Switch locations ______	Switch locations ______	Switch locations ______
Security locks? ______	Security locks? ______	Security locks? ______
Services	Services	Services
Concierge ______	Concierge ______	Concierge ______
Room-service times ___	Room-service times ___	Room-service times ___
Turndown ______	Turndown ______	Turndown ______
Ice machine ______	Ice machine ______	Ice machine ______
Soft-drink machine ___	Soft-drink machine ___	Soft-drink machine ___
Wake-up ______	Wake-up ______	Wake-up ______

(continued)

Property 1	Property 2	Property 3
Laundry ______	Laundry ______	Laundry ______
Valet ______	Valet ______	Valet ______
Other (list)	Other (list)	Other (list)
______ ______	______ ______	______ ______
______ ______	______ ______	______ ______
______ ______	______ ______	______ ______
Maid service	Maid service	Maid service
Rooms per maid ______	Rooms per maid ______	Rooms per maid ______
Time per room ______	Time per room ______	Time per room ______
Daily vacuum ______	Daily vacuum ______	Daily vacuum ______
Normal gratuity ______	Normal gratuity ______	Normal gratuity ______
Total of ratings for sleeping rooms ______	Total of ratings for sleeping rooms ______	Total of ratings for sleeping rooms ______

Meeting Rooms

Names	Dimensions	Rate	Names	Dimensions	Rate	Names	Dimensions	Rate

Individual Room Analysis: (One form per property. Use ratings for each item.)

PROPERTY 1

Name	Acoustics	Heat/Cool Controls	Decor	Lighting	Phone	Lighting Controls	Ceiling Height	Distractions	Proximity to Kitchen

PROPERTY 2

Name	Acoustics	Heat/Cool Controls	Decor	Lighting	Phone	Lighting Controls	Ceiling Height	Distractions	Proximity to Kitchen

PROPERTY 3

Name	Acoustics	Heat/Cool Controls	Decor	Lighting	Phone	Lighting Controls	Ceiling Height	Distractions	Proximity to Kitchen

Location and adequacy of restrooms.

Property 1 Rating ___	Property 2 Rating ___	Property 3 Rating ___
Comments. ___	___	___
___	___	___
___	___	___
___	___	___
Additional meeting-room considerations		
Electric service amps ___ Rating ___	Electric service amps ___ Rating ___	Electric service amps ___ Rating ___
Freight elevator	Freight elevator	Freight elevator
Door size ___ Rating ___	Door size ___ Rating ___	Door size ___ Rating ___
Wt. capacity ___ Rating ___	Wt. capacity ___ Rating ___	Wt. capacity ___ Rating ___
Stage area size ___ Rating ___	Stage area size ___ Rating ___	Stage area size ___ Rating ___
Loading dock size ___ Rating ___	Loading dock size ___ Rating ___	Loading dock size ___ Rating ___
Chairs # ___ Size ___ Rating ___	Chairs # ___ Size ___ Rating ___	Chairs # ___ Size ___ Rating ___
Tables	Tables	Tables
Size ___ # ___ Rating ___	Size ___ # ___ Rating ___	Size ___ # ___ Rating ___
Size ___ # ___ Rating ___	Size ___ # ___ Rating ___	Size ___ # ___ Rating ___
Size ___ # ___ Rating ___	Size ___ # ___ Rating ___	Size ___ # ___ Rating ___
Size ___ # ___ Rating ___	Size ___ # ___ Rating ___	Size ___ # ___ Rating ___
Lecterns (table) # ___ Rating ___	Lecterns (table) # ___ Rating ___	Lecterns (table) # ___ Rating ___
Podiums (floor) # ___ Rating ___	Podiums (floor) # ___ Rating ___	Podiums (floor) # ___ Rating ___
Screens (pulldown or portable)	Screens (pulldown or portable)	Screens (pulldown or portable)
Size ___ Rating ___	Size ___ Rating ___	Size ___ Rating ___
Size ___ Rating ___	Size ___ Rating ___	Size ___ Rating ___
Size ___ Rating ___	Size ___ Rating ___	Size ___ Rating ___
Other audiovisual in house	Other audiovisual in house	Other audiovisual in house
Microphones	Microphones	Microphones
Lavaliere # ___ Cost ___ Rating ___	Lavaliere # ___ Cost ___ Rating ___	Lavaliere # ___ Cost ___ Rating ___
Roving # ___ Cost ___ Rating ___	Roving # ___ Cost ___ Rating ___	Roving # ___ Cost ___ Rating ___
Standing # ___ Cost ___ Rating ___	Standing # ___ Cost ___ Rating ___	Standing # ___ Cost ___ Rating ___
Table # ___ Cost ___ Rating ___	Table # ___ Cost ___ Rating ___	Table # ___ Cost ___ Rating ___
Cordless # ___ Cost ___ Rating ___	Cordless # ___ Cost ___ Rating ___	Cordless # ___ Cost ___ Rating ___

Projectors
Overhead # __ Cost __ Rating __
Opaque # __ Cost __ Rating __
16 mm # __ Cost __ Rating __
2 × 2 # __ Cost __ Rating __
Carousel # __ Cost __ Rating __
Filmstrip # __ Cost __ Rating __
Rear Projection
__ Cost __ Rating __
VCRs # __ Cost __ Rating __
Flip charts # __ Cost __ Rating __
Easels # __ Cost __ Rating __
Chalk-boards # __ Cost __ Rating __
Pointer (elec.) # __ Cost __ Rating __
Pointer (hand) # __ Cost __ Rating __

Room Lighting
Rheostat-controlled __ Rating __
(List rooms without)
Gooseneck spots __ Rating __

Mirrors:* # __ Rating __
Ornate Wall Decorations* __ Rating __
Ventilator Noise* __ Rating __
Chandeliers* __ Rating __
Blackout curtains* __ Rating __
Low Ceilings* __ Rating __
Columns* __ Rating __
Tier seating __ Rating __

Riser:
Dimensions Rating __
Number Rating __
Covering Rating __
Skirting Rating __

Dance Floor:
Type __ Rating __

Projectors
Overhead # __ Cost __ Rating __
Opaque # __ Cost __ Rating __
16 mm # __ Cost __ Rating __
2 × 2 # __ Cost __ Rating __
Carousel # __ Cost __ Rating __
Filmstrip # __ Cost __ Rating __
Rear Projection
__ Cost __ Rating __
VCRs # __ Cost __ Rating __
Flip charts # __ Cost __ Rating __
Easels # __ Cost __ Rating __
Chalk-boards # __ Cost __ Rating __
Pointer (elec.) # __ Cost __ Rating __
Pointer (hand) # __ Cost __ Rating __

Room Lighting
Rheostat-controlled __ Rating __
(List rooms without)
Gooseneck spots __ Rating __

Mirrors:* # __ Rating __
Ornate Wall Decorations* __ Rating __
Ventilator Noise* __ Rating __
Chandeliers* __ Rating __
Blackout curtains* __ Rating __
Low Ceilings* __ Rating __
Columns* __ Rating __
Tier seating __ Rating __

Riser:
Dimensions Rating __
Number Rating __
Covering Rating __
Skirting Rating __

Dance Floor:
Type __ Rating __

Projectors
Overhead # __ Cost __ Rating __
Opaque # __ Cost __ Rating __
16 mm # __ Cost __ Rating __
2 × 2 # __ Cost __ Rating __
Carousel # __ Cost __ Rating __
Filmstrip # __ Cost __ Rating __
Rear Projection
__ Cost __ Rating __
VCRs # __ Cost __ Rating __
Flip charts # __ Cost __ Rating __
Easels # __ Cost __ Rating __
Chalk-boards # __ Cost __ Rating __
Pointer (elec.) # __ Cost __ Rating __
Pointer (hand) # __ Cost __ Rating __

Room Lighting
Rheostat-controlled __ Rating __
(List rooms without)
Gooseneck spots __ Rating __

Mirrors:* # __ Rating __
Ornate Wall Decorations* __ Rating __
Ventilator Noise* __ Rating __
Chandeliers* __ Rating __
Blackout curtains* __ Rating __
Low Ceilings* __ Rating __
Columns* __ Rating __
Tier seating __ Rating __

Riser:
Dimensions Rating __
Number Rating __
Covering Rating __
Skirting Rating __

Dance Floor:
Type __ Rating __

*Indicates the needs for a separate list of those without.

(*continued*)

Location and adequacy of restrooms (*Continued*)

Property 1	Property 2	Property 3
Dimensions ___ Rating ___	Dimensions ___ Rating ___	Dimensions ___ Rating ___
Simultaneous translation Rating ___	Simultaneous translation Rating ___	Simultaneous translation Rating ___
Portable steps:	Portable steps:	Portable steps:
Number ___ Rating ___	Number ___ Rating ___	Number ___ Rating ___
Dimensions ___ Rating ___	Dimensions ___ Rating ___	Dimensions ___ Rating ___
Rails ___ Rating ___	Rails ___ Rating ___	Rails ___ Rating ___
Covering ___ Rating ___	Covering ___ Rating ___	Covering ___ Rating ___
Ramps:	Ramps:	Ramps:
Number ___ Rating ___	Number ___ Rating ___	Number ___ Rating ___
Covering ___ Rating ___	Covering ___ Rating ___	Covering ___ Rating ___
Rails ___ Rating ___	Rails ___ Rating ___	Rails ___ Rating ___
Staging area (performers) Rating ___	Staging area (performers) Rating ___	Staging area (performers) Rating ___
Reception area: Rating ___	Reception area: Rating ___	Reception area: Rating ___
Emergency exits: Rating ___	Emergency exits: Rating ___	Emergency exits: Rating ___
Fire/smoke detectors: Rating ___	Fire/smoke detectors: Rating ___	Fire/smoke detectors: Rating ___
Sprinkler system: Rating ___	Sprinkler system: Rating ___	Sprinkler system: Rating ___
Total of ratings for meeting rooms ___	Total of ratings for meeting rooms ___	Total of ratings for meeting rooms ___
	Kitchens	
Cleanliness:	Cleanliness:	Cleanliness:
Grills: Rating ___	Grills: Rating ___	Grills: Rating ___
Hoods: Rating ___	Hoods: Rating ___	Hoods: Rating ___
Floors: Rating ___	Floors: Rating ___	Floors: Rating ___
Prep area: Rating ___	Prep area: Rating ___	Prep area: Rating ___
Employees:	Employees:	Employees:
Hair Covers: Rating ___	Hair Covers: Rating ___	Hair Covers: Rating ___
Clothing: Rating ___	Clothing: Rating ___	Clothing: Rating ___
Utensils: Rating ___	Utensils: Rating ___	Utensils: Rating ___
Service tables: Rating ___	Service tables: Rating ___	Service tables: Rating ___
Efficiency of layout: Rating: ___	Efficiency of layout: Rating: ___	Efficiency of layout: Rating: ___
Total of ratings for kitchen ___	Total of ratings for kitchen ___	Total of ratings for kitchen ___
	Recreation	
Exercise Area:	Exercise Area:	Exercise Area:
Type ________ Cost ___ Rating ___	Type ________ Cost ___ Rating ___	Type ________ Cost ___ Rating ___
Type ________ Cost ___ Rating ___	Type ________ Cost ___ Rating ___	Type ________ Cost ___ Rating ___
Type ________ Cost ___ Rating ___	Type ________ Cost ___ Rating ___	Type ________ Cost ___ Rating ___
Type ________ Cost ___ Rating ___	Type ________ Cost ___ Rating ___	Type ________ Cost ___ Rating ___

Property 1	Property 2	Property 3
Rec. Supervision Available:	Rec. Supervision Available:	Rec. Supervision Available:
Cost ___ Rating ___	Cost ___ Rating ___	Cost ___ Rating ___
Total of ratings for recreation ___	___	___
	General Hotel	
Liquor policies?	Liquor policies?	Liquor policies?
In writing? ___ Rating ___	In writing? ___ Rating ___	In writing? ___ Rating ___
Local taxes:	Local taxes:	Local taxes:
Room tax: ___	Room tax: ___	Room tax: ___
Telephone Charges: ___	Telephone Charges: ___	Telephone Charges: ___
Parking: ___	Parking: ___	Parking: ___
Food Tax: ___	Food Tax: ___	Food Tax: ___
Beverage Tax: ___	Beverage Tax: ___	Beverage Tax: ___
Gratuities: ___	Gratuities: ___	Gratuities: ___
Door/bellpersons	Door/bellpersons	Door/bellpersons
Customary charges ___	Customary charges ___	Customary charges ___
Special charges (list)	Special charges (list)	Special charges (list)
______________________	______________________	______________________
______________________	______________________	______________________
______________________	______________________	______________________
Special charge rating ___	Special charge rating ___	Special charge rating ___
Deposit policies (Write) rating ___	Deposit policies (Write) rating ___	Deposit policies (Write) rating ___
Distances:	Distances:	Distances:
Airport ___ Rating ___	Airport ___ Rating ___	Airport ___ Rating ___
Public transport ___ Rating ___	Public transport ___ Rating ___	Public transport ___ Rating ___
Overflow housing ___ Rating ___	Overflow housing ___ Rating ___	Overflow housing ___ Rating ___
Shipping and receiving ___ Rating ___	Shipping and receiving ___ Rating ___	Shipping and receiving ___ Rating ___
Neighborhood rating ___	Neighborhood rating ___	Neighborhood rating ___
Personnel attitude rating ___	Personnel attitude rating ___	Personnel attitude rating ___
Total of general hotel ratings ___	___	___

GRAND TOTAL OF *ALL* PROPERTY RATINGS

Property 1		Property 2		Property 3	
Sleeping rooms	______	Sleeping rooms	______	Sleeping rooms	______
Meeting rooms	______	Meeting rooms	______	Meeting rooms	______
Kitchen	______	Kitchen	______	Kitchen	______
Recreation	______	Recreation	______	Recreation	______

(continued)

Location and adequacy of restrooms (*Continued*)

Property 1	Property 2	Property 3
General hotel ______	General hotel ______	General hotel ______
Grand total ______	Grand total ______	Grand total ______
Average	Average	Average
$\frac{\text{Grand total}}{6}$ = ______	$\frac{\text{Grand total}}{6}$ = ______	$\frac{\text{Grand total}}{6}$ = ______

Notes ____

Attach to this form a list similar to the following one for each property.

KEY HOTEL PERSONNEL

Service	Daytime	Extension	Nightime	Extension	Notes
Airline reservations					
Auditor					
Audiovisual					
Banquet manager					
Bell captain					
Carpenter					
Car rental					
Catering manager					
Chef					
Convention services					
Decorating firm					
Drayage firm					
Electrician					
Engineer					
Florist					
Food and beverage manager					
Garage manager					
General manager					
Golf starter					
Golf pro shop					
House doctor					
Housekeeper					
Maitre d'hotel					
Messenger service					
Parking garage manager					
Photographer					
Projectionist					
Receiving/shipping					
Recreation director					
Reservations					
Sales director					
Security office					
Setup crew manager					

(continued)

KEY HOTEL PERSONNEL (*Continued*)

Service	Daytime	Extension	Nightime	Extension	Notes
Sound person					
Stenographer					
Recreation director					
Taxi					
Tennis pro					
Other staff Names needed					

Off-shore Property Evaluation

When planning an off-shore meeting, consider the following checklist when doing your site inspection:

Electrical

Voltage ______ 110 ______ 208 ______ Other.
Are voltage converters available ______ Cost (US $) ______
Electrical capacity in amps of property ______
Electrical receptacles. ______ 2-prong ______ 3-prong

Gratuities

______ Included in cost? ______ Additional

Currency

Units? (francs, marks, pesos, colones, etc.) ______
Exchange rate: (You may buy in United States at a good rate long before your meeting.) ______
Closest currency exchanges to property ______________________________
____

Clothing (Check local customs and attitudes. Avoid cultural differences that would shock locals.)

Acceptable daytime attire: ______ suits, etc. ______ informal
______ casual ______ shorts, etc?
Acceptable nighttime attire: ______ Formal (tuxedo, evening dress)
______ Semiformal (suits, dresses, slack suits)
______ Casual (sport coats, slacks, sweaters)

Transfers from airport

______ Costs ______ Types
Schedules:

Customs procedures

Visas Required? ______ Innoculations? ______ Passports? ______

Any special local laws?

Staff English capabilities

______ General manager
______ Sales director
______ Convention services
______ Reservations manager
______ Front desk clerks
______ Catering manager
______ Beverage manager
______ Sommelier
______ Maitre d'hotel
______ Electrician
______ Chef(s)
______ Dining room captains
______ Bell captains
______ Bellpersons
______ Recreation director(s)
______ Tour directors
______ Transportation manager
______ Sales manager
______ Head houseperson
______ Front desk manager
______ Telephone operator(s)
______ Baggage person(s)
______ Server(s)
______ Security officer
______ Engineer
______ Setup manager
______ Housekeeper(s)
______ Accountant
______ Night manager(s)
______ Sound person
______ House doctor
______ Car-rental manager

Special notes on unique characteristics of property and destination

Appendix H

Cost-Saver Tips for Meeting Manager

No-Show Count Is Vital for Accurate Guarantees

Research your past performance.

Collect and keep tickets from meeting to meeting.

Color-code tickets by function.

Check number of *beds* being occupied in the hotel (it is more accurate than a room count to get *potentials* at a food function).

Ask the hotel front desk: How many arriving? How many departing? Do this on a day-by-day basis.

Consider weather and competing events that might draw attendees away from your food function.

Consider having an *exchange* ticket they have to pick up sometime in advance in order to attend.

Design an emergency reserve in the event your guarantee is low. (The hotel usually has chickens in the freezer.)

Keep Food Costs in Line

Work with the chef on menu selection.

Arrange a "colorful," but moderately priced, plate.

Taste-test the meal.

Select foods that are abundant, in season, or peculiar to the area.

Try juggling menus *between meals* if attendees aren't eating a certain food.

Buy hors d'oeuvre by the piece and have them served. (People eat more from a buffet.)

Stay away from high-labor-cost hors d'oeuvre (those that have to be stuffed).

Avoid continental breakfasts for large groups (too much food waste).

Don't go overboard on luncheon menus (either cost or size).

Avoid French or Russian service.

Avoid buffets unless you do careful planning.

Consider a catered meal either outside or from outside the property.

Solicit meal sponsorships.

Control Your Bar Costs

Stay away from salty items such as salty nuts, pretzels, anchovies. (They can double your bar tab.)

Calculate 5 to 6 hors d'oeuvre per person per hour.

Arrange for a complete audit of liquor used for a reception or hosted bar.

Provide drink tickets and let attendee pay for additional drinks if you have a tight budget.

Pay by the person, by the hour, by the drink, or by the bottle, but get an agreement before the function.

Close the bar on time. (This can't be emphasized enough.)

Double-check dram (or grog) shop laws. Learn property "corkage" rules.

Save on Promotions

Remember, some promotionals are needed even when attendance is guaranteed.

Use "shells" provided by hotels, cities, convention bureaus.

Plan mailings in advance to get bulk printing savings and save on postage.

Use cut stock wherever possible.

Consider art students at local college. (They are getting more expensive.)

Print newsletter letterheads in quantity so you just have to run those you use for each mailing and don't have to reprint letterhead.

Use airlines and telephone canvassing with a toll-free number, and use fliers.

Use postage imprints and stickers on all regular and meeting mail.

Write a collection of fillers, and send them to magazines and newspapers that reach your potential attendees.

Have people on hand from next year's meeting destination to promote that conference at this year's conference.

Submit your signage list well in advance to save increased cost of crash printing.

Make up your press kits well in advance.

Negotiate with photographers. (Many will work on a speculation basis.)

In resort areas, negotiate a working vacation for your speakers and reduce speaker fees.

Try a simple, brief, pocket-sized program that attendees can carry easily.

Photo-reduce the agenda onto a name tag.

Control Entertainment Costs

Don't exceed the number of musicians required for certain ballrooms.

Don't pay more than current union rates.

Consider a community group or dinner-theater cast.

Use a reliable agent, broker, or bureau for established entertainers.

Determine regular hours for property electricians and make entertainers rehearse during regular work hours. (You save a lot on the electrician's overtime.)

Some General Ideas for Reducing Cost

Work with other meeting managers to coordinate arrangements—perhaps two or three could book a whole hotel at reduced costs.

Try dealing with a hotel chain if you have a series of meetings to get chain rates rather than individual property rates. (Also, this can save you a lot of negotiating.)

Consider the package concept in properties (one price includes room, certain meals, etc.)

Gear your meeting to the area. Take advantage of local attractions.

Try packaging your meetings. Put several meetings in the same property and perhaps book that property for a month.

Be certain to encourage group travel and take advantage of the lower fare and tour conductor passes.

Take the time to obtain comparative prices. Use bids and proposals.

Bibliography

This bibliography is designed for ready reference to subjects that relate to meeting management. It begins with those books that relate to general meeting management. The categories are:

- General meeting management
- Audiovisual
- Budgeting and financial management
- Communication
- Evaluation
- Food and beverage
- Hotel and hospitality management
- Law
- Negotiation
- Planning
- Programming and adult learning
- Promotion
- Teleconferencing
- Travel/transportation

A separate section lists periodicals with which meeting professionals should be familiar. Each issue updates the meeting profession and it would not be wise to list specific articles, since their subject matter or approaches become out-of-date within a short period of time.

General Meeting Management

American Society of Association Executives. *Guidelines for Effective Conventions and Meetings.* 2 vols. Information Central, ASAE, Washington, D.C., 1981.

Auger, B. Y. *How To Run Better Business Meetings.* Audiovisual Division, 3M, St. Paul, Minn., 1985.

Bradford, Leland P. *Making Meetings Work: A Guide for Leaders and Group Members.* University Associates, San Diego, Calif., 1976.

Burke, W. W., and R. Beckhard. *Conference Planning.* University Associates, La Jolla, Calif., 1976.

Caruso, Frederick C. *The Challenge of Association Management.* Insight Press, Englewood, Colo., 1977.

Cavalier, Richard. *Achieving Objectives in Meetings.* Corporate Movement, Inc., New York, 1973.

Comstock, T. W. *Modern Supervision.* Delmar Publications, Inc., Albany, N.Y., 1987.

Convention Liaison Council. *Convention Liaison Manual.* 4th ed. Convention Liaison Council, Washington, D.C., 1985.

Cooper, S., and C. Heenan. *Preparing, Designing, and Leading Workshops: A Humanistic Approach.* CBI Publishing Col, Boston, 1980.

Doyle, M., and D. Strauss. *How to Make Meetings Work: The New Interaction Method.* Wyden Books, Ridgefield, Conn., 1976.

DuBey, R. E., et al. *A Practical Guide for Dynamic Conferences.* University Press of America, Lanham, Md., 1982.

Ferrell, R. *Field Managers Guide to Successful Meetings.* Successful Meetings Book Division, New York, 1977.

Fiedler, F. E., and M. M. Chemers. *Leadership and Effective Management.* Scott Foresman Publishing Co., Glenview, Ill.

Finkel, C. *Professional Guide to Successful Meetings.* Successful Meetings Book Division, New York, 1976.

Hart, L. B., and J. G. Schleicher. *A Conference and Workshop Planners Manual,* AMACOM, New York, 1979.

Jones, James E. *Meeting Management: A Professional Approach.* Bayard Publications, Stamford, Conn., 1978.

Jones, M. *How to Organize Meetings: A Handbook for Better Workshop, Seminar and Conference Management,* Beaufort Books, New York, 1981.

Lawson, F. *Conference, Convention and Exhibition Facilities.* Nichols Publishing Co., New York, 1982.

Lemp, Helena. *Manual for the Organization of Scientific Congresses.* S. Karger Publishers, Inc., New York, 1979.

Lobinger, J. L. *Business Meetings that Make Business.* Macmillan Co., New York, 1969.

Lord, Robert. *Running Conventions, Conferences and Meetings.* AMACOM, New York, 1981.

Meeting Planners International. *General Meeting Management.* 2 vols. Meeting Planners International, Dallas, Tex., 1986.

Myers, Helen. *The Business of Seminars.* Center for Seminar Management, Las Vegas, Nev., 1982.

Nadler, A., and Z. Nadler. *The Conference Book.* Gulf Publishing Co., Houston, Tex., 1977.

Nichols, Barbara, ed. *Professional Meeting Management.* Professional Convention Management Association, Birmingham, Ala., 1985.

Odiorne, George S. *Management by Objectives*. Pitman Publishing Corp., New York, 1965.

Preston, Paul, and Thomas W. Zimmer. *Management for Supervisors*. 2d ed. Prentice Hall, Englewood Cliffs, N.J., 1983.

Public Management Institute Staff. *Successful Seminars, Conferences, and Workshops*. Public Management Institute, San Francisco, Calif., 1980.

Reynolds, Helen, and Mary E. Trauel. *Executive Time Management*. Prentice Hall, Englewood Cliffs, N.J., 1979.

Schindler-Rainman, E., and J. Cole. Rev. ed. *Taking Your Meetings Out of the Doldrums*. University Associates, Inc., San Diego, Calif., 1988.

Seekings, David. *How to Organize Meetings*. Nichols Publishing, Co., New York, 1981.

Smith, H. *Organizing for Better Meetings*. Sales and Marketing Management, Sales Builders Division, New York, 1977.

Stogdill, Ralph M. *Handbook for Leadership*. The Free Press, New York, 1974.

Successful Meetings. *Planning and Staging Company Meetings*. Successful Meetings, Bill Publications, Philadelphia, Pa., 1974.

This, Leslie. *The Small Meeting Planner*. 2d. ed. Gulf Publishing Co., Houston, Tex., 1979.

Tippers International. *Guide for Tipping*. Tippers International, Oshkosh, Wis., 1982.

Workman, M. S., and F. Luthans. *Emerging Concepts in Management*. Macmillan, New York, 1970.

Audiovisual

Jeffries, James R. *The Executives Guide to Meeting, Conferences, and Audiovisual Presentations*. McGraw-Hill, New York, 1983.

Kenny, M. F., and R. F. Schmitt. *Images, Images, Images*. 3d ed. Eastman Kodak Company, Rochester, N.Y., 1983.

McBride, Dennis. *How to Make Visual Presentations*. Art Direction Book Co., New York, 1982.

Budgeting and Financial Management

Dudick, Thomas S. *Inventory Control and the Financial Executive*. John Wiley, New York, 1979.

Evans-Hemming, D. F. *Flexible Budgetary Control and Standard Costs*. MacDonald and Evans, Ltd., London, England, 1952.

Goodman, Sam R. *Effective Control of Administrative Costs*. Prentice Hall, Englewood Cliffs, N.J., 1972.

Hinricks, Harley H., and Graeme M. Taylor. *Systematic Analysis: A Primer on Benefit Cost Analysis and Program Evaluation*. Goodyear Publishing, Pacific Palisade, Calif., 1972.

Jones, Reginald L., and George Trentin. *Budgeting: Key to Planning and Control*. American Management Association, New York, 1971.

Maciariello, Joseph A. *Program Management Control Systems*. John Wiley, New York, 1978.

Phyrr, P. A. *Zero-Based Budgeting*. John Wiley, New York, 1973.

Slavin, Albert. *Basic Accounting for Managerial and Financial Control.* Dryden Press, Hinsdale, Ill., 1972.

Sweeney, A., and J. N. Wisner, Jr. *Budgeting Fundamentals for Non-Financial Executives.* AMACOM, New York, 1975.

Communication

Adams, Gay B. *A Bibliography on a Human Theory of Organization.* Council of Planning Librarians, Monticello, Ill., 1977.

Burgoon, M., et al. *Small Group Communication: A Functional Approach.* Holt, Rinehart, and Winston, New York, 1974.

Dessler, Gary. *Applied Human Relations.* Reston Publishing Company, Reston, Va., 1983.

Filley, Alan C. *Interpersonal Conflict Resolution.* Scott Foresman, Glenview, Ill., 1975.

Koneya, M., and A. Barbour. *Louder Than Words—Nonverbal Communication.* Charles E. Merrill, Columbus, Ohio, 1976.

Luthans, F., and R. Kreitner. *Organizational Behavior Modification.* Scott Foresman, Glenview, Ill., 1975.

Phillips, Gerald M. *Communication and the Small Group.* Bobbs-Merrill, New York, 1966.

Patton, Bobby R., and Bonnie R. Patton. *Living Together: Female/Male Communication.* Charles E. Merrill, Columbus, Ohio, 1976.

Pickens, J. E. *Without Bias: A Guidebook for Nondiscriminatory Communication.* 2d ed. International Association of Business Communicators, San Francisco, 1982.

Rosenfeld, L. B. *Human Interaction in the Small Group Setting.* Charles E. Merrill, Columbus, Ohio, 1973.

Rothstein, Jerome. *Communication, Organization, and Service.* Falcon's Wing Press, Indian Hills, Colo., 1958.

Tubbs, S. L., and J. W. Baird. *The Open Person.* Charles E. Merrill, Columbus, Ohio, 1976.

Wiley, J. Barron. *Communication for Modern Management.* Business Press, Elmhurst, Ill., 1966.

Evaluation

Ciarlo, James A. *Utilizing Evaluations.* Sage Publications, Beverly Hills, Calif., 1981.

Davis, L. M. *Planning, Conducting and Evaluating Workshops.* Learning Concepts, Austin, Tex., 1979.

Epstein, Irwin. *Research Techniques for Program Planning, Monitoring, and Evaluating.* Columbia University Press, New York, 1977.

Furst, Edward J. *Constructing Evaluation Instruments.* D. McKay Co., New York, 1958.

Gabriel, Richard A. *Program Evaluation: A Social Science Approach.* MSS Information Corp., New York, 1975.

Spitze, Hazel T., and Mildred B. Griggs. *Choosing Evaluation Techniques.* Home Economics Education Association, Washington, D.C., 1976.

Weiss, Carol H. *Evaluation Research: Methods for Assessing Program Effectiveness.* Prentice Hall, Englewood Cliffs, N.J., 1972.

Food and Beverage

Bell, Donald. *Food and Beverage Cost Control.* McCutchen Publishing Co., Berkeley, Calif., 1984.

Bottom Line Personal. *The Book of Inside Information.* Boardroom Classics, New York, 1988.

Houston, Joseph. *The Professional Service of Food and Beverage.* Batsford Academic and Educational, Ltd., London, 1982.

Johnson, F. E. *The Professional Wine Reference.* Beverage Media, Ltd., New York, 1977.

Keister, Douglas C. *Food and Beverage Control.* Prentice Hall, Englewood Cliffs, N.J., 1977.

Kowalski, R. E. *The 8-Week Cholestrol Cure.* Harper and Row, New York, 1987.

Wurtman, J. J. *Managing Your Mind and Mood Through Food.* Rawson Associates, New York, 1986.

Hotel and Hospitality Management

American Hotel and Motel Association. *A Meeting Planner's Guide to Master Account Billing.* American Hotel and Motel Association, East Lansing, Mich., 1980.

Brymer, Robert A. *Introduction to Hotel and Restaurant Management.* 3d ed. Kendall/Hunt Publishing Company, Dubuque, Iowa, 1981.

Henry, Ben. *The Young Supervisor's Manual.* Mr. Zippy/Printers, Dunwoody, Ga., 1986.

Hotel Sales Management Association. *Glossary of Hotel/Motel Terms.* Publications Office, Hotel Sales Management Association, Margate, N.J.

Kalt, Nathan. *Introduction to the Hospitality Industry.* Bobbs-Merrill, Indianapolis, Ind., 1971.

Lane, H. E., and Mark von Hartesvelt. *Essentials of Hospitality Administration.* Reston Publishing Company, Reston, Va., 1983.

Lattin, Gerald. *Modern Hotel and Motel Management.* W. H. Freeman and Company, Publishers, San Francisco, 1968.

Law

Cournoyer, Norman G. *Hotel, Restaurant and Travel Law.* Duxbury Press, North Scituate, Mass., 1978.

English, Robert J. *Business Contract Forms.* John Wiley, New York, 1984.

Filler, Lon L. *Basic Contract Law.* West Publishing Co., St. Paul, Minn., 1972.

Goodwin, J., and J. M. Rorelstad. *Travel and Lodging Law.* John Wiley, New York, 1980.

Jacobs, Jerald A. *Association Law Handbook.* The Bureau of National Affairs, Washington, D.C., 1981.

U.S. Office of Federal Contract Compliance. *Manual.* Employment Standards Administration, Office of Federal Contract Compliance Programs, Washington, D.C. (continuously updated)

Negotiation

Fisher, Roger, and William Ury. *Getting to Yes*. Penguin Books, New York, 1983.

Karrass, Chester L. *Give and Take*. Thomas Y. Crowell, New York, 1974.

Karrass, Chester L. *The Negotiating Game*. Thomas Y. Crowell. New York, 1970.

Levin, Edward. *Negotiating Tactics*. Fawcett Columbine, New York, 1980.

Nirenberg, Gerald I. *Fundamentals of Negotiating*. Hawthorne/Duttin, New York, 1973.

Richardson, J., and Joel Margulis. *The Business of Negotiation*. Avon Books, New York, 1981.

Planning

Cook, Desmond L. *Program Evaluation and Review Technique: Applications in Education*. University Press, Lanham, Md., 1979.

Evarts, H. F. *Introduction to Pert*. Allyn and Bacon, Boston, 1966.

Gantt, Henry L. *Gantt on Management; Guidelines for Today's Executive*. American Management Association, New York, 1961.

Hansen, B. J. *Practical PERT: Including Critical Path Method*. American House, Washington, D.C., 1965.

Horowitz, J. *Critical Path Scheduling: Management Control Through CPM and PERT*. The Ronald Press Company, New York, 1967.

Levin, R. I., and C. A. Kirkpatrick. *Planning and Control with PERT, CPM*. McGraw-Hill, New York, 1966.

Pitman, N. J. *PERT-GANTT and the Good Use of Time*. Educational Improvement Center, 1977.

Rook, Dana C. *Program Evaluation Review Technique, An Annotated Bibliography, 1962–1974*. Council of Planning Librarians, Monticello, Ill., 1976.

Programming and Adult Learning

Brookfield, Stephen. *Understanding and Facilitating Adult Learning*. Jossey-Bass, San Francisco, 1986.

Delbecq, A. L., et al. *Group Techniques for Program Planning*. Scott Foresman, Glenview, Ill., 1975.

Deloz, Laurent. *Effective Teaching and Monitoring*. Jossey-Bass, San Francisco, 1986.

Director of Program Development. *Readings in Program Development*. Office of Continuing Education and Public Service, University of Illinois, Champaign, Ill.

Iannone, A. L. *Management Program Planning and Control*. Prentice Hall, Englewood Cliffs, N.J., 1967.

Jarvis, Peter. *Adult Learning in the Social Context*. Corwn Helm, New York, 1987.

Jenkins, Janet, and Donald H. Brundage. *Adult Learning Principles and Their Application to Program Planning*. Ontario Ministry of Education, Toronto, Ont., 1980.

Knowles, M. S. *The Modern Practice of Adult Education*. Rev. ed. Follett Publishing Co., Chicago, Ill., 1980.

Mager, Robert F. *Preparing Instructional Objectives*. 2d rev. ed. D.S. Lake Publications, Belmont, Calif., 1985.

Smith, Robert M. *Learning How to Learn.* Follette Publishing Co., Chicago, Ill., 1982.

Sprague, S. K., and J. N. Becker. *Planning Effective Programs.* New Ventures, Oakland, Calif., 1979.

Training Magazine. Adult Learning in Your Classroom. Minneapolis, Minn., 1982.

Promotion

Astroff, M. T., and J. R. Abbey. *Convention Sales and Services,* Wm. C. Brown Publishers, Dubuque, Ia., 1978.

Engel, James F., et al. *Promotional Strategy: Managing the Marketing.* 5th ed. R. D. Irwin, Homewood, Ill., 1983.

Kress, G. *Marketing Research.* 2d ed. Reston Publishing Co., Reston, Va., 1982.

Mass, Jane. *Better Brochures, Catalogs, and Mailing Pieces.* St. Martin's Press, Inc., New York, 1981.

Winston, M. B. *Getting Publicity.* John Wiley, New York, N.Y., 1982.

Woods, Robert, ed. *Printing and Production for Promotional Materials.* Van Nostrand Reinhold, New York, 1987.

Teleconferencing

Bronstein, R., J. Gill, and E. W. Koneman. *Teleconferencing: A Practical Guide to Teaching by Telephone.* ASCP Press, Chicago, Ill., 1982.

Johansen, R., J. Vallee, and K. Spangler. *Electronic Meetings.* Addison-Wesley, Reading, Mass., 1979.

Travel/Transportation

Harris, G., and K. M. Katz. *Promoting International Tourism.* The Americas Group, Los Angeles, 1986.

Henry, Ben. *Fundamentals of Travel and Tourism.* Mr. Zippy/Printers, Dunwoody, Ga., 1986.

Hudman, L. E. *Tourism; a Shrinking World.* Grid Publishing, Inc., Columbus, Ohio, 1980.

Lehmann, A. D. *Travel and Tourism.* Bobbs-Merrill, Indianapolis, Ind., 1979.

Lundberg, D. *International Travel and Tourism.* John Wiley, New York, 1985.

Lundberg, D. *The Tourist Business.* 4th ed. CBI Publishing Company, Inc., Boston, 1980.

McIntosh, R. W., and C. R. Goeldner. *Tourism: Princples, Practices, Philosophies.* Grid Publishing, Columbus, Ohio, 1984.

Periodicals

Association and Society Manager. Barrington Publications, Los Angeles.

Association Management. American Society of Association Executives, Washington, D.C.

Best's Insurance Convention Guide. A.M. Best Co., Oldwick, N.J.

Business Travel News. CMP Publications, Manhasset, N.Y.

Communication Monographs. Speech Communication Association, Annandale, Va.

Corporate Meetings and Incentives. Harcourt Brace Jovanovich Publications, New York.

Corporate Travel. Gralla Publications, New York.

Health Care Conference Planner. Bayard Publications, Inc., Stamford, Ct.

Insurance Conference Planner. Bayard Publications, Inc., Stamford, Ct.

Medical Meetings. Laux Company, Inc., Harvard Mass.

Meeting News. Gralla Publications, New York.

Meeting Manager. Meeting Planners International, Dallas, Tex.

Meetings & Conventions. Ziff-Davis Publishing Co., Secaucus, N.J.

Meetings & Incentive Travel. Southam Communications, Ltd., Ontario, Canada.

Quarterly Journal of Speech. Speech Communication Association, Annandale, Va.

Successful Meetings. Bill Publications, Inc., New York.

Training. Lakewood Publications, Minneapolis, Minn.

Training and Development Journal. American Society for Training and Development, Washington, D.C.

Index

A

B

C

D

E

F

G

H

I

N

O

T

U

V

W